Left, Right, Wrong

POLITICS HAS LOST ITS WAY: A ROUTE MAP FOR CHANGE

Left, Right, Wrong

POLITICS HAS LOST ITS WAY:
A ROUTE MAP FOR CHANGE

Sir Robin Wales and Clive Furness

The Book Guild Ltd

First published in Great Britain in 2023 by
The Book Guild Ltd
Unit E2 Airfield Business Park,
Harrison Road, Market Harborough,
Leicestershire. LE16 7UL
Tel: 0116 2792299
www.bookguild.co.uk
Email: info@bookguild.co.uk
Twitter: @bookguild

Typeset in 11pt Minion Pro

Printed on FSC accredited paper
Printed and bound in Great Britain by 4edge Limited

ISBN 978 1915603 937

British Library Cataloguing in Publication Data.
A catalogue record for this book is available from the British Library.

To Bill and Jean Furness.

From my father I learned that right and wrong were as clear as black and white; from my mother, that where people are concerned, there are infinite shades of grey.

And to Lily, Allanah, Freya and Cole for making life brighter.

INTRODUCTION

*Although the big word on the Left is 'compassion', the big
agenda on the Left is dependency.*
(Thomas Sowell)

Continuous improvement is better than delayed perfection.
(Mark Twain)

Social democracy is under threat around the globe, and not
solely from the rising tide of Right-wing populism that in the
past decade has elected Donald Trump in the United States, Jair
Bolsonaro in Brazil and Viktor Orbán in Hungary.

Rather, the threat to progressive centre-Left politics also
comes from the twenty-first century's strange incarnations
of ideologies that identify themselves as Left. The rise of
Corbynistas in the United Kingdom following Jeremy Corbyn's
surprise victory in the 2015 Labour Party leadership election,
fuelled by campaign groups such as Momentum, highlighted
the vulnerability of the Labour Party to the superficial appeal of
middle-class ideologues as much as to empty-headed populists.

Politics is changing fast. In just ten years, what we took for
granted was rejected in the UK, Italy and the US to name just a
few. Yet, in this book, we argue that genuine social democracy
still has much to offer and was dismissed too easily following

the global economic crash of 2008. How do we know? Because not only did we see the benefits of social democracy in action; we led an entire area committed to it as a political creed which, while imperfect, delivered significant improvements to a large number of citizens. And we delivered those benefits across a London borough that had faced some of the biggest public policy challenges in history.

The inspiration for this book lies in our achievements at Newham Council in East London between 1996 and 2018. As anybody familiar with this extraordinary part of Western Europe's biggest metropolis will know, Newham faced a daunting mixture of social and economic challenges throughout the twentieth century: poverty, low-quality housing, mass immigration, poor public health, low educational standards and aspiration, and higher-than-average crime rates. We believe that the achievements described in this book will impress unbiased reviewers. More importantly, however, we hope that they will make people think again about the direction in which the political Left is heading.

This book will also explain *why* we focused on specific areas of public policy in Newham. Through that analysis, we hope readers will understand the true benefits of progressive social democracy over what we consider the superficial or posturing preoccupations of the statist Left and the woke wannabe revolutionaries.

Most books that tackle politics and the problems we face today start with the author's analysis: often insightful and exciting; sometimes banal. They usually end with exhortations about what we should change without explaining how to achieve that change; generally preferring to utter some pious platitudes. As we try to show in this book, this is not the fault of those authors, but it reflects the current political culture. We come from a different place. We are clear about what we want to achieve and how to achieve it. Instead of creating the new man (or new woman), as revolutionaries often suppose they can do, we describe a process that we believe needs to be applied to public service and leadership. Our objective is to support the development of *resilience*: the ability of people to deal with whatever life throws at us. This is contrary to the current Leftist obsession with victimhood.

A key theme throughout this book is the need to apply scientific methods to public policy. Too often, policy at a national and local level fails because it does not rest on empirical evidence and, when implemented, is not subject to robust review. This is the antithesis of what became the 'Newham Approach'. Our approach worked because it could be measured and compared. Unlike other authors who exhort us to oppose or support a new way of doing things without evidence, we also demonstrate what we did to address Newham's problems. These actions and policies, while never perfect, had a major impact on local people, transforming the life chances of one of London's poorest populations. Action rather than exhortation has always been our approach.

What has been done in one place can be done elsewhere if the evidence can be measured and the practical lessons learned. So, this book is not a policy blueprint. Instead it is an invitation to change thinking to restore social democratic traditions that work. The prioritisation of practical application is much underrated in our society, especially across the political sphere. Just as in science, theories stand or fall on experimental results, and much of the thinking in this book has been governed by that practice. But our initiatives also shared a common root in our desire to improve our population's personal, economic and community resilience. They were not implemented in a lab under test conditions, but in the real world. As such, we believe the results are particularly valid. We are now keen to see these initiatives tested within other settings to see whether, with some variation based on local requirements, successes can be replicated. We are confident they can be.

In this book, we detail our experiences and identify a set of hypotheses and lessons based on them. We encourage other political leaders and policy wonks to do the same and to compare our experience with theirs: Newham was not the only local authority to do amazing things! If you hail from a different council, at this point you are probably harrumphing and asking, 'What was so special about Newham?' The answer is not that we ran services better, though we did well at that. What was 'special' was that we tried to change the experience of local people; to encourage them to behave differently by supporting the development of capacity or resilience. One of the current political buzzwords is 'empowerment'. It's not a word we generally used, but it was key to people developing resilience. Few councils, if any, adopt this approach as coherently and systematically as we did; something we hope to illustrate in this book. We encourage readers to challenge our experiences and findings based on empirical evidence and not just political prejudice.

Between us, authors Sir Robin Wales and Clive Furness have been members of the Labour Party for almost a century. We were both active in local government for more than twenty years, and racked up half a century of public service.

Robin was first elected as a Newham councillor in 1982 and became leader of the authority in 1995. In 2002 he became the borough's first directly elected Mayor – a position which enjoyed significant local autonomy – and he won further elections in 2006, 2010 and 2014. In 2000 he received a knighthood for services to local government. Not bad for a kid from a council estate in Kilmarnock, Scotland ('Onthank', for those readers familiar with the BBC Scotland programme *The Scheme*)!

Clive became a Newham councillor in 1997, and variously served in regeneration, and as head of community engagement, finance and health – all critical local government portfolios. He spent most of his working life in the voluntary sector and, in

1992, helped establish Newham's first night shelter for homeless people. He has worked with the homeless as a volunteer ever since. Clive is also a youth worker and, in 2017, was awarded the British Empire Medal for his work with young people across Newham.

Between 1998 and 2002, Robin and Clive represented the same Canning Town ward in Newham, and during this period we developed clear ideas about tackling the borough's most pressing needs.

Early in public office, we learned many lessons that cynics warned us about. One in particular stands out: at the political level, actors' motivations are mixed, and lack of ability should not be considered a hindrance to political ambition. Here, Mark Twain's comment always seemed remarkably apt: 'All you need in this life is ignorance and confidence, and then success is sure.' Does the name Liz Truss (though perhaps too much ignorance means you get found out very quickly) ring any bells?

But the ignorant confidence of others was not our only hurdle. When we took over in Newham, a comic refrain, probably coined by council officers, was: 'Councillors spend hours discussing sandwich fillings or choosing biscuits for meetings, but sign off in mere minutes spending plans costing several million pounds.' While this was never entirely true, the saying contained a grain of truth. Upon taking office, we found that in complex and challenging matters, other decision makers had often found it easier to defer to full-time council officers: the assumed experts. In too many UK councils, the officers were, and are, 'in control'. We hope you will find in these pages an explanation of why that is generally a bad thing. We also hope that it will begin a conversation about the politicians who run councils and also with Members of Parliament. Unless such leaders are willing to take considered risks with public policy, nothing will change.

How do we create an environment in which it is easier to develop initiatives that improve people's lives, and that people value? According to national surveys, the approach we took in Newham made us the most popular council in the country. So, in terms of incentives, following our approach would seem to offer some help to local politicians struggling to convince residents of their worth. The other side of the coin is that, where people do not believe their politicians are delivering for them, they can turn very quickly against the party in power – just look at the sizeable loss of Labour's 'Red Wall' seats in the UK's 2019 general election.

Both authors of this book are shamelessly on the moderate Left of the political spectrum. We have been since childhood, though Clive had a dalliance with Trotskyism in his late teens! Our sympathies are with those not born with silver spoons in their mouths; who often spend their lives struggling to make ends meet, but who continue to play by the rules of society. Newham is full of such folk. So, we suspect, are most boroughs and shires in the country. Such people often work for low wages, take responsibility for their family and community seriously, don't fiddle their taxes, and are law-abiding. If the government asks them to stay at home for the nation's health, they don't drive forty miles to test their eyesight. Such people come in every shape and colour. They are quintessentially modern Britons. But, too often, such people lack a political voice. We entered politics to make a difference on their behalf. That used to be what the Labour Party was for. But, even with the political demise of Jeremy Corbyn, the Labour Party currently remains populated by graduates from grievance studies courses; those for whom debates about whether a particular female journalist at the BBC should be paid £300,000 annually, rather than £150,000, are more important than assisting five hundred female cleaners on minimum wage and insecure contracts. We're too old to get overexcited about pulling down statues of long-dead men with sometimes dubious personal histories. But over the past decade, as a more populist brand has swamped movements on the Left and Right, that is where the excitement of contemporary politics seems to lie. We think this approach is a distraction from goals that will ultimately benefit wider society. Even if this modern-day posturing has virtue – and we are far from convinced that it does – the spray-painting and statue-tumbling nihilism of contemporary revolutionaries does nothing for most of the people we seek to support.

Social democracy has become a sad and aged relative of refreshed populist demands to tear up existing orders; the currently unpopular 'middle-aged parent' of the political world. Yet we believe it remains the single best hope for the people and communities described above, and for broader society. Social democracy *should* be dynamic, challenging and exciting, and provide a vision for the energetic and enthusiastic young people who really want to change the world. During our time in Newham, it was all those things and more; an exciting time to be involved in local government. Who'd have thought it?

A thought: what is it that excites you about politics? Is it the emotional high of today's fashionable protest? Or is it making a positive change in the lives of real people? Tedious though they may seem to current populists, it is social democrats who have changed the world for the better, while revolutionaries and statists have left a trail of destruction in their wake. Want to tackle global warming? Then look at what can *really* be achieved and subject your ideas to proper scrutiny. Clive lives in Canning Town, a traditionally blue-collar area of Newham populated by the sort of hard-working families and young professionals we like. In October 2019, his neighbours demonstrated their attitude towards the middle-class environmental warriors of Extinction Rebellion when protesters at Canning Town Tube Station inadvisably tried to prevent them from getting to work. The intervention was brought to a swift conclusion when locals – not the police – matter-of-factly removed protesters from train rooftops and then, with little fuss, carried on about their daily business. We do not condone physical clashes between citizens. But the whole incident reflected the present divide between the middle-class dilettantes of the activist Left and regular working people who may even share the activists' environmental concerns and vote for the same political party.

Posturing versus pragmatism has become a new divide on the Left and across the political spectrum. We believe it is essential that pragmatism wins this battle, because it leads to outcomes that give the biggest benefit to the largest number of people, not just a tiny and angry mob of self-proclaimed messiahs. A minority of environmentalists believe that disrupting roads and public transport on a wet Wednesday is a victory in 'their' battle to save the planet. This is a symptom of the politics which views the world through a single lens. How to deliver more carbon reduction without hitting the economy and living standards is the debate we need to have, rather than the virtue-signalling disruption imposed by those who believe that only their opinions matter. Extinction Rebellion and their acolytes seem wedded to a twenty-first-century form of hair-shirt Luddism. We suspect that technology will be a major factor in combating the causes of global warming, not political self-flagellation.

The subtext of environmental and 'social justice' warriors is the overthrow of capitalism. This is where we, and other social democrats, differ from those on the Left with revolutionary fervour. The revolutionary overthrow of an existing order involves enormous suffering. Alas, it is all too easy to find examples of supposed Left-wing revolutions replacing an existing corrupt tyranny with a new one, only worse. Throughout history and in our own lifetimes, we have seen many existing orders overturned. But we struggle to identify one where such change led to sustained improvements for most people. The persistent denial of this by the Left suggests an attachment to fantasy over experience. Those on the hard Left who counter that 'real' revolutionary socialism has never been tried are simply wrong. It has been tested repeatedly, and failed each time. The proponents of revolution could perhaps consider whether the model for achieving it might be systemically flawed. If we believe in empirical evidence, there is little supporting the proposition that revolutionary socialism will benefit most people. But then, reason and empiricism are products of what critical race theory (CRT) advocates now term 'whiteness', and, as such, are enemies of the intersectional mob.

One of the themes in these pages is that social democracy is not about managing capitalism better than the Conservatives – another poor critique of moderates offered by the hard Left. (Although it does help to be provably better at managing the excesses of capitalism than the Tories or any other party.) Rather, we argue that social democracy remains the best mechanism yet devised for using the wealth generated in our societies to improve the lives of ordinary people. We know what can be done because we did it, and in these very pages, we show how. At its best, social democracy can and should be radical: it should challenge the bureaucracies which govern our public services (and larger private sector companies); it should employ the rigour of empiricism and challenge the shibboleths of the Left which sound good but fail to deliver on their promises.

But threats to social democracy are numerous and can be seen across the political spectrum. While the populist Right has thrived politically in recent years, the woke Left has established a cultural hegemony that too often promotes fashion over policy and narrative over objectivity. We attempt to show how a different approach could work – and did in Newham.

Adlai Stevenson said of Eleanor Roosevelt, 'She would rather light candles than curse the darkness.' It's an adage that we found helpful. Our experience was that incremental steps made a significant difference in the lived experience of our residents. Indeed, we might labour the point and say that the candle was replaced by a light bulb and then by LEDs. Social democracy is the system that fights to ensure that the benefits which arise from scientific innovation are ultimately shared more fairly than unregulated capitalism allows. Social democracy built council houses after World War II. Social democracy established a free-at-the-point-of-use National Health Service. Social democracy established a welfare state that, while it has problems, massively addressed deep-rooted poverty.

Yet in more recent years, social democracy has suffered from having become the public policy establishment throughout Britain and the rest of Europe after 1945. Impatient new generations, who failed to understand that no political system resolves all ills in a world of finite resources, turned their backs on undynamic social democracies that had become stale and failed to deliver. But did that mean that the philosophy was wrong and the entire concept could be cast aside? As social democracy in the UK has weakened, so bigger (and unresolved) challenges have emerged:

- Intergenerational inequality and debt burdens.
- Not enough housing and affordable homes.
- Global warming.
- Destruction of the skills base across a state which led the world.
- The growth of bureaucracies which squander resources and hinder progress.
- A graduate class struggling to land jobs beyond Uber and McDonald's.
- Cancel culture that challenges our right to freedom of speech and thought.

These are significant societal issues, and our response needs to be one of scale. When a council or government initiates a small-scale improvement and then trumpets its achievement, that, in our view, is avoiding the bigger challenges facing society today. Good small-scale initiatives are always welcome – you will read about some in this book. But they should always be considered against the totality of the challenge; local or national. If something works at ward level, or even across a borough, think about what's needed to scale up that response and achieve more comprehensive benefits.

For example, as you will read later, Newham was the first council in the country to fund free school meals for all primary-school children, resulting in an improvement in education outcomes, particularly for the more disadvantaged children. It costs, sure, but given the evidence, why has government not implemented the initiative across the country? In Newham, our view was that if we were going to do something, it had to be applied across the council. But often national governments initiate pilot schemes across a local authority (through centralised funding) and, even where a pilot is successful, choose not to roll it out more widely. This was the case with Newham's free school meals. Why? If something made a difference in Newham, then our mantra was that it was immoral not to offer it to everyone. Hence, teach *every* kid to play a musical instrument. License *every* private sector landlord. Provide 'early years' guarantees to *every* resident. The central purpose of this book is to argue that government now needs to adopt or encourage this Newham Approach – this social democratic approach – across the UK.

We recognise that this book will be published a while after we left office. For this, we apologise. But for a time we struggled to position what we did in Newham to make it relevant to a national audience. We hope we have now achieved this but, if not, there is no refund policy.

The dominant Left narrative requires obeisance to the view that the West is the root of all ills; that white people are inherently racist; that recitation of a contemporary creed is more important than what you do. It is a dualist dogma in which the West, capitalism and even democracy are the roots of all evil; and victimhood, as espoused by any other group or system, however authoritarian or barbaric, is therefore a source of political virtue. This is nonsense, of course.

We happen to like Britain. It isn't perfect, but we struggle to think of somewhere we would rather be. We like our history and are proud of it, warts and all. We like the quirkiness of its Parliament and the incomprehensibility of its constitution. We like the Britain we grew up in and the Britain that has emerged in the twenty-first century. We like its vibrancy and its stability. We like its cities and its countryside. We like the safety it gives to residents and the disproportionate and positive role it plays on the world stage. We like the UK's general tolerance, justice and humanity. But we are in danger of losing much of what makes Britain great. We believe Britain can be better. We hope that this book highlights ways in which that could be achieved.

Chapter 1

SOCIAL DEMOCRACY UNDER FIRE: RESILIENCE VERSUS VICTIMHOOD

These politically correct language initiatives are misguided and harmful. They create highly entitled professional "victims" who expect to be free from any offense, and they engender a stifling atmosphere where all individuals walk on eggshells lest they might commit a linguistic capital crime.
(Gad Saad)

I have not failed. I've just found 10,000 ways that won't work.
(Thomas A. Edison)

There is a nihilism that has infused contemporary politics. It has seeped into the politics of the Right and Left, and imbues the current activity of the young. This book does not attempt to determine the psychology of these movements. Instead, we simply note – with regret – their existence.

The UK Labour Party is failing. As the collapse of the so-called 'Red Wall' vote in the 2019 general election showed, it has alienated traditional supporters and abandoned its founding principles. In a rush to become 'relevant' and fill lost voids, it has embraced fashionable zeitgeists without considering their philosophical roots or the practical consequences of such support.

In more recent months, and possibly due to the Covid-19 pandemic, the casual revolutionaries and the statue-topplers seem to have taken a rest and the field has been vacated for the supposed intelligentsia of the new woke Left movements who are now embedded in every area of the arts, media, education and public service.

In the decades after 1945, the world experienced the most significant and most equitable growth in wealth in its history. Yet following the 2008 financial crash caused by banking greed, there seems to have been a desire to ditch the guiding principles behind this most successful economic system; those principles which delivered the greatest freedom to the greatest number, together with the greatest opportunity for self-actualisation. Contrary to simplistic revolutionary narratives, these principles were not those of pure capitalism. Rather, they were those of a regulated free market in a representative democratic state that operated under the rule of law. Such principles worked best where states institutionalised the values of the Enlightenment with an independent judiciary and separation of powers; where values such as liberty, freedom of thought, and freedom of speech were protected.

It is a matter of concern that we now see these basic tenets of our society under assault from those who claim to be on the Left. Capitalism is once again the enemy. Little lip service is paid to concepts such as the rule of law or even democracy. You only have to observe much of the Left's refusal to accept the UK's exit from the European Union – where Leave won a majority – to see this in action. Neither author of this book supported Brexit, but that misses the point: too many on the posturing Left simply refused to accept that 'we' (Remainers) had lost the battle, and so tried to undermine a democratic mandate.

Today we see the Left split into three. Firstly, the traditional statist Left, still straining under the burden of proving that the writings of Marx continue to be correct 170 years later. They want to replace capitalism with a system in which they (the party) dictate to the working class. Secondly, the new woke Left, who do not strain under any such intellectual burden but carry a list of contemporary assertions and simply state that their lived experience is sufficient proof of their rightness. They want to abolish capitalism because it sounds good. Quite what thought they have given to an alternative economic theory is unknown, but they *know* that it would be a good thing. And thirdly, there is the bloodied infantry of the social democratic Left, who think that changing the lives of working people for the better is an admirable objective and of itself worth fighting for.

To be fair to the statist and woke Left, there are many examples of unbridled capitalism doing harm because capitalism is not a moral system. Classically, Leftists have always argued that capitalism fails those at the bottom of society. To an extent, they are right. But we find it ironic that the most remarkable progress in raising people from poverty in the past hundred years has been the introduction of a largely unregulated free market to the People's Republic of China. While Mao's Cultural Revolution and centralised Great Leap Forward lost the lives of forty-five million Chinese people to brutality and starvation, the economic restructuring begun under Deng Xiaoping and intensified under Xi Jinping has lifted some 875 million people out of extreme poverty – more than the entire population of Europe, including Brexit Britain. Just how, we wonder, would the overthrow of capitalism in China improve the lives of 1.4 billion Chinese?

Much antipathy to capitalism is expressed in opposition to corruption and/or exploitation. Yet these flaws are hardly unique to capitalism. See, for example, Britain's pre-capitalist colonial history, or the way China currently operates economically in Africa. While African coltan miners are subject to a pre-feudal system of exploitation, the product of their efforts makes possible the iPhones of the protesters who demand an end to capitalism. We rather suspect that these labourers would welcome rather more regulated capitalism with regular wages and safe working conditions. In truth, corruption is an abhorrent part of the human condition. But where there is no rule of law, no free expression and no effective democracy, the potential for corruption becomes greater. Where there are no institutions that attempt to hold people to account, corruption flourishes. Yet, where these institutions exist, corruption appears worse because a light is shone on it. Where the courts effectively operate as an arm of the state, there is no check on members of the executive looting the coffers. Russian President Vladimir Putin is reputed to have acquired tens of billions of dollars. The list of dictators in Asia, South America and Africa who have gained vast personal fortunes is staggering. Beside them, the corruption which exists among UK parliamentarians looks pathetically amateurish.

While the UK's anti-capitalist protesters appear to suffer from a form of cognitive dissonance, on a macro scale, free-market capitalism continues to improve much of the global population's material wealth, living standards, and life expectancy; a fact conveniently ignored by many of its detractors. Quite the opposite is true of every socialist or communist state that took power through warfare or revolution. True, the Cubans claim to have an outstanding health system. But recent history has shown that sustainable improvements to living standards within states deemed politically 'communist' have only been achieved by adopting a capitalist market economy feeding that political structure.

We are genuinely puzzled about the form of society and economy that contemporary anti-capitalist protesters desire. The utopian experiments of the twentieth century were not promising. We are not ideologically committed to capitalism, but no one has yet demonstrated a better alternative. As social democrats, though, we believe governments should intervene to mitigate the worst excesses of capitalism and, where possible, improve life for the majority of people by providing a welfare net, education, healthcare, safe workspaces and the like. Social democrats within the trade union movement forced the first big improvements in the UK's working conditions, and it was social democracy that most effectively challenged untrammelled capitalism. For many social democrats, the purpose of the battle was to introduce greater equality in the distribution of the fruits of their labour – to ensure that people with less power and wealth obtained a larger, fairer share of the cake.

Social democracy reached its zenith in Britain post World War II. The creation of the NHS and the modern welfare state, plus a massive expansion of council housing, represented a significant redistribution of wealth and addressed many problems the Labour Party was established to tackle. Indeed, so successful was social democracy that even political opponents adopted its key tenets. In addition, the trade unions had a considerable and positive impact on living standards and working conditions. But this was when between nine and ten million people were trade union members and two thirds were in the private sector. Now, just 6.3 million workers are unionised and over half work in the public sphere. These raw figures also hide the fact that the working population in 1950 was twenty-three million; yet in 2018 it was 27.5 million. So, as the working population has increased, the number of unionised workers has dropped.

Increasingly, organised labour has become a pressure group dominated by the far Left representing workers in the public rather than the private sector. More often than not these days, unions' conflicts are with the taxpayer and not with industrialists and plutocrats. Yet, in recent years, economic, social and cultural changes have altered the economic and working landscape considerably, and social democracy has not responded well. Too often, it has been slow to reform, and – having for decades grown wealthy and comfortable on its benefits, such as good jobs and disposable income – people have forgotten what it delivered and what it rescued us from. Consequently, across Europe social democracy has failed to respond effectively to changing environments and has come under enormous pressure from populist movements on the Right and Left. What we called social democracy no longer seems to have the cachet or excitement necessary to bring young people onto the streets.

However, we will seek to demonstrate that it does retain the ability to deliver a politics that improves people's lives. It is not about sloganeering, and it will largely fail to fill the emotional void that is satisfied by ecstatic dancing with a can of spray paint or (for those of a more sedentary disposition) gluing yourself to the tarmac in front of ambulances. But it still provides the best mechanism to improve the lives of real people.

In thinking about current protests and movements, which are all too often based upon a self-declared identity, we ask a fundamental question about the UK today: are we a single community or a conglomeration of communities? The former suggests a community of individuals with different interests but who are unified in belonging to something greater (the UK). It signifies both a geographical area and a set of unifying principles. The latter suggests competing interest groups with little, if any, unifying identity.

Politicians frequently appeal to the first definition, however cynically. When former Prime Minister David Cameron claimed during the dark days of austerity that 'We're all in this together', it was a lie. While many people in steerage faced disproportionate impacts from spending cuts, those in first class continued to splash the cash. If people feel that they are being taken for mugs, they may look elsewhere for groups or organisations with easy – sometimes superficial – answers. Such groups often support the idea that the UK is a conglomeration of competing communities, and reach for simplistic narratives which primarily benefit their congregation. So, we can see how supposedly radical or populist solutions from either Right or Left become more enticing when those in power create mistrust.

From the Left there are essentially two ideologies competing with social democracy. The first is what we'd consider a classic statist Left critique. While for social democrats demanding better wages and greater equality are positives in their own right, for the fifty-seven varieties of Trotskyists and what remains of the Communist Party, better wages and conditions are merely 'transitional demands' in the march towards revolution and a glorious centrally planned future. A second threat to social democracy has been a little more nuanced. As material wealth has increased in Western societies, cultural issues have grown in importance, and so class has reduced in political significance. Neo-Marxists therefore often abandon a critique of the social-economic base in favour of claims about the cultural superstructure of society. When mixed with vacuous declarations by postmodernist thinkers, in which truth is a charade and reason merely the vehicle to promote oppression, we arrive at the devil's brew that now dominates the media and the syllabi of humanities departments. This is who we mean when we talk of the woke Left. In the past decade social democrats have had no answer to these threats. Perhaps they suffered a crisis of conviction that rendered them dumb in the face of these challenges? Flat-footed they may have been, but they need to start moving or abandon the field altogether to the contemporary nihilists. In his trenchant and heartfelt essay for the *New Statesman* in March 2020, former Labour MP Phil Wilson said:

> We also need to go further. Dig deeper, beyond even our purpose and search once again for a beginning. We need to ask ourselves if the Labour Party was created today, at the start of the third decade of the twenty-first century,

what would it look like? Where would our strength come from? How would you root a new Labour Party in our communities? The world that created the Labour Party has gone, but a Labour Party is still needed because the values we hold are for all time. Our quest is to make them relevant once more for the here and now, not the age of once upon a time.

The issues which created the Labour Party have indeed changed dramatically in recent years – particularly those involving work, wealth and representation. Yet social democrats have not adapted to these changes as quickly as other, flawed ideologies, mainly because we have not been clear on how to apply progressive values to the current situation.

In his book *The Road to Somewhere*, journalist and thinker David Goodhart describes a new, essentially cultural fault line in the British population between Somewheres and Anywheres. Anywheres are the liberal, Europhile middle class. They are comfortable with immigration and globalisation, value academic qualifications, and support most forms of equality – though not necessarily economic. They see themselves as citizens of the world, and value mobility and novelty. They are on the Left and generally vote Labour, Liberal Democrat or Green. Somewheres generally voted to leave the EU and are often far from Central London, though many live in the capital's outer boroughs. In East London, for example, Barking and Dagenham, Bexley, and Havering voted Leave, while Redbridge, Bromley and Newham had Remain majorities of only 8%, 2% and 6% respectively. They are culturally conservative but socially liberal, communitarian, patriotic, and proud of Britain and its history. They are rooted in the place where they live. As Goodhart explains, Somewheres can be working-class northerners or *Daily Mail* readers from the Home Counties. What unites them is a shared set of cultural values.

The desertion of the working-class Somewheres resulted in Labour's rout at the 2019 general election. We contend that the current woke agenda is that of the Anywheres. Their political approach is rooted in a superficial view of the world based on what they can see or feel. Like most Britons, they do not like unfairness, so visible equality matters. However, their response today is often based on symbolic activity rather than meaningful action that will bring about the changes they profess to care about. This approach is described by the author Thomas Frank in *What's the Matter with Kansas?*, who asserts that Left-wing politics has become:

> *A matter of shallow appearances, or fatuous self-righteousness... a politics in which the beautiful and wellborn tell the unwashed and the beaten-down and the funny-looking how they ought to behave.*

Somewheres value aspiration and hard work. If they like their area, they don't see why change should be encouraged. If they think their area is not prospering, they want to know why and what is being done. Societal change is inevitable, but the headlong rush to change inspired by Anywhere cosmopolitan policies has accelerated the pace. Change has arrived cloaked in the language of caring, but it is often not care extended to those who were already there. For example, in the early days of mass immigration, there was a reaction often steeped in racism, and 'white flight' from many areas, particularly the old East End of London. However, opinions and perceptions have changed and racism is, across the UK, on the retreat and has been for some time. New communities have brought elements of their culture with them, and most people defend that right. But why can indigenous culture not be accorded the same privilege? The desire to live in a place you like and don't want to see changed beyond recognition is not racist.

During the Corbyn years, the Labour Party embraced the cultural values of university-educated Anywheres while holding tight to the economic statism of the 1940s. The economic approach of the statist Left maintains a reverence for a planned, centralised state that borders on religion. Our approach is somewhat more pragmatic. For the state, there is the Hobbesian role of protecting the borders and the citizenry. There are services – health and prisons, for example – for which the social contract requires that the state is the provider (or at least the commissioner) of those services.

When we were young (and naive), we *wanted* to believe that central planning worked. A third of the world's population lived in planned economies. The Soviet Union, which funded numerous liberation movements but often acted entirely undemocratically (the annexation of Czechoslovakia and Hungary, to name but two examples), was given considerable leeway by the Left – to the eternal shame of people like us who failed to hold them to the standards we should have; a failing that was identified years ago by Nick Cohen in books such as *What's Left*. As Lefty youngsters, we criticised the United States for supporting some obnoxious leaders in Latin America. But we were largely silent on the abusive actions of liberation movements and revolutionary governments.

The economic model of socialised central planning continued as an alternative to the free markets of the West. It was surely a better, less exploitative model than free-market capitalism, right? Except, it wasn't. To be fair, after World War II it appeared obvious to many on the Left that central planning and delivery was the way to improve production. The Soviet Union, with its planned economy, had played a huge part in defeating Nazism, while production in Britain had been centralised and helped deliver victory on the Western Front. Unfortunately, in the post-war scramble to get societies moving again, not enough Lefties looked at the experience of the US and its extraordinary increases in production. Actually, for some it wasn't even that unfortunate: the oversight was by design. For many on the statist Left, their hatred of capitalist models precluded recognising the success of a country with many faults which had nonetheless become the most powerful example of democracy and freedom in history. Europe's experience of the war was different, however, and more local. So, understandably, social democrats initially supported nationalisation and central control, which, as the years passed, became demonstrably less efficient at organising national economies. We learned from our mistakes. Social democrats grew up. The zealots did not.

Our concerns about statism are manyfold. Foremost is that, in the UK, past performance of nationalised industries should have taught us something about government trying to control large bureaucracies. The inefficiencies, failures to invest, and subjection of economic priorities to political ones across these industries – British Rail, BT, coal and steel, for instance – were obvious. In contrast, the performance of privatised companies was generally better. As the distinguished political scientists Anthony King and Ivor Crewe put it:

> *The privatised companies were at least as effective – and in a majority of cases far more efficient – than their nationalised predecessors.*

Elsewhere in this book, we describe the problems facing large and inflexible bureaucracies, and particularly government bureaucracies. Yet there is still a significant part of the statist Left which sees this model as the mechanism for delivering socialist nirvana. It isn't. In contrast, the success of social democracy was its incrementalism and flexibility. Over time, incremental improvements – tried and tested on the ground – were shaped into a significant body of progress.

But not all of the contemporary Left has explicitly embraced the statism associated with past failures, partly because when they abandoned an analysis based upon class, they also abandoned economics. In its place, the woke Left have built a politics of nihilism, based upon identity and victimology. The nihilism of the Right is exemplified by a statement made by Steve Bannon, former strategist at Donald Trump's White House: 'I am a Leninist. Lenin wanted to destroy the state. That's my goal too. I want to bring everything crashing down and destroy all of today's establishment.' It is a revealing comment. In contrast, the nihilism of the Left is exemplified by a placard at a Black Lives Matter rally in 2020: 'New Gen, New System'. The struggle for a poorly identified future is predicated upon a perceived state of victimhood. We prefer politics based upon agency.

The woke Left is essentially a new religion; one that divides humanity into victims and their abusers. We have original sin in a peculiar form of (inverted) racism. It is currently identified as 'whiteness'. It is not entirely clear whether this is exemplified in the inherent racism of the transatlantic slave trade or caused by it. And whilst this original sin can be passed down through the generations, within secular religion, there is no place for redemption. But this sin and victimology is determined selectively, and absolutely does not include the Holocaust or the millennia of slavery that preceded and followed it. There is a catechism that must be taken on faith, giving primacy to the personal experience of a virtuous few rather than evidence; and which requires the persecution of any unbelievers.

Writing in 1901, Vladimir Lenin asked the infamous question: *What is to be Done?* At the time, that question concerned *how* the working class could move from merely fighting employers over wages and conditions, to actively embracing a broader political philosophy and movement. We believe Lenin's question is still the right one to ask of labour movements, even if our answers will be very different to his (which, unsurprisingly, involved the creation of an undemocratic vanguard that centralised power).

In 1995, the Labour Party introduced a new Clause Four of its constitution, which for almost a hundred years had called for the common ownership of industry. Under the reformist zeal of Tony Blair, that totemic old Labour definition of socialism was replaced with a paean to resilience that stated:

> *The Labour Party is a democratic socialist party. It believes that by the strength of our common endeavour we achieve more than we achieve alone, so as to create for each of us the means to realise our true potential and for all of us a community in which power, wealth and opportunity are in the hands of the many not the few; where the rights we enjoy reflect the duties we owe and where we live together freely, in a spirit of solidarity, tolerance and respect.*

Out went the commitment to nationalised industry; a stance that, while heavily criticised by the party's hard Left, has survived even beyond Jeremy Corbyn's worship of statist Labour.

What is it Labour wants to be in government to do? Is it, as Lenin believed, about a grand plan to introduce a 'socialist' programme? Inevitably that requires that we insist that the population does what it is told. The people may not want to be a part of the new millennium. Tough. If we have a programme that is the correct one, they will have to adapt until their consciousness has risen to an appropriate level. And if a person's consciousness fails to rise, well, that's what you have a Gulag for.

Except that we never believed in such statism. Newham was and is one of the poorest boroughs in the UK. We were in politics to make a difference to the lives of the people who lived there. The approach favoured by the statist Left suggested that we should be the provider of an ever-increasing bundle of services. We demurred. We were not going to take the mini-statist approach of doing everything for people, but we did want to create the infrastructure that enabled people to help themselves. If they chose to. If we were to achieve this ambition, it meant ensuring that each person had the capacity to make choices and decisions. It meant supporting the development of 'resilience': having sufficient understanding to exercise control, and then having the means and capacity to make informed choices. In 2011, following a major public (and internal party) consultation, we outlined our guiding principles in a document called *Quid Pro Quo*:

> *Resilience is much more than an ability to bounce back from a single damaging event. It is about possessing a set of skills and having access to the resources that allow us to negotiate the challenges that we all experience but also that allow people to overcome the more difficult circumstances many [face]… the approach builds on concepts such as capabilities, empowerment and research on social mobility.*
>
> *Our personal skills, experiences and upbringing are essential to our resilience, but these are intertwined with the resilience of the communities we live in and the economic circumstances we face. On the flip side, it is also vital to recognise the importance of character and personal responsibility and to ask more of people as citizens. There must be give and take, or a quid pro quo, for a fuller offer of support from the welfare state.*
>
> *That applies to all people, not just those at the bottom. The welfare state has always been about pooling and insuring against risk, but it should also be something more: a means by which we collectively support each other to achieve our potential in a way that we could not do alone. A good society and one that fairly reflects the contribution of all must also offer support to people higher*

up the income spectrum. Those who whilst not in crisis, nevertheless, need a leg up. Put simply the state should be there for people at times of success as well as need.

Income matters and is at the root of many of the challenges our residents and people across the UK face, particularly now as slow wage growth and inflation put ever more pressure on family budgets. But once the damage of living in poverty is done, it takes more than money to cultivate social mobility. We believe a lack of resilience and its key components – being able to bounce back from adversity, but also to access and use resources to help you succeed – keeps our residents and communities disadvantaged. It is important to be clear that resilience is not just about individual characteristics; it is also about whether our community and our economy make people stronger. A new welfare state must embody our collective values of fairness and reciprocity but also build that resilience and genuinely seek to overcome disadvantage, not just to ameliorate it.

There are many challenges for the welfare state. It should be more localised so that it is more accountable and responsive to local needs. Service boundaries must be broken down so that across the public sector we work together to deliver shared goals. However, in this paper we focus on the need for a more reciprocal welfare deal. We believe greater emphasis on reciprocity and reward for contribution will make the welfare state fairer and more effective in supporting and encouraging individuals and communities to build their resilience and capacity to succeed independently.

That's a long citation, but it hammers home the point about how we perceived the need for resilience, and how it informed our policy thinking.

Getting the most out of life is also about the economic environment. Hence, access to employment and a regular income is a critical part of resilience. However, economic resilience is not just about finance: work also gives our lives meaning and a sense of dignity. Indeed, it is intrinsic to good mental and physical health. Thus, personal and economic resilience are two sides of the same coin: we need both to thrive as individuals. So, for social democrats, redistributing income and wealth, while important, should not be the whole story. Individuals need to be encouraged and supported to develop the skills and capacity which will enable them to operate more effectively in our society. Only in this way will we genuinely increase levels of equality across society.

We believe that personal responsibility is a virtue. It is not the only one, but it is one that the contemporary Left often decries. But none of us exists as an island. We live in family groups and in communities. There is an enrichment to life and security in knowing that we are part of a wider group sharing life's joys and burdens. The state is the overarching representation of that community; it exists to protect and serve the wider community, not the other way around. That is a crucial difference between what social democrats believe and the views of top-down statists.

In our view, social policy should aim to support individual agency and independence. The principles underlying that policy should be to assist those who are able to get into active and productive life as soon as possible. In short, we believe strongly in putting some bounce back into the welfare safety net. In recent decades, however, a mindset of dependency has been created whereby, too often, someone else is expected to sort out problems. For example, in Newham we amended our housing allocation policy at a local level. Typically, Labour councils were inclined to offer access to subsidised housing based on need. It sounds good, eh? Those who didn't need subsidised housing didn't get it. But the result – nationally and locally – of this long-term policy had been to create social housing ghettos. A UK government-commissioned review of social housing by the academic John Hills identified this in 2007, but national politicians did little in response. The apparently rational, and even noble, needs-based sentiment had masked problems local people had known and complained about for decades. We saw it expressed in the following ways.

A couple decide to limit their family to two children because they know that is the number they can afford and support. Under a 'needs-based' scheme, they are unlikely ever to get help from the council. Next door, another couple, in all other respects identical to their neighbours, choose to have five children. They become eligible for help because of 'need' – because of overcrowding. Rightly or wrongly, in Newham many residents experienced this as queue-jumping. But worse fallout was to come. Frequently families originally from the Asian subcontinent were larger. So, the needs-based policy was perceived as giving preferential treatment to those families, and led to suggestions that some populations within the local community were being deliberately favoured. Of course, there was no such favouritism. But the lesson of the policy was clear: never underestimate the law of unintended consequences. People who had lived in Newham for generations saw new arrivals issued with access to housing that was denied to their children. The modern Left dismissed their criticisms as racist. They were wrong; but it was an easy and unthinking observation often made by those with comfortable incomes who owned their homes.

Another problem with the needs-based policy was that it mitigated against the sort of personal responsibility we wanted to support people to develop. Partly this was a political choice: most locals worked hard for forty years, and our view was that we should support them. Partly it was pragmatic: we had a waiting list of more than twenty-three thousand applicants and just over thirty thousand council and housing association properties. Only a few hundred of these homes became available each year, and we could never meet the excess demand. State support is effectively rationed. The unelectable statist Left can happily argue for expenditure on anything and everything (as Jeremy Corbyn did in 2019). But in the real world, support is rationed, and distributing it is challenging. Who should benefit from the limited subsidy available for housing? If one person benefits, another does not. That is the challenge of scarcity, and addressing that dilemma is real-world politics. Later, we discuss housing and demonstrate an approach to solve some of these problems, but it will take decades. Decades might seem too long, but Right to Buy took decades to destroy what our forebears had created.

As Newham's Mayor, Robin held regular surgeries. During one, a young man came to see him. He'd been in the care system, and had been provided with a one-bed council flat once he was of age. Now, aged about twenty-three and with no qualifications or job, he wanted to know when we would give him a house. He had never worked, and social services had never thought it necessary enough to help him get a job. What was to be done? Well, the council gave the appearance of caring. But in truth didn't. Newham Council had ticked all the relevant boxes in assisting this young man but had not equipped him with the personal tools necessary to make his way in the world. Worse, a mindset had been created in which the council, not the individual, was responsible for his future well-being.

As elected politicians, and as we saw it representatives of the community, we wanted to be there for the care leaver throughout his life, but we wanted that for all the borough's residents. We did not wish to dole out largesse, but to support people in meeting their needs and aspirations. Our view was that where people look to the state for support, they must be seen as individuals, and support must be properly tailored. Currently, public service is too often about ticking that box. Do you qualify as X or Y? It is not enough to treat an individual as a member of a disadvantaged group – we have gone past the era of the one-size-fits-all approach. Rather, we should be supporting people with singular development requirements or support needs. This might be basic maths and English, or a suit in which to attend an interview, or learning how to cook for yourself, or a low-cost loan to furnish your flat, or reconnecting with parents and family.

This is not to belittle the efforts of those working in public bodies to help individuals. But the systems, tools and philosophy currently in vogue are flawed. If lasting and meaningful change is to be achieved, virtues such as personal responsibility must be prioritised. As far as is possible, the language of needs should be confined to the dustbin of history. If someone only comes to the council when they need something, this will sustain a relationship of dependence (and in truth, only a minority of people benefit from such a system). It is a model which simply replaces the squire with the state. As people on the sensible Left, that's not a model we find attractive. But if the council is where someone goes to get *support* to achieve something, then the relationship could become more positive. We need a language of hope and realistic encouragement allied to genuine, tailored support to help someone overcome their challenges. We wanted to offer a hand up, not a handout. Essentially, we must place the individual at the centre of government efforts to support them to realise their full potential. There is also a need to support the development of community and social bonds that contribute to this aim. The eventual goal must be to encourage people to exercise control over their own environment. This requires that the individual be challenged and that councils care enough to help people change their lives, not just coddle them. We already do this with our own children: encouraging and challenging them to do better at school, to help them gain new skills in the hope that this will provide them with better options later in life.

As we have moved away from the battleground of class and the economy, the contemporary Left has sought to assert its moral ascendance because, in theory, we 'care' for people more than our political rivals. That care is illustrated by how we are willing to spend more (of taxpayers' money) on a particular group or service, or at least promise to do so. Caring and spending have become synonymous. But they shouldn't always be. In politics, spending can too easily be a way to buy off or avert criticism. It can also be an expression of that current fixation of the Left: virtue-signalling, or parading one's caring credentials without actually doing the work needed to solve the problem. A pound spent on Problem X is always a pound unavailable to address Problem Y. This is true in times of plenty and times of hardship. Before we spend any pound raised through someone else's hard work, we have a responsibility to make sure it has a chance of making things better. Historically, throwing money at an immediate problem has been an approach used by both the Left and the Right. We understand why: it often buys time or diverts criticism. But it is not always a way to solve underlying problems, the roots of which are usually more complex than a mere lack of resources.

Resilience is an attempt to bring about greater equality by working with the individual to develop skills that enable them to access more of what society offers. It's a simple example, but the ability to cook nutritious meals is a cheaper alternative than buying pre-prepared food, and can provide a better life without changing the broader economic situation of an individual or family.

But why do some people survive on (what are hardly generous) benefits, while others dependent on welfare are always in difficulty? The answer to such questions is never simple. While we'd be fools to ignore the fact that resources remain important, we must go beyond the economic when confronting problems. When discussing equality, personal capacity should also be a key consideration. Resilience can be expressed in the language of rights and responsibilities. People should have rights to services which will help them to progress, but must also play their part and take their own responsibilities seriously. This is related to the concept of agency, or the ability and responsibility to act. Resilience is a means to provide the practical, personal and psychological support to realise agency within our population. It has an added advantage in that it is seen to be fair. It builds on the idea that rights are allied to responsibilities. The British public believes that we should help others, but they also think that others should help themselves. In the 2015 Britain Uncovered survey, 95% of respondents thought it was important that healthcare should be free (78% very; 17% quite). Yet, interestingly, some 78% thought that where treatment was required as a result of alcohol or drug abuse (including smoking), individuals should pay (22% always; 56% sometimes). Despite the fondness for the NHS within the majority of the population, there is still a desire to see elements of reciprocity. People think that is only fair.

In Newham, through personal capacity development we sought to place the power to make decisions in an individual's hands. We wanted people to work: it was the only route out of poverty for most, but it was also an expression of their taking responsibility for their lives and the lives of those around them. But it is incumbent on society to ensure that people at work receive a wage that enables them to benefit from employment.

Resilience is also a powerful argument for Labour to support the principle behind Universal Credit – if not the appalling and stupid way in which it was implemented. The idea that, if we work, we get to share in some of the benefits of society seems unanswerable. However, the response from some on the Left was to call for the abolition of Universal Credit rather than its reform – they would rather virtue-signal than work out how to effectively implement policies that make a real difference to working people; criticise rather than improve. Surely when the gig economy is making wage packets less predictable, proper support for workers should be a rallying cry for social democrats?

For the sake of clarity, and to address the intellectual miasma that has clouded Left-wing thinking since the 1960s, the implications of this need to be stressed: we believe that those who work, or who seek to work, should receive greater support than those who do not. And just to avoid the inevitable criticism that this will generate, we are talking about a comparison of like with like: a seventeen-year-old male with a seventeen-year-old male; a wheelchair user with a wheelchair user; a blind woman with a blind woman. This is not an argument for restricting support or services to those who need them. Everyone who wants to improve their life should be supported irrespective of their abilities. Nor is it about imposing moral judgements or differential benefit levels. It is about ensuring that those who wish to change their circumstances are helped by the state to do so.

The objective of social democrats should be to ensure that through the development of resilience, everybody who can be helped into some form of work, (and hence some form of contribution to society), should be. The provisions in the welfare state were always meant to provide a safety net to support people in difficult times, for a limited time, except in particular cases where there was an ongoing problem. Potentially, the concept of supporting workers is a powerful weapon for social democrats. The ability to say that the state supports people in helping themselves detoxifies the welfare benefits debate and makes it politically possible to offer a more generous entitlement for those who genuinely cannot work. However, if people are trying and social democrats are not there for them, they can hardly be blamed for losing faith. If we cannot deliver that which makes a difference to people's lives, then what is the point of social democracy? Social democrats have not been critical enough of our own failures; nor faced up to the implication that if we continue to operate as we have done – without reforming systems that have not worked, or that have become outdated – then it is not in the electorate's interest to support us.

Social democrats have historically pursued policies that support aspirational people who, in turn, have rewarded us with votes. When this group is no longer our top priority, when our focus is somewhere else (for example on any number of self-identifying victim groups), then the bond is broken, and their support and their votes go elsewhere. It was our experience that this approach was approved of by our voters: the work described in the following chapters resulted in residents' satisfaction levels with our council services surging to 81% locally, with only 6% expressing dissatisfaction. Incredibly, that meant that even some local Tory voters must have liked what the council was doing! Indeed, our residents' satisfaction levels compared favourably with other parts of the country. Polling by the Local Government Association found that average satisfaction levels for councils were around 64%. What made Newham's outperformance even more impressive was highlighted by work undertaken by the independent polling firm Ipsos MORI, which produced an Area Challenge Index estimating the ease of achieving positive perceptions given local circumstances. Newham had a MORI index score of one hundred, indicating that it was *the* most challenging place in the country to achieve satisfaction among residents. The council in the next most difficult area had an index score of eighty-eight. So, Newham really was in a league of its own in terms of resident satisfaction.

A major contribution to satisfaction is the extent to which people feel they can influence the council. We adopted a simple (but some might say radical) approach to this issue by asking people what was important to them and then responding. You might think that sounds obvious. But believe us, organisations and political leaderships wedded to dogma or tradition, rather than committed to continuous improvement, are not exactly good at listening to voters' concerns. And we didn't just listen in the way that some inept politicians do, by only organising 'community' meetings with the same small but committed group of activists. Newham is home to one third of a million people from all over the world. We quickly recognised that discussions with the same small group would not provide a representative sample of the community's voice. Of course, we held meetings, focus groups and personal interviews when specific groups of people were affected by particular proposals – for example, changes to housing estates or parking schemes. But we wanted more. Our answer was to survey independently, regularly and often, to ensure that a broader range of local views was fully understood. So, we introduced regular and ad hoc surveys focusing on residents, tenants, leaseholders, young people and other groups. In addition, we introduced a major 'longitudinal survey' of residents that we believe was unique among UK councils. Indeed, we thought so highly of the views reflected in that survey that it became the only area of council planning in which Robin insisted on being the first person to see the results. All other policy proposals involved officer input, but we firmly believed that elected representatives should interpret residents' views without prior screening by officers.

From the early days of the mayoralty, listening to people and responding to what they said was central to our approach. So, in 2009 Andy Byrom, the associate director of MORI, reported that:

Ratings are higher in the London Borough of Newham for feelings of influence than anywhere else in England.

After seven years of the mayoralty, people knew that they were being listened to, and they appreciated it. Only when we explain this background do people grasp why support for the council exceeded 80%. Outsiders found it hard to believe, but we also expanded some areas of our work while making savings elsewhere. The resilience agenda was never about cost-cutting. It was a means to deliver services and programmes that our residents needed, and at the optimum cost.

Chapter 2

DELIVERING IN NEWHAM: BETTER SERVICES FOR LESS

There are two times when you should outsource. When the private sector can do the same job more cheaply and when they can do it better. If neither of these things were true, why would you bother?
(Richard Gooding, former chief executive of London City Airport)

The language of priorities is the religion of socialism.
(Nye Bevan)

Newham is north of the Thames, in the east of London between the Lea and Roding rivers. Casual readers may know it as the home of West Ham United Football Club and the Queen Elizabeth Olympic Park.

Historically the area was the south-western limit of the Danelaw. London lay across the Lea to the west, while East Ham and West Ham were mainly in Essex. And so they remained until local government reorganisation in the 1960s merged the two county boroughs into a single London borough with the inspired name of Newham. The nineteenth century saw rapid growth locally, which transformed a collection of scattered hamlets into an industrial heartland driven by engineering and trade, the beating heart of which was the Royal Docks. The docks generated wealth, but the area surrounding them was riven by poverty. After World War II, containerisation moved trade towards the coast, and the docks closed in the 1970s. This was the beginning of a blight of unemployment that would dog the area for decades.

Cheap housing in the 1960s made the area attractive to new immigrants, making Newham the most diverse community on the planet. Other areas of London, including Brent and Haringey, also lay claim to this accolade but, of course, they are wrong. There is a dynamism about Newham that comes from the mixture of its people and customs which makes it an exciting place to be; where people with radically different outlooks and backgrounds seek to work out how to occupy the same space. For example, the 2011 census recorded Newham as the most religious borough in the country. But even local experts would be hard pushed to name every religion it celebrates. With a population of 350,000, Newham is also one of the most populous boroughs in London – and this figure is expected to rise to 450,000. Too, it has one of London's youngest populations, with almost half of residents aged under thirty.

For decades, Newham has been one of the poorest areas of London, with unemployment rates above the capital's average. It also consistently ranked among the lowest on indices of multiple deprivations. For decades, poverty was rife, and the unpopular local council was nowhere to be seen. When Newham entered a new decade in 1990, just 40% of residents thought the authority was doing 'a good job', and only 28% thought it was 'efficient and well run'. Hostility towards the borough was often merited. In the 1980s and '90s, Newham's children performed poorly in educational achievement. There was, of course, a vigorous defence by educationalists claiming that education was not really about getting qualifications, but about learning for its own sake. Such people argued that we should not measure local achievement by exam passes. As young politicos, we thought this was nonsense. It was a theory attractive to education unions, but not necessarily to people like us, who cared about changing the life chances of disadvantaged children. But by the early 1990s, it was not just the local education sector that was poorly run. The local environment was poor too; yet, due to internal issues, council resources were not always targeted on improvement. For example, before London City Airport was built, cleansing staff cleaned the large site and received a special payment for their labour. After the airport was built, staff no longer had to clear the area – but continued to receive the bonus regardless. A huge waste of local taxpayers' money, and cash that could have been spent on improving other parts of the borough.

In the early '90s, a common set of performance indicators for London's boroughs showed Newham in the bottom three for almost all services. Aggregating the league placings for each measure, Newham ranked as the third worst of the capital's thirty-two boroughs – just above Lambeth and Hackney. Newham Council was complacent, ineffective and inefficient, and staggered from crisis to crisis with no overarching vision. Around this time, several like-minded Labour Party members decided enough was enough. We believed the time had come for radical action to improve matters.

In November 1995, Robin was elected as leader of Newham. Over the next few years, we began to consolidate our hold on the council. In 1997, the election of Tony Blair's New Labour government – an identifiably social democratic movement – meant that our local change agenda matched that sweeping through the corridors of power. Clive was elected in a Newham by-election on the same evening that Blair swept to power.

We are politicians of the liberal Left. Historically, the liberal Left was free-thinking. It opposed dogmatism, whether that came from the church or the organs of the state. It supported the poor, but did so to help people get out of poverty. It believed in many freedoms: personal, physical, and of thought and speech. To the liberal Left, ultimately, what you did allowed someone to judge your character, and your character was more important than the way in which you phrased something. Martin Luther King's words still resonate for us: we seek to judge people by the content of their character rather than the colour of their skin – or, for that matter, the school they attended, the football team they support, the job they do, the way they worship, or the party they voted for.

For clarity, there has also always been an illiberal Left. The history of the twentieth century is littered with the bodies of the 'beneficiaries' of authoritarian Left-wing governments. Generally expressed in terms of their application of Marxism, such regimes have variously sought to create the 'new man' or rebuild society from scratch.

Assuming that at least some of our readers may be under thirty years old and, as such, somewhat less familiar with the history of the Left, we will pause here to provide much-abbreviated 'highlights'. The principal date is 1917, the year of the Russian Revolution's overthrow of the autocratic Tsarist state. Unfortunately, the communist alternative turned out to be in many ways worse than the Tsarist autocracy it replaced. Not only was it more brutal – in its use of Gulags, for example – but it demonstrated that 'benign' central planning was neither benign nor very good at planning. The brutality of Left-wing governments towards their own people was, and remains, staggering. 'But so,' we hear you say, 'has been the brutality of corrupt dictatorships, tribal despots and theocratic tyrannies.' True. But they are not – and never claimed to be – democratic. Japan, the Republic of Korea, and Taiwan show how autocratic regimes can transition, but Pol Pot's Year Zero experiment and the Laotian People's Republic suggest that communism was never the answer.

None of the shortcomings of democracies have come close to authoritarian regimes when it comes to brutality. Democracy, for all its failings, remains the least worst of political systems currently on offer. Those countries that embrace it score better on both freedom and material wealth indices. This is why our social democrats in Newham have always been wary of dogma, even when it is espoused by those who operate within democratic states. Dogmatists seek to impose both a direction of travel and how it must be achieved. If they do not get to their destination, that failure is blamed on somebody else. It is never the fault of the dogma, nor of those giving the orders.

Our approach was always more pragmatic. In Left-wing circles, pragmatism is nearly always referred to negatively. By contrast, ideology is set on a pedestal. It is the subject of endless debate, schism and conflict. Ideology contains a purity, an ideal, and a permanent (and, we would argue, always unrealised) promise of a better tomorrow. Those unswervingly committed to it become good at making abstruse points, not because they understand an issue, but because they spend more time down rabbit holes, endlessly arguing about what constitutes the purest commitment to their particular ideology. But most people spend their lives above ground and away from rabbit holes. They don't think in purely ideological terms, and nor should they, because they live and work in the real world. While workers, the unemployed, the mentally ill or immigrants are often central to the narrative of the dogmatic Left, such groups rarely benefit from the practical implementation of hard-Left policy. Instead, the language of care is deployed to demonstrate virtue even as a pragmatic approach to improving individuals' lives is eschewed.

Pragmatism, by contrast, should be the product of political principle – by dealing with the mundane world in which one generation or group actually seeks to make things better for those who follow. On taking over a poor-performing Newham Council, we purposefully adopted a pragmatic approach to running the borough and sought to apply the principles of scientific method to the development and implementation of policy, so that what we did could be tested and assessed to make it work.

For the ideologue, if something doesn't work, someone must be blamed – usually somebody who does not espouse quite the same ideology. At Newham, particularly in the early days of our leadership, such attitudes were often demonstrated by long-serving councillors who did not share our pragmatism. When confronted with a local problem, one woke councillor (who shall remain anonymous) declared to us, 'I don't care how you plan to fix it; I just want to know who to blame.' It summed up the attitude behind the many problems we had inherited. For the pragmatist, if you try something new and it does not work, you don't blame somebody. Instead, you have increased your knowledge base and simply try something different and better.

When we entered politics, it was to improve the world around us. But failures are part of politics, and you learn how to avoid them through being flexible, pragmatic, determined and undogmatic. Some of the things we wanted to do forty years ago, we would not want to do now, because we now understand that they don't work. We learned from our own experiences and mistakes, and those of others. And one of the biggest things we learned was that people are more important than ideology or dogma.

That is not to say that we were not tribal. We were and still are. When we took office, our core constituency was people like our parents: those who worked hard, played by the rules, and took responsibility for their actions and families. Their religion, skin colour or sex did not matter (of course, all of them do matter, but not in this equation). Their willingness to be part of a dynamic Britain and play an active part in their local community mattered. Our people rarely scaled glittering heights or earned millions. But they were the backbone of this country and every country. Such people formed the majority of Newham's population.

This did not mean that we were oblivious to other members of our community. But the well-off didn't really need us (save to improve their children's schools, fix the roads that took them to their well-paid jobs, and keep their streets clean). Those who were poor did. So, our aim was to set a policy framework that worked across every department, seeking to encourage locals to become more self-reliant. This was a matter of principle and pragmatism. Benefits, for example, were necessary but not sufficient. The way out of poverty was for people to make a decision to change; we aimed to support them, but we could not do it for them. There was a quid pro quo.

In this regard, we were the antithesis of the current woke/ intersectional agenda. Our reading of the intersectional agenda is that the greater the number of intersecting 'oppressions' you have, the greater the degree to which somebody else should bail you out. In stark contrast, we sought to build agency. It is not that we didn't believe that the wider community should offer support to its members in hard times; we absolutely did. But we didn't believe in rewarding victimhood, real or imagined. We were ready to offer extra help to those in our community who needed it – but they had to be willing to make an effort to take up the offer. Ultimately, this support was an extra cost borne by the wider community. But we believed it was worth it, both in terms of long-term savings to the public purse (for example, by helping people develop skills that helped them land jobs and thus reducing welfare bills) and because it helped people live more fulfilling lives.

We saw ourselves as representatives of the community. We believed, and still do, that the community would always support initiatives that genuinely change people's life chances. You only have to look at responses to the Covid-19 pandemic to see the true nature of people and how they look out for each other. This was the policy of resilience described in the previous chapter. If people are to be able to exercise genuine choice, they need a reasonable income sufficient to live on, a bit with which to enjoy themselves, and some, perhaps, to save. To achieve this, they need a job. We set ourselves firmly on the pragmatic path to support people to increase their resilience and thereby the options available to them. Initially, we focused on driving up standards of public service in the borough. Our approach was pretty routine for a New Labour-led council at the time, being essentially managerialist. Our analysis of Newham Council was that it had been poorly managed with little focus on delivering quality services in a cost-effective manner. So, we focused on outcomes and demanded more from the entire organisation. 'What gets measured, gets managed' became a key motto as we sought to drive up performance standards. Another mantra, 'What matters is what works', has since been discredited in Labour circles – and to our shame, because it focused minds on success in circumstances in which public services had previously been so poor. Revisionists to the Left of us scoffed, but that approach to delivery worked because it recognised that services are for people not bureaucracies, and need to be the best they can be, irrespective of how well funded they are. It was a soundbite, yes, but also a response to the long and bitter experience of public services failing to deliver what people deserved: a pragmatic response.

And we were not the only group to succeed through this approach. The broader Blair government went against Labour orthodoxy and introduced the concept of best value: delivering quality services at the best price even if that meant using private companies. Despite initiating steady improvements across health and education, the government was damned for this heresy by particular forces on the 'Left' which claimed to care about public services such as the NHS.

Public services are constrained by two competing dogmas. The first asserts that only bodies managed within the public sector can or should provide services. This was the traditional, pre-Blairite view of delivery within Labour, and returned during the recent Corbyn years. The second states that 'Private is always better'; a view often espoused by the Thatcherite wing of Conservatism which repeatedly sought to roll back the frontiers of the state.

The reality, of course, is that neither view is accurate. We found, early in our tenure, that what matters is what works. Without question, some state-provided services worked well. But equally, we found that outsourcing to high-quality private partners produced results when contracts were well managed. For a brief period from the late 1990s through to the 2010s, this 'mixed economy' approach was largely promoted within Labour. But, as with so many social democratic successes, the idea began to fall out of favour after the financial crash of 2008. As a consequence, the Labour Party has still not, deep in its psyche, fully resolved its issues with outsourcing and privatisation.

Outsourcing was, initially, hugely successful in driving down costs and driving up quality. Those who remember the disgraceful state of direct labour organisations before privatisation owe it to younger people to tell the truth. As an example, for years, politicians in London did little about the Inner London Education Authority (ILEA), then one of the most expensive and worst-performing education authorities in the UK. Despite high spending, results for children across the ILEA were far below England's national average. To explain the underperformance, it was said that schools were working in difficult circumstances with many difficult children. But those very same schools, teachers and children saw results improve dramatically under Education Secretary David Blunkett's more flexible initiatives. It transpired that it wasn't the kids who couldn't learn, nor the teachers who couldn't teach. Rather, it was the education sector's leadership who talked the talk but failed to walk the walk. They lacked ambition for the children under their care. As a 1980 report by the Education Inspectorate said:

Too many secondary schools expect too little from their pupils at all levels.

With the benefit of hindsight, many in local government would admit that the inefficiencies of the 1980s were legion. Across education and other sectors, the introduction of competition and outsourcing drove down costs through increased efficiency and, in part, assaults on workers' terms and conditions. However, nothing stands still and each action in politics has a reaction (not necessarily equal, but a reaction nonetheless). In response to competitive pressure, many local authorities upped their game. They improved delivery to ensure that in-house service provision became more competitive. At the same time, there was a reaction across the private sector. Easy profits gleaned from trumping previously poor in-house services led to larger and less efficient companies growing fat and lazy on the back of generous public contracts. In particular, the natural result of competition was to create an ever-smaller number of companies that did not necessarily favour the competition that would drive both service improvement *and* lower cost.

The Right, of course, wanting to minimise the state's size for ideological reasons, has always been interested in driving down the cost and range of public services as a matter of dogma. As a result, instead of debating what people wanted to achieve through public services and focusing on how to drive improvement and efficiency, the Right has tended to focus on an ideological 'big state becoming little' top-down approach. Those on the Right often lack a clear narrative about what they think we should seek to achieve through the state. Consequently, on this issue, they are intellectually bankrupt. So, having driven efficiencies through the intensification of outsourcing, many on the Right have simply vacated the field.

But we digress.

In Newham, we found that the 'private versus public'

debate was sterile and pointless. Irrespective of who owned the delivery vehicle, the key was to focus on *what* was to be delivered: outcomes, not inputs. Translating requirements into clear objectives, with equally clear incentives and disincentives for delivery organisations, determined service quality. Either you believe that services are for the public, in which case you examine the options, or you follow your chosen dogma and, since you are not open to effective scrutiny, make mistakes and ultimately achieve nothing. By pursuing an outcomes-based approach and not being dogmatic about provision, we improved to become the highest-rated council in London according to the common set of measurements mentioned earlier.

But it was not all plain sailing. We experimented with some outsourcing which proved a mistake. For example, our in-house Housing Benefit service had performed less than satisfactorily for many years. We were keen to improve the service and drive down costs, and the obvious way (or so we initially thought) was to get the private sector to run the operation more efficiently. So, we determined to outsource the service, against some political opposition from dogmatic 'Old Labour' councillors. The results were eyebrow-raising – but in all the wrong ways. The outsourcing giant Capita made an already poor situation much worse. So much worse, in fact, that we had to perform a swift U-turn and bring the service back in-house. It was a salutary lesson that changed our understanding of service delivery and influenced our future delivery models. We came to understand that external competition had become limited, even though in-house delivery mechanisms left much to be desired. As far as Housing Benefit was concerned, neither public nor private provision seemed too enticing. What to do in that situation? The answer was staring us in the face: become the improvement. In these particular circumstances, the advantage of in-house provision was that we could drive improvements by exercising active and continuous pressure on the department. But we only arrived at that hands-on model through trial and error – and the flexibility which comes from avoiding dogma.

In Newham, our view was that public services exist to serve the public (the clue is in the name!). What was paramount was the benefit to residents and taxpayers, not the council's proprietorial interests, nor those of the people delivering the services. And we were prepared to fight for that concept. We started to describe residents as 'customers'. Again, some on the hard Left scoffed at the term, but we wanted to imply that residents exercised choice over the services we provided, and that they were central to our thinking, rather than mere passive recipients of council benevolence (which they had paid for). Around the same time, some state organisations outside Newham began to use the term 'clients' to replace 'residents'. But for us, 'client' smacked of dependency. We wanted to place less emphasis on dependency and instead encourage the idea that residents should be empowered.

In addition to driving service improvements, we recognised that when paying for services we were dealing with other people's money. That meant we had to have a good reason for taking money off people, particularly when the instrument of taxation – council tax – was the most regressive in the UK. Additionally, there was a determination to ensure that when public money was spent, it was spent effectively. People earn money; it belongs to them. It is essential that when money is taken from them through tax or fees, there is a demonstrable reason for, and an outcome from, that action.

You would be surprised how many politicians do not actually agree with this. A constant refrain from the middle-class Anywheres and from our Corbynite wing was that council tax, which hits the working poor hardest, should be increased to provide well-paid middle-class jobs in public service. That's not quite how they phrased it, but it was the reality of their desire. According to an Institute for Fiscal Studies report published in 2019:

The system of direct taxes (income tax, NICs[1] and council tax) and benefits reduces inequality... But council tax is regressive. Even after accounting for council tax support (which reduces council tax liabilities for low income families), the poorest tenth of the population pay 8% of their income in council tax, while the next 50% pay 4–5% and the richest 40% pay 2–3%.

This concerned us, given our population. So, for ten years, we froze council tax in Newham until residents were paying the third-lowest average council tax in the country. It was, unsurprisingly, electorally popular. But when the Corbyn-inspired Labour council that eventually replaced us came to power, it reported that the poor council had suffered as a result of the freeze. Its report stated:

This has contributed to Newham having the lowest council tax in outer London but had council tax been increased by the maximum amount available in each of those years the council would have collected c£82m additional cash over the period and would now be receiving an additional c£19m per year in its ongoing budget.

We were more than a little alarmed to read such nonsense. In our view, the council should not be seen as having a life of its own. It is – or should be – the expression of community will. Any resources or assets it holds, it does so on behalf of the community. The reality is that people in Newham, a very poor area, kept £82 million in their pockets. It was their money, but the current generation of woke Newham councillors and leaders think that the cash somehow belonged to them. There is something contemptuous about an attitude in politicians that

---

1   National Insurance contributions.

views residents simply as the means to facilitate their spending plans. It also hides an unwillingness or inability to manage both budgets and organisations. For many people on low incomes in Newham and elsewhere, council tax represents their biggest and most obvious tax burden. While in office, we felt it was right to ease that burden.

But even as the current Tory government has been putting a greater burden on the poorest by cutting government support, we find it interesting that the new generation of middle-class and Corbynite 'socialists' in Newham wanted to increase spending using a tax that hits the working poor hardest. Those who assert most loudly that they champion the interests of the working class seem more than happy to pursue economic policies which hurt that same demographic the most. In Newham we experienced pressure from within the party to increase council tax, and there remain those for whom increasing taxes is more popular than the work of making services more efficient. We suspect that this is a symptom of a national phenomenon.

Having said that, we recognise that the provision of public services is necessary in a civilised society. Indeed, the smooth working of our economy necessitates high-quality and adequately funded services. The Right is fundamentally opposed to state intervention, regarding it as costly and unnecessary. The hard Left is ideologically programmed to support public spending, irrespective of outcome. Both views are wrong. It is when the spending is not rigorously tested, and the benefits of it not examined, that public expenditure becomes an unnecessary burden. When that burden is exercised through council tax, then truly it is 'for the few, not the many' – even if implemented under the banner of the red rose.

So, we were proud to have frozen council tax for much of our time in office. And what's more, over that period, there were no meaningful service cuts in Newham other than those we wanted to make for their own sake. Our income was constrained by a self-imposed council tax ceiling; yet we nevertheless drove improvements because we focused on value for money and identifying more efficient ways to deliver without pulling front-line services. It can be done, but you must manage that process carefully.

Since we left office, we'd argue that subsequent increases in Newham's council tax have not led to improved services. Instead, they have been used to cover the budget deficits of the new Labour-led administration, which has also implemented substantial cuts. In our view, the new regime has failed to effectively monitor its performance and delivery. Its hands are not on the steering wheel.

In reviewing an early draft of this book, we were reminded by a friend of some words that were purportedly spoken by Charles I: 'There is more to the doing than bidding it be done.' Without the means to deliver them, great ideas are so much wishful thinking. Our achievements in Newham reflected our belief in the scientific method as applied to public service. We know that method works; we see the results of its application elsewhere in everyday life. Ask a question, research it, propose a hypothesis, test your hypothesis, record and analyse, draw conclusions, act, measure, and test again. Yet there have been few serious attempts to apply this approach to public policy – and Newham, among other political bodies, appears recently to have cast it aside in favour of a return to dogma or old ways of attempting public service delivery. In the absence of scientific-style measurement and assessment, that's akin to crossing one's fingers and hoping that things work out.

The market provides a mechanism that delivers an objective value of something. But government is about more than producing widgets for the lowest price. Some externalities can only be addressed by public policy. For example, what are the environmental costs of different production processes, and how do we ensure that these costs are properly included in the final price? How do you ensure, for example, that carbon costs are factored into a final price? Public policy in this area, particularly taxation, should seek to address these issues. Taxing externalities provides an incentive for scientific advance. However, public service often has no easy way of measuring outcomes, especially when dealing with people. There are many services competing for resources; hence the resonance of Bevan's quote about priorities at the beginning of this chapter. We need a way of evaluating outcomes that is as objective as possible – which is extraordinarily difficult.

This was what gave our approach to resilience resonance. If you believe resilience is what needs to be delivered, then you have something against which you can measure outcomes and apply empirical methods. When we determined that resilience was our objective, we spent some time explaining what that meant for the council's approach to residents. We wanted, and got, genuine buy-in from officers and like-minded councillors; and spent time explaining it to, and in turn getting support from, the local Labour Party. Critically important was that since executive members of the council were signed up to the principle, they acted as community representatives rather than as mouthpieces for services. That gave us a language to use when evaluating initiatives and services. The most important driver of services and financial savings in the mid noughties was achieving consensus across the council, which meant that everything we did begged the question: 'Is it delivering increased resilience?'

One problem created by virtue-signalling that bedevils politics is that everything becomes a priority. When the United Nations set its infamous Sustainable Development Goals – measures and targets to 'transform the world' by 2030 – it listed seventeen key goals and an incredible 169 priorities for investment. 169 priorities! That meant, in effect, that nothing was a priority because almost everything was deemed equally important. Funnily enough, the world has since struggled to deliver the UN's goals. The paradox was that, in showing that it cared about so many issues equally, the UN failed to prioritise, and delivered much less than it might have done. In office, we wanted to avoid such mistakes. It takes courage to defend priorities, as Nye Bevan realised. Resilience gave us a yardstick to measure priorities and actions.

Delivery of services by the state is confounded by a profusion of objectives and targets, and consequently it is difficult to identify poor performance. Every time another objective is added, it makes it harder for management to deliver and provides another excuse for not delivering what is really important. This is not to say that there shouldn't be objectives; just that there should not be too many. To achieve this, there needs to be clarity about priorities and the people in charge of commissioning services need to know what they want. But, as we discovered early on in Newham, those two things are often not in place.

Another problem we had to avoid when it came to targets or priorities was that people asked to deliver political priorities often developed a tendency to 'game' any measurements to produce the desired result – an approach of little benefit to any service or community. For example, when Blair's government first introduced the four-hour target for hospital accident and emergency (A&E) waiting times, it undoubtedly improved performance. However, over time bureaucrats sought to game the system rather than face the penalties and opprobrium of failure. So, corners began to be cut. Patients were not registered when they first arrived at A&E, or were kept outside in ambulances or sometimes admitted on trollies in pop-up wards; all tricks designed to help officials meet their target, but of absolutely no use whatsoever to patients or taxpayers.

Problems with metrics to control outcomes are now so well understood that we have even seen the development of 'laws' to describe them. Campbell's Law, for example, states that

'The more any quantitative social indicator is used for social decision-making, the more subject it will be to corruption pressures and the more apt it will be to distort and corrupt the social processes it is intended to monitor.' The British version – Goodhart's Law – states that 'any observed statistical regularity will tend to collapse once pressure is placed upon it for control purposes'. What these laws do not say, however, is that a measure will only distort when incentives are distorted. If you own a small company and a measure is vital to that company's financial success, you will pay great attention to it. You are hardly likely to game it to convince yourself that your finances are better than they are (though we accept that this rule does not apply to larger companies). By contrast, if you work in a bureaucracy, it is more likely that all that matters is to hit your target, no matter the implications for the long-term health of the company.

The most important measure for any company, and (usually) even for the public sector, is finance. Almost all organisations have substantial internal or external teams that monitor their spending (finance officers, auditors etc.). They usually also have clear desired outcomes (such as reducing debt) linked to their budget. They pay great attention to these figures because they know that the organisation is toast if they muck up their finances over the long term. So, if this approach works for finance, why not for other key measures?

Obviously, as the number of measures increases, any monitoring programme becomes onerous, and you have to ensure that you avoid measuring things badly. The infrastructure necessary to monitor finance alone is considerable. But we strongly believed that if we identified the key measures that would build resilience and improve outcomes for locals, then it would be possible to monitor and improve them. For different levels of management, key measures will be different. The person in charge of many operations must see what is going on at a strategic level, while managers delivering services need other measures to tell them what is happening day-to-day. In either scenario, too many indicators lead to an unfocused manager chasing too many targets.

In science, objective measurement is prized. As the Royal Society's website explains, the organisation's motto, 'Nullius in verba', is taken to mean 'Take nobody's word for it.' It is an expression of scientists' determination to withstand authority and verify all statements by facts determined by experiment. That approach contrasts with the current zeitgeist that elevates the value of 'lived experience' as a way of evaluating policy. Which is correct? Next time you start your car engine, get a vaccination, or even log into Twitter to describe how your lived experience is more important than empiricism, it's worth reflecting for a few seconds on how many of these inventions were the product of someone's lived experience rather than years of dedicated testing and experimentation. There is a point to the Western obsession with measurement and detail.

In our view, measurement of systems also needs to be (as far as possible) replicable and subject to scrutiny. Delivering effectively within a complex organisation requires an independent monitoring system that identifies and negates potential gaming. This thinking is not new. For years, it has been understood that it is important to focus on what is important. As Mark Twain said:

Behold, the fool saith, "Put not all thine eggs in the one basket" – which is but a manner of saying, "Scatter your money and your attention"; but the wise man saith, "Put all your eggs in the one basket and WATCH THAT BASKET."

Focus on what is important and do not allow any element of gaming the figures to creep in.

This is where our commitment to resilience comes in. By requiring our services to focus on delivering resilience, we had a good reason to reduce the volume of measures or targets locally. This was crucial to Newham: build systems informed by evidence and focused on policy outcomes.

In the early years of this experiment, we endured some criticism that Newham had significant ambition that was not being fully realised. Through our managerial approach, we had created relatively efficient services and raised Newham to the same standard as the best councils across the country. Recognising that efficiency was important, we had also created a stable financial environment which meant that council tax was relatively low. But we were not yet changing lives – and that's what we had entered politics to achieve. So we felt we had not yet succeeded. But as local resilience developed in areas such as employment and skills, our approach began to pay off. The determination to save money and still deliver quality services was a powerful combination that supported our resilience ambitions. Several robust initiatives were pursued, supported by a cadre of council officers who gradually understood what we were trying to achieve.

For example, the most important single initiative we undertook was the purchase of large new council offices in 2010 and the move away from several older sites. At first, this initiative – which brought many of our staff under one roof – was criticised by our opponents. But by 2018, Newham had saved £70 million in accommodation costs alone; money that could be reinvested in front-line services. By bringing together the council's operation in one place, a wide range of further efficiency savings and service quality improvements were made possible. Subsequently, many UK councils have copied Newham and sought to bring their services closer together physically speaking.

As we developed our thinking around resilience, it became clear that we would need new resources. Not only did we want to deliver high-quality existing services, but we wanted to expand into new areas of delivery to support even greater local resilience. After the financial crash in 2008, it was also clear that some form of austerity was coming and central government support (usually paid to councils in the form of grants) would be rationed. It was a shrewd prediction: Newham eventually faced central government funding cuts of £138 million between 2010 and 2021. The borough responded by identifying savings of more than £200 million, meaning we could implement changes without slashing our most essential services. Many councils saw their core Whitehall grants cut by more than 50%, failed to plan effectively, and watched as primary local services took a hit. Thus, if we wanted to continue to provide the services we valued across Newham, we had to consider radical changes to the ways in which we delivered those services. As a council unafraid to explain our priorities, we also bit the bullet and, in an age of austerity, asked tough questions to identify which activities were of no value. After the financial crash, we quickly realised that 'business as usual' would not create the savings necessary to retain all of Newham's services – particularly when demand for, and the cost of providing, adults' and children's social services soared due to austerity. This required a radical look at how Newham delivered vital services.

We determined that we could not make intelligent decisions on spending unless we knew the fine details of key services' cost and likely outcomes. It was clear that while we had made progress on this in our early years, we still had a way to go in this new landscape of scarcity. We were used to dealing with large budgets which covered several 'main' services and hid a multitude of additional (often unproductive) support services. We knew the gross sums but not the detail. Consequently, no one could tell us what we were buying or exactly how much it cost. We believe this remains an all-too-common situation for politicians and many officials at a local and a national level. But if we were going to make rational spending decisions, we needed to know the facts.

Our solution was to approach each area of the council's spending and service provision as if it were an independent business. That is not to say that we treated elderly residents with Alzheimer's in the same way that we looked to purchase new dustbin lorries. But just as we specified what we wanted for refuse lorries, we could specify what we wanted in services for elderly and disabled adults. Often, we found that we were paying for things that we didn't want or need – especially when it came to those hidden 'extra' service requirements. But more of that later.

Essentially, our programme recognised that delivery needed to be tied to performance. To do that, there needed to be a few clear objectives measured by a small number of performance measures. Achieving those objectives had to include incentives for the workforce. Getting agreement on that necessity was enormously time-consuming and required considerable political input. But priorities should be the business of politicians.

The problems that face large bureaucracies and inevitably lead to sclerosis are well documented and you will revisit many of them in this text. But we believe the only way to challenge this and drive efficiency in the public sector is through genuine competition. For that competition to be real, there must be a penalty for the losers and rewards for the winners. That doesn't mean the workforce should pay the price, as it often does. It means that the people who run the businesses – the senior managers and executives who have replaced owners as the people who control businesses – must be accountable for their actions. Both positive and negative incentives are required. Large pay packets should be justified by meaningful results instead of being given simply for administering. These people might work incredibly hard – but so did Sisyphus. The entrepreneur who bets their shirt on a business that succeeds deserves a reward. The chief executive who takes over a company created by previous generations should have to *provably* deliver something extra before they receive their mouth-watering pay packet. With higher pay should come more significant risk. Yet in recent years, the risk/reward equation seems to have been inverted. The current imbalance in the system was perhaps best exemplified during the financial crisis of 2008/09, in which the people responsible for the crash appeared not to pay the price; an unfairness that still resonates with the public and drives belief that the current system is corrupted and benefits those in positions of power.

Yet in the private sector there is (or should be) a greater understanding of the company's objectives. If a company wants to be in business tomorrow, it needs to make a profit. They might sacrifice some profit today to generate profits tomorrow, but without any profit the company cannot exist. The incentives are clear. Unfortunately, large bureaucracies have a different incentive: the rewarding of the *manageriat*. Increasingly, those who run the organisation look after themselves with obscene payments, yet often their contribution is simply one of steady administration.

In the public sector there is little downside for failing to deliver, though the lower-paid workers can be and are sacked for poor performance. There are few penalties for failure at higher management levels, and substantial pay-offs and juicy consultancies beckon for the incompetent. We could identify a number of individuals from failed councils who continue to work as well-paid consultants, but we see no reason to sacrifice whatever profit we might make from this book to fight defamation suits.

So, in Newham, we recognised that large bureaucracies would be unable to deliver what was required. Instead, we determined to create small, nimble organisations; properly incentivised mutuals/cooperatives in which rewards were matched to the achievement of performance, and where, if they succeeded, they could compete for work in other parts of the public or private sector. This was the application of resilience to the workplace: encouraging people to take more control over their day-to-day working life, but within a framework that encouraged and rewarded success. As we described above, our view was that those who earn most should assume the greatest risk. Our ultimate aim was to create a number of mutuals to deliver services, jointly owned by the workforce and the council and with a profit-sharing mechanism that encouraged efficient work practices. So, we drove ahead with what we believed was the largest mutual/cooperative programme in the country. Alas, when offered the opportunity of increased worker participation and joint worker/council co-ops, the 'old' Left in Newham defaulted to in-house provision; the classic statist response, and a model that was not as flexible, cost-effective or popular as its alternative. But it met the dogma criteria to which the hard Left remained wedded.

Prior to floating as a mutual, it was necessary to do a root-and-branch analysis of the business unit. This was done through the Council Services to Small Business (CSSB) programme. *The London Borough of Newham Efficiency Plan 2016–2020* described the benefits of those parts of programme that had been realised:

It is anticipated that these… will deliver £8m of savings in addition to the £12m savings delivered as at April 2016.

By May 2018, savings of £22 million had been, or were in the process of being, realised – far outstripping the original estimate. By that same date, twelve businesses had been established and (although owned by the council) were to all intents and purposes independent. The process towards independence was incremental, but it gave us the greatest chance of success. Two organisations were owned by the membership and one, The Language Shop, was 51% owned by the workers and 49% by the council. The ultimate aim, of course, was for the majority to be co-owned by workers and the council. The companies were making considerable profits: £1.4 million for 2017/18, rising to an estimated £5 million by 2020/21. When polled, 72% of transferred employees said they would recommend the approach to colleagues.

What the savings figures do not include is the reduction in middle management. As part of the programme, when companies were established, higher management functions were not required: the companies managed themselves. Consequently, Newham was able to carry out a series of reorganisations which reduced management levels. We initiated a management transformation programme in 2017/18 with projected savings of £12.7 million by 2020/21. By the time the programme was stopped after we left office, £4.7 million had already been saved. By May 2018, the programme had only really looked at between a quarter and a third of the council, although the pace at which the work was being done was increasing and significant further savings were anticipated. The change of (Labour) administration brought this programme to an abrupt end. It seems that this was done to appease the statists within the new leadership and was carried out without realising the implications. Service improvement and financial savings ended abruptly, and Newham is currently paying the price.

As we prepared this book, we received the following comment from Frances Gordon, one of the key officers involved in the programme:

For me, it was about changing the "norm"; trying to change the mindset of what a council should look like and how it should be run. We were, for all intents and purposes, a traditionally run council, doing the same thing as every other council. The vision of the CSSB programme was to create council services that were efficient, lean, slick and provided a better-quality service but at a much cheaper cost.

You were being radical and a lot of people (mainly from inside the council) didn't like it. We were meant to be the first ever council to take such an approach to restructuring council services... It was difficult to take people on that journey because it hadn't been done before and people were (rightly so) nervous about it. Managers were worried and effectively stopped working with the Programme Team... I remember how difficult it would be for them to get answers from officers about their services. The Language Shop proved it could be done. It was a huge success.

The CSSB initiative delivered millions in savings, improved services, and removed the bureaucracies which were not delivering services effectively. Lengthy discussions about what was to be delivered, followed by rigorous reviews of what was actually being delivered, provided an understanding that was used to make savings and improve services. Creating co-ops and mutuals as viable businesses, properly incentivised, ensured significant savings for the council which considerably exceeded the figures which had initially been predicted.

Every local authority wants to save money and deliver better services, but the two objectives often seem contradictory. Consequently, many councils engage in the same behaviours: annual spending cuts slicing X% off budgets to save money, and hoping that simultaneous ill-conceived or untried improvement programmes will work. We're minded here to recall the famous quote often attributed to Einstein:

The definition of insanity is doing the same thing over and over again but expecting different results.

While Einstein may not have said it, by attributing it to him it makes it harder for ordinary mortals to disagree.

It accurately depicts the work often carried out in large, bureaucratic organisations – often, but not always, those in the public sector. Rather than repeat those same failures, Newham's CSSB programme identified a different way of working. It is not an easy path to tread. Still, it is one that promises significant improvement in public services and benefits for residents. Although our experiment with the programme was shorter than we would have liked, we believe we showed that, if implemented correctly, it can be popular with staff and be effective.

An example of how to deliver savings

We mentioned above that Newham worked hard to overcome the austerity that swamped the public sector – and the wider global economy – after 2008/09. Many of our initiatives, such as the small business/co-op programme, were radical and new. But we also realised that we had to deliver more traditional cost savings: those delivered throughout the same period by many hard-working councils across the UK. So let us give you an example.

The way council housing rent was traditionally collected in Newham was in cash at council offices. Following an extensive period of consultation, payments were transferred to PayPoint, a private provider offering automated services at multiple locations, and our rent offices were closed. In practice, this meant that rent could be paid at more places around the borough, and so the service to residents improved. With such a significant change to a vital service, we expected some local resistance. But there was not a single complaint at any of the Mayor's surgeries.

The Left of the Labour Party continues to moan about councils making savings and regularly blames someone else for such necessities. At the same time, our Left-leaning comrades like to express, in the most vocal terms, just how much they *care* for the citizens they represent while they cut services. Virtue-signalling, and sometimes just outright whingeing, replace policy and praxis (see next chapter).

Additionally, in Newham we faced central government funding discrepancies that arose between Inner and Outer London boroughs. The details of this dispute are dry, so we'll spare readers the minutiae. But essentially, it boiled down to the fact that Newham was considered an Inner London borough in every single measure except finance. The separation of the Danelaw from the Anglo-Saxons had repercussions a millennium later in deciding where the border between 'Inner' and 'Outer' London lay. The county boroughs were the administrative successors of the Danelaw, when England was divided between the Anglo-Saxon children of immigrants, who'd been around for some 500 years and the rather aggressive new immigrant community from the edges of the Baltic. Meanwhile, the poor Britons were shunted off to the northern and western fringes. The wholly unanticipated result of King Alfred's legacy meant that a millennia later, Newham missed out on the largesse of inner-city status. If only Alfred had chosen to battle the Danes a couple of miles to the east – say, along Barking Creek instead of the Lea – then our lives would have been so much easier, and Newham would have been better off to the tune of £70 million per annum.

So, for many years, the indefensible annual underfunding of Newham was the focus of a campaign, Newham Needs, to try to change the way in which central government allocated funding. Politically, it placed Newham in the role of perpetual supplicant; in hock to the whims of Whitehall wonks. The way the council had long (before us) presented this to locals was that our failures were the failures of national government policy. Blaming someone else became a perpetual 'get out of jail free' card. But, never a mayoralty to navel-gaze, we felt that a victimhood stance masked some inefficient approaches to local finances. So, we resolved to take a different approach. We would no longer present Newham as a victim. We certainly wanted the additional money that we believed we were due; it was neither rational nor fair that an area with our economic and social deprivation levels was treated unfavourably compared with our Inner London neighbours. But this would not stop us from taking action to improve our residents' lives. We did continue to lobby government privately, and a number of senior ministers recognised the justice of our case. But as they noted, had we received the fair amount, it would have had to come from the existing budgets of the other Inner London authorities. There are frequently times when fairness gives way to expediency. This was one of them. It's worth reflecting, though, on the fact that whatever we achieved, we did it with £70 million less per annum than our neighbouring councils.

Before we embarked on changes, there were three questions we asked:

1. **What were we spending money on?** We wanted to know not just the amount on a budget line, but what that budget line purchased and what we got back in terms of results for Newham's residents.

2. **Was the money being spent on things we wanted?** Was cash simply being spent because we'd spent the same amount last year, or was it contributing to our resilience agenda? If not the latter, why were we spending it?

3. Lastly, if a service or programme was something we decided should continue, **was there a way of doing it better or cheaper?**

Let's give an example of how this worked. Looking at our renovation grant process, we asked our three key questions and got the following answers:

1. Every year we spent some £1.7 million on improvement grants. That sounded good. We could pat ourselves on the back. We were helping people.

2. Making it possible for disabled residents and their families to live together in decent accommodation clearly met our resilience requirements.

3. Then we looked deeper. Of that £1.7 million, £800,000 was spent on in-house admin, design, surveying and monitoring. An entire internal department had grown incrementally over time and now swallowed up almost 50% of the budget.

Consequently, we opted to provide grants directly to homeowners, who would be responsible for commissioning the work (following consultations with occupational therapists). Undeniably, our solution shifted some of the risk from the council to the homeowner. But it also allowed for greater flexibility and speed than council-directed services provided. To mitigate the risk, homeowners were encouraged to use an approved local builder. Inclusion on that approved list therefore became a priority for local contractors. Complaints or a failure to remedy defects jeopardised their continued inclusion. So, almost at the stroke of a pen, we made a significant saving without cutting the service. In fact, we believed we had enhanced an essential service and given residents more control over their future. Lo and behold, satisfaction increased.

This three-question initiative was deployed throughout the council. It lay behind many service improvements and enabled significant savings to be spent on our priorities. Incidentally, it also reduced the backlog for most of its services from over a year to a few weeks – perhaps a lesson for the NHS as it faces enormous backlogs: less bureaucracy, perhaps? It was the resilience agenda in action.

Chapter 3

DELIVERING IN NEWHAM:
LESSONS LEARNED AND APPLIED

It isn't sufficient just to want. You've got to ask yourself what
you are going to do to get the things you want.
(Franklin D. Roosevelt)

Show me the incentive and I will show you the outcome.
(Charlie Munger)

Praxis – the practical implementation of policy – is the key to change. The huge range of policy initiatives successfully implemented by Newham Council and described in the succeeding chapters demonstrates an understanding of praxis which could be successfully exported elsewhere. The political world is replete with grand ideas, but without an understanding of how to implement policy, nothing will change.

Generally, we found two significant impediments to improving services. One is political. The posturing, virtue-signalling and ineptitude of many politicians make effective delivery extremely difficult. Politicians are supposed to provide the vision; the direction of travel. In the last analysis, it is the job of politicians to specify clearly what should be achieved. It is they who should set the objectives and measures to determine success. Failure to do so leads to confusion and non-delivery.

We faced internal opposition on several fronts. There were those on the statist Left, for whom ownership and control were more important than outcomes. There were those on what we would now call the woke Left, for whom the narrative was more important than delivery, and for whom it was better to complain and blame than to effect change. Lastly, there were those for whom engagement in council politics was simply a well-paid hobby – they lacked any semblance of a coherent approach to council work, but were very active on items of personal or communitarian interest.

There exists, certainly in Left-leaning councils, a desire to avoid censure for factors or outcomes for which others can be blamed. So, in this mindset, when central government cuts several million pounds from annual council grants, it is clearly Westminster's fault. And if cash shortages are the fault of the government, so are the consequences of those cuts, whatever they arc. This assumes that the role of government is perpetually to improve the financial lot of councils. It isn't and they won't. But the response of many councils has often been to default to the traditional blame game.

An example at Newham. It was one of the older leaders of our internal opposition who demanded that, when seeking to save cash at budget time, we exemplify what potential cuts of 1%, 2% or 3% would look like, as had been traditional in his day. We pointed out that in his day, a typical 1% cut meant stationery savings, a 2% cut meant the odd low-paid member of staff being axed, and 3% meant 'dead babies in the street'. (It was a metaphor, of course, meaning that a catastrophic service reduction would lead to worst-case outcomes.) These would be the arguments used by Labour traditionalists, partly so that they could then attack central government for foisting such cuts upon us at a local level. Such narratives created the central government demon that the statist Left needed. It was a good way to persuade themselves that they were doing something about their tight financial situation. But it was no way to run effective local services, and we had no time for such an approach.

Many readers will be familiar with the 'salami-slicing' model response to cuts. For the uninitiated, this meant that if a decision was taken to cut the council's total budget by 3%, each department would simply cut its expenditure by 3%. For years in local government, this simplistic model became a common way to share the pain of cuts across major organisations. But, again, it was no way to organise service delivery or deliver political priorities. That required a different mindset; one that focused on what we could do, not what we couldn't. At Newham, we took big decisions such as moving to a new headquarters, which saved millions and helped us to identify other efficiencies and income streams across the council that would otherwise have been missed or overlooked. The mutual and co-op programme (badged internally as the small business programme) enabled us to target expenditure much more effectively. And any budget reductions, we insisted, would follow our principles and objectives rather than adopt half-baked requirements for salami-sliced cuts across all departments, which effectively left officers in charge of our priorities. The results speak for themselves.

As an aside, we would say that the Blair government demonstrated similar political courage and priorities, which helped to dramatically improve public services in the country after years of underfunding – though the woke and the statist Left will never give due credit for that. As we have pointed out, for different reasons, they are less interested in improving services and hence can happily cooperate in destroying the fabric of public services. Indeed, when the narrative becomes more important than the services you deliver to people, it can be quite useful to have an evil (usually Tory; sometimes Blairite) government to blame.

Politically and practically, the Blair government was impressive when it came to public service reform, initially pouring billions into services and improving outcomes. But as time passed, even Blair's reformist zeal ran into the problems of bureaucracy which pervade many public institutions and afflict services. In response, the government generated more performance measures to try to force continued improvements on stale bureaucracies. Local government in particular became bogged down by the centre's obsession with targets, with hundreds of performance measures assessed by taxpayer-funded watchdogs such as the Audit Commission. Ultimately, such moves were expensive and self-defeating, and hindered councils. Political and managerial 'bandwidth' is limited. It is possible to focus on a few areas and drive improvement, but sustaining that improvement usually requires continued effort. The greater the number of priorities, the more thinly focus is spread and the less impact is made. But we learned from the experience. We realised that we needed an approach which would encourage delivery of the services we wanted without trying to resort to self-defeating micromanagement.

An additional problem is that bureaucrats build safety-first structures designed to cover their backs and spend their time talking to each other. The people who inhabit these structures speak the same language, and the cultural hegemony within the organisations reinforces belief in their rectitude. Such a structure makes the organisation ripe for woke ideology. People will demonstrate their loyalty to the new ideology even though they may not believe it. As in the Soviet era, people are adept at saying the right thing while believing something different. It is the job of politicians to challenge the bureaucrats, which requires an understanding of the services (hence the small business/co-op programme) and courage. Overwhelmingly, it requires the courage to say no to professional officers. To be fair, and in the interest of full disclosure, at Newham our approach to tackling bureaucracy was supported by some senior officers who wanted to be part of something different and exciting that delivered major service improvements. In the end, many became our co-conspirators rather than the opposition – that was left to our Left-wing opposition allied to an Islamist communitarian front.[2]

Private organisations focused on the bottom line and profit can avoid the worst excesses of bureaucracy, though as managerial capitalism replaces old-style capitalism the rigours of the market can get lost. Adam Smith expressed just this in *The Wealth of Nations*:

> *The directors of such companies, however, being the managers rather of other people's money than of their own, it cannot well be expected that they should watch over it with the same anxious vigilance with which the partners in a private copartnery frequently watch over their own.*

Or, as we would say, bureaucracies exist to serve themselves. The Right have O'Sullivan's Law:

> *All organisations that are not explicitly right-wing will over time become left-wing.*

We think this is just a way of the Right saying that bureaucracies serve themselves, but that the Right interprets anything different to the Right as a move to the Left. On some level, they may be correct, for there are certainly many examples of organisations moving from their original objectives. Amnesty International,

---

2   We are not particularly interested in criticising the current Newham administration here, disappointing though it is. The website Open Newham catalogues the disasters of the current administration, and if you are interested it can be found at https://www.opennewham.co.uk/

which sacrificed its unique moral high ground to campaign for whatever political causes are currently in fashion; the similar move by the National Council for Civil Liberties as it morphed into Liberty; the National Trust, which seems to be sharing the expanded mission of publicly owned museums and galleries to engage their audiences in collective guilt; and the decline of BBC news coverage, whereby objective reporting has sometimes been sacrificed on the altar of diversity, equity and inclusion. It might simply be 'mission creep'. But if it is, then it is mission creep heavily influenced by the Marxism of the later twentieth century. The core objective is not to improve society; it is to undermine it.

But now we are in danger of straying from the core of our argument.

We assume that readers will have some sympathy for the idea of incremental improvements to society, and that this includes better ways to deliver public services. In this book we try to show how clarity of objective is critical to delivering effective, high quality services. The importance of ensuring that any objective has measurable outcomes has been stressed, alongside empirical observation and the scientific method. With this clarity, it is possible to apply suitable incentives to achieve desired outcomes. In addition, such clarity will enhance public discourse since, when objectives are clear, it is possible to have a sensible argument about the purpose of a particular approach and how you will know whether you have achieved it.

An example of public discourse being enhanced by clear objectives is Universal Credit. In an article for *The Guardian* by Patrick Butler discussing a critique of the benefits system regime by Jonathon Reynolds, 'Labour' is quoted as saying:

[T]he current system means that a single parent working 30 hours a week on the national living wage loses £573 a month of their universal credit entitlement – equivalent to

a marginal tax rate of 75%. It contrasts this with the 47% marginal tax rate faced by people earning over £150,000 a year, such as the prime minister.

We have long argued that Universal Credit has the benefit of clarity, since it makes clear the marginal rate of tax and, properly funded, is designed to help people in work (unlike the opaque system it replaced). As a result, it allows people to see the reality of the welfare system. The decision by the Labour Party to abolish Universal Credit was an example of a knee-jerk reaction against a system which, if properly used, can transform public attitudes to welfare and contribute significantly to a growth in resilience. The failure to ensure clarity in the public discourse and thereby hold politicians to account helps to sustain existing bureaucracies. If there is no clarity of outcome or assessment, they cannot be held accountable. However, wherever there is a degree of clarity, issues and facts become easier to discuss politically.

Two examples reinforce this point. Firstly, when Prime Minister Boris Johnson set ambitious targets for Covid-19 vaccinations across the UK, they were not always hit but the overall outcome was still spectacular. In politics, people will forgive a near miss, especially if the original target was tough. So, they rightly credited Johnson's government with a significant achievement. Secondly, we have witnessed a significant increase in the number of immigrants taking huge risks to escape from France and across the English Channel to the land of milk and honey known as Kent. The UK government long ago stated that it wanted to reduce the number of modern-day 'boat people'. Whether one agrees with the policy or not is irrelevant: ministers' inability to deliver what was promised is rightly seen as an example of incompetence. As an emergency measure, the largely successful vaccination programme sat outside normal policy channels, while people crossing the Channel were targeted by arguably the most incompetent department (and bureaucracy) in government: the Home Office.

It is one thing to have bureaucratic management structures in a repetitive manufacturing process, though we are unconvinced that it necessarily provides the most efficient approach. But when dealing with public services like social care, education and health, we recognise the importance of training skilled practitioners like social workers, nurses, GPs etc.; yet we proceed to undermine their professionalism through excessive bureaucracy – not for its own sake, but largely because we are afraid of the risk. And not the risk to an abused child, for example, but the risk to those in authority if the press gets to hear about it.

We are reminded of the words, attributed to both Peter Parker and Winston Churchill (though probably pre-dating both…):

Where there is great power there is great responsibility, where there is less power there is less responsibility, and where there is no power there can, I think, be no responsibility.

To focus on the last part of that quote, it is surely true that if you do not give someone power to deliver you cannot, in good conscience, hold them responsible for that delivery. Bureaucracies are, by their very nature, organisations in which power is hierarchical and diffuse. It is only at the very top that power comes together in one place, and given the size of many organisations, the chief executive or leader can get away with saying that they cannot know about everything that is happening. It follows, therefore, that there is little or no accountability in a large bureaucratic structure – so how the hell do we deliver decent public services when we regularly design delivery mechanisms and organisations which cannot be held to account? If, for example, we wish to protect children, surely it is necessary to have social workers who exercise judgement? If that is the case, how do monolithic bureaucratic structures benefit social work practice? Some form of quality check is necessary, but layers of management who both do the work and then check their own work are a recipe for failure. Of course, this situation is often made worse by the fact that we do not have a clue what we are trying to achieve. The mantra is that young people must be kept safe – but what does that even mean? How will we measure safety? How will we know when we have achieved it? And what of the development of personal skills, abilities and resilience? How do we measure what has been put in place to test whether young people are helped to develop rich and fulfilling lives?

In Newham, changing delivery structures was critical. We applied a number of lessons and principles equally to the delivery of services, whether they were delivered locally, by national government or by quangos. We outline four key principles and seven observations below. These combine to become our 'Eleven Rules', because books that have a clearly defined number of rules sell better. Jordan Peterson made a fortune with *12 Rules for Life*, while Moses only had Ten Commandments. So, we think eleven is a happy midpoint!

Four key principles of public service delivery

1. The most important element in the delivery of services is the **application of scientific method** to policy formulation and implementation. There is plenty of talk about evidence-based policymaking in local government, but precious little of it in practice.

To us, this approach meant that policies must be subject to widespread discussion and peer review prior to implementation. We even tried to involve our (internal) opposition in the hope that they would find flaws in our approach which, in being corrected, would improve delivery. Alas, virtue-signalling is much too attractive and easy, while thinking through ways to ensure delivery can be difficult. Once implemented, the outcomes were constantly reviewed to ensure that the results were as anticipated. If they were not, then change had to be implemented and the whole cycle repeated. Elsewhere in this book, we point out the dangers of working to performance indicators that are subject to gaming, or that don't measure the outcomes they are intended to measure. We also discuss elsewhere the success of the fixed-odds betting terminals campaign run by Newham. This was necessary because legislation under the Blair government did not work as intended but there was no mechanism to review outcomes and correct mistakes.

Workplace, the largest local authority jobs brokerage scheme in the country, was perhaps the most significant achievement in Newham during our period in office, providing internal statistics demonstrating significant success. In addition, employment figures produced by the government were regularly scrutinised to see if there was a real-world impact. In particular, when the Index of Multiple Deprivation was published we saw the outstanding success of the programme in practice rather than in internal statistics. Newham had moved up twenty-two places, from third bottom to twenty-fifth.

Prior to implementing the first borough-wide private rental licensing scheme in the country (a programme to improve the quality of private rented properties in the borough through the targeting of bad and criminal landlords), a pilot project was run for eighteen months to ensure that lessons were learned before any full roll-out.

Of course, the downside of this experimental approach is that when mistakes are made – and they always are – admitting them results in political fallout. It requires courage in politics to put ideas and actions to the test and learn from them through admitting to your mistakes. But if you are in politics to change things, it is the only proven way to get results. On the other hand, if you are not interested in change, or lack courage, the scientific method holds nothing for you. Which is why, we suspect, it is not applied widely in politics.

2. **Keep it simple**. The more complexity is built into a system, the more likely it is to fail. This means that we should have the minimum necessary number of key indicators to watch, and then we should *watch those indicators*.

When we were considering a pilot using a small business to transform long-term home (social) care, there were only three required objectives:

i.   Control of finance was a given, as it is in any business.

ii. Compliance. The operation had to comply with the requirements of the Care Quality Commission to ensure the satisfaction of minimum professional standards.

iii. Customer satisfaction. Were the people we were serving (or their families) happy with the service?

Incentives were then aligned with these measures.

Previously, we spent many hours in discussions about how to ensure that the itemised lists in care plans were delivered, and that staff arrived on time and didn't leave before their allotted hour was up. But ultimately, we wanted a service that was more 'human'; in which the people who were receiving the service felt that they were respected and genuinely 'cared about', rather than just 'cared for'. In the end, we also decided to build in some flexibility, allowing the carer and the person receiving care to interact as people, rather than as client and carer. It might mean that on a random Tuesday, the living-room floor didn't get hoovered. But on that day, for our carers and residents, sitting and talking over a cup of tea may have been far more important.

Our feedback mechanism – our gauge of whether all of this worked and improved the service – was the satisfaction of the client and his or her family.

3. **Incentives need to work** for both individuals and organisations. Bus lane and parking enforcement have generated large sums for councils, which have therefore enthusiastically kept their eye on those issues. Individuals and organisations, even public ones, respond to incentives. There are thousands of statutory duties on local authorities, the police, the NHS etc., and all such organisations are under financial pressure. If something is not a priority for an organisation, then it will not do it – unless an incentive is provided. Saying something is a statutory duty for an organisation may make legislators feel better, but unless it is embedded in the service delivery of the organisation, and incentivised within it, then such statutory duties risk being gamed by those charged with delivery and becoming objects of virtue-signalling by those at the top, who simply pass a motion or spend more of the community's money to demonstrate their goodness.

4. **Responsibilities should be devolved** to the lowest democratic structure possible. Much of this expenditure is directed at a national level by huge bureaucracies, yet delivered locally – delivering services to an area (refuse collection, parks, housing maintenance, transport etc.) or to people (health, education, benefits, housing allocations etc.). The vast government bureaucracies which are established to deliver these local services are the chief culprits in failing to deliver what is promised (often at exorbitant cost). Devolving powers closer to the front line, where staff and politicians should be more familiar with what works locally, does not guarantee success; however, providing government exercises effective scrutiny, challenges with appropriate incentives, and eschews micromanagement, it should improve our public services.

So, to recap: apply the scientific method, keep it simple, incentivise results, and devolve. We firmly believe that any organisation that follows these four golden rules is most likely to improve its service delivery. But hot on the heels of our four key principles, we also make…

Seven further observations

1. **Organisational interfaces**. In the delivery of public services, problems invariably occur where different organisations interface, especially when those organisations have different incentives.

One problem we faced at Newham, as did many UK councils, was the so-called 'delayed discharge' from hospital of older people. Elderly patients were often kept in hospital for longer than they needed to be because there wasn't the support at home that made it safe to discharge them. Hospitals across the country were desperate to free up beds but, prior to the establishment of the Better Care Fund (BCF), there was no real incentive for care commissioners to facilitate this. If the local authority improved care services (at a cost), it was the NHS that reaped the financial benefits. It was a social good, but the financial incentives were not aligned with outcomes.

For some years after the introduction of health and well-being boards, our adult social care department and the local clinical commissioning group (CCG) operated a 'virtual' pooled budget. Long before the introduction of the BCF, we looked at funding not on an organisational level, but from the point of view of the borough's residents. By focusing beyond our organisational boundaries, we developed shared priorities and a shared agenda. This did not end difficult decisions about spending, but it put them in a context in which spending was only justifiable if it contributed to the priorities of the health and well-being board. Whether it was the borough or the CCG that paid for something became increasingly irrelevant, given our commitment to a shared agenda. What was important locally was the degree to which spending furthered the health and social care priorities to which both bodies had signed up. So, in the case of delayed discharge the question for us became: how do we facilitate discharge at the time when it is clinically most beneficial to the patient?

The answer took multiple forms; all small, local services which contributed to a much greater whole. For example, Newham Council commissioned social workers to assess patients and ensure their safe transition home. These staff were based not in a local adult care body, but in the local hospital. A small handyman team was also created to ensure that minor safety improvements within the patients' homes were undertaken. The team generally responded and completed work tasked by the social workers within twenty-four hours, paving the way for patients to be allowed home sooner. Where patients did not have someone at home with them, Newham commissioned the local branch of Age UK to provide a resettlement service. Staff and volunteers from Age UK would be at the patient's home when he or she returned from hospital, often with the kettle on. Age UK staff also visited regularly and were available to the former patient for up to a month after discharge. And it did not end there. Newham's adult social care teams operated a well-developed telecare service which provided ongoing support in addition to any other service the resident was receiving.

Two NHS trusts, the CCG, the voluntary sector and the local authority. It sounds like a recipe for confusion and disaster. But because the incentives had been aligned beforehand, different parts of a much broader service pulled together, not apart. It worked superbly.

2. **Unintended consequences** are a perennial problem. When implementing a policy there is usually an accompanying narrative.

For example, years ago when the government wanted to change drinking hours, politicians pushed the idea that it might lead to a 'French-style café culture' on the streets of London and boost business. It didn't. But what it did do in many local areas was usher in a period in which neighbours' complaints about licensed premises increased. Likewise, when national government legislation allowed bookmakers to install multiple fixed-odds betting terminals with a maximum prize of £100 per spin, it became economically viable to open more betting shops next to each other. The opportunities for gambling large sums of money increased, and the viability, diversity and vibrancy of local high streets declined.

When any policy is implemented, it is essential that decision makers are prepared to quickly address the unintended consequences that frequently arise. Failure to do so merely exacerbates the problem and undermines reforms.

3. Cuts are always implemented as far away as possible from the body holding the budget, which results in **unintended cuts or costs** elsewhere. You would be hard pressed to find a local authority in the country that hasn't cut a voluntary sector organisation that was doing useful work, simply because it protected a department's direct spend.

The closure of a local magistrates' court saved the court system some money. However, as a result, Newham police officers had to travel much further to give evidence, and that meant a reduction in the time they had available for other duties.

4. Central government says it wants to work with local authorities but, when push comes to shove, **the civil service is resistant**. (This point is linked to Point 3.)

For example, it was agreed that a work programme would be devolved to several East London boroughs for implementation. When the proposal was revealed, it required the boroughs to select an organisation (from an approved list) to carry out the work based on criteria set by the civil service. Newham, with the best jobs programme in the country, was not allowed to use its own service, Workplace. Unsurprisingly, we turned down the money on offer.

5. **One size does not fit all.** Within any local authority area there are vast differences in population, economy and culture. Across the country, there are enormous differences. But since civil servants and politicians tend to live in the same sort of places (the Home Counties, or posh North London boroughs), their understanding of a problem is often coloured by their 'lived experience', which is the antithesis of the scientific method.

But we repeat ourselves.

In 2018 Robin spoke on housing policy panels at the Labour and Conservative Party conferences. What struck him was that in both meetings people meant well and were keen to see more housing built. At the Tory conference the discussion centred around the difficulties of developing green-belt land, and at the Labour conference the subject of greatest interest was brownfield development. Each audience came with the problems they experienced in their local area uppermost in their minds. Of course, both issues need to be dealt with if we are to meet housing need – but too often we interpret problems through our own experiences and not through a proper analysis of all of the information available. Relying on an individual's 'lived experience' to determine policy is a recipe for disaster.

6. **Data is badly used in government.** The private sector has shown the power of data, which, if properly used, can transform services. Most councils have now created good-quality, front-end websites – but they are still some way off making effective use of data.

In Newham we developed a data warehouse without which the private sector licensing scheme would not have worked. We planned to apply the same approach to identify where young people were most at risk.

7. **The offender (or polluter) should pay.** Linked to this is the concept that compliance must be incentivised if behaviour is to be changed. For some crimes, we consider removing a person's liberty, and discuss extensively how far the punishment acts as a deterrent. For businesses, and people with assets, financial disincentives can be very powerful, but only if they provide a sufficient deterrent. Essentially, we need to break the business model of any antisocial or criminal enterprise.

For example, several waste removal businesses operate on the basis of simply dumping waste, at a huge cost to local taxpayers. This problem is not unique to any local authority. A professional fly tipper often hides behind the protection afforded by a limited company. We experienced a similar problem in relation to the licensing of private sector accommodation. We had no problem with landlords who provided clean and secure properties that were adequately maintained. Our problem was that significant numbers didn't. For those with a business model wherein fines were simply a cost of doing business, it was clear that the law was not acting as a deterrent. If the cost of acting badly is less than the cost of acting properly, there is little incentive for the reckless landlord or waste carrier to improve their behaviour.

The question is, how much should we fine? Robin and Clive have different views on this. Clive believes that fines should be substantial, even to the point of confiscating entire businesses. Robin is more draconian, and says that people who break laws should pay the costs of enforcement, to the extent that potentially all their personal assets should be confiscated. It does seem perverse that people operating in a particular area – e.g., good landlords (within a landlord licensing scheme), or innocent taxpayers – must pay the cost of an enforcement scheme when, if everybody played by the rules, there would be no need for enforcement. It seems fairer that those who create the problem should be responsible for the cost of mitigating it. In reality, however, since judges and politicians don't generally live where the effects of bad behaviour can be seen, they can afford to be 'reasonable' when dealing with criminals who have contempt for normal behaviour, and everybody else pays the price.

As an aside, one principle we tried to apply was that any attempt to reduce bad behaviour should include a determination to minimise the impact on good people. Why should people who do the right thing have their lives made worse because of bad behaviour by others? The Home Office would have done well to apply this philosophy when considering their response to the Windrush issue.

Chapter 4

DELIVERING RESILIENCE: WORKPLACE

By 2010, Newham will be a major business location where
people choose to live and work.
(Vision adopted by Newham Council in the late 1990s)

When Newham adopted its vision, the word 'choose' was included to stress the importance of developing the personal and economic capacity to exercise choice. The vision was a precursor to the concept of resilience adopted somewhat later.

Work is critical both to a person's view of themselves and to providing them with a means by which to exercise choice. It instils pride and a sense of purpose. You only need to read the studies published by Professor Sir Michael Marmot, director of University College London's Institute of Health Equity, to understand that work is key to improving a person's physical and mental health. Aspiration requires a belief that you can do something for yourself – indeed, that you *must* do something for yourself. Resilience – the building of aspirational capacity – is therefore the opposite of victimhood. It is an approach that is both radical and effective. It is a message of hope, and applies to all sections of the community. It is also the antithesis of the nihilism of what passes for Left-wing politics today.

The issues involved in resilience are thrown into sharp relief by different approaches to our welfare system. Initially seen as a form of insurance for people who got into difficulties – support while they got back on their feet – the welfare system no longer has a clear purpose other than to stop people starving. Of itself, this is a worthy ambition, and one to which we are most assuredly not hostile. But beyond that staple function of welfare, what does Britain really offer? While Anywheres take a relaxed approach to the distribution of benefits, Somewheres consider it important that people exercise personal responsibility and that there should be a reward for doing so. For example, they believe that it is wrong to take benefits and not work – that it is wrong to take something for nothing. That's only fair. They believe in common provision, and that society should support people doing the right thing. In this, they reject Thatcher's claim that there is 'no such thing as society' (she didn't say exactly that, but it's a useful, if lazy, way to raise relevant issues here), and support a vision of solidarity and community.

As David Goodhart notes:

> *Somewheres are comfortable with differentiating between the deserving and less deserving – among highly-paid financiers as well as the welfare dependant... Somewheres tend towards a 'club membership' rather than a 'need' view of welfare as preferred by many Anywheres.*

Incidentally, support for the deserving, rather than the undeserving, has a long history in the Labour Party. Keir Hardie, founder of the Labour Party and MP for West Ham, delivered his maiden speech in Parliament in 1893, and called for employment for the deserving but not the undeserving poor. He observed:

[Those] without visible means of subsistence, not because of any fault on their part, but because our present land and industrial system denies them the opportunity of working for a living… This does not refer to those who are casually employed, and it does not refer to those usually spoken of as loafers and criminals. It refers exclusively to bona fide working men who have been thrown out of employment in consequence of bad trade.

Hell, even Lenin had something to say on the subject:

He who does not work shall not eat.

But the concept of aspiration, particularly work-based aspiration, has fallen by the wayside within the Labour Party in recent years – and we believe that this has had electoral consequences. In Deborah Mattinson's book *Beyond the Red Wall*, the following was said by a focus group member discussing why Labour lost the 2019 election:

[The Labour Party] is for young people and students, and the unemployed. It used to be for normal working people, who pay for their house, pay for their car.

In other words, Labour was no longer the party for the aspirational working class. The virtues of personal responsibility and fairness seemed to have been displaced.

This feedback echoes concerns expressed by Tony Blair in his 2010 memoir *Tony Blair: A Journey*:

A person who is poor first needs someone to care about it and then to act; but when no longer poor their objective may then become to be well off. In other words, for such a person it is about aspiration, ambition, getting on and going up, making some money, keeping their family in good style, having their children do better than them.

Many people are happy to work long hours in low-paid jobs in the hope that they are providing the basis of a better life for their children. But in our view, these people have been abandoned by the Labour Party. In *The Tribe*, the author and former Labour activist Ben Cobley notes that the 2017 Labour Party rule book contains:

- Twenty-six references to 'gender'.
- Forty-one references to 'BAME'[3].
- Forty-three references to 'ethnic' background.
- Eleven references to 'race'.
- And two references to 'black' and 'Asian' respectively.

Yet there were just two references to 'class' in the entire ninety-one-page document from the party established to represent the working class.

Building capacity so that people can get more out of life and supporting people's ambition to improve their lives should be at the core of social democracy. But there can be little wonder that a large percentage of the low-paid white population no longer feels that Labour works for them. Increasingly, significant sections of minority communities also feel that, given the social values espoused by Labour, the party no longer speaks for them. The landscape has become something of a mess.

Democracy requires an opposition party that can articulate an alternative solution for a critical mass of people, and one which occasionally seems fit for government. Following Boris Johnson's failures and the election of Liz Truss, Labour's poll lead leaped, but this was more because the Tories have worked

---

3   Black, Asian and minority ethnic.

hard to make themselves unelectable than because of any vision or confidence in Labour's ability to govern.

Of course, different people have different capacities. Wherever people are in their lives, the state should be willing to support them in achieving as much as possible. There must be rewards for people who try, and support for people who struggle. Resilience is a call for people to take responsibility for their own lives as far as they can, in the knowledge that the state will stand behind them when they attempt to change their lives for the better. The state is neither 'Big Brother' nor 'nanny' in this equation, but it is possibly 'best mate'. When we say that social democracy is the truly radical approach of the Left, we are referring to just this sort of point. And it runs directly counter to the approach of the woke.

Of course, the identity politics of the Left and the rise of political correctness started with the best of intentions. In addressing issues and people ignored for too long, society was forced to look at the (sometimes deliberate and sometimes unintentional) marginalisation of certain groups. The underlying political principles of critical theory and intersectionality have their roots in the far Left. But however it is framed, their aim is not to improve democratic societies, but to undermine them. This builds on the familiar Marxist dialectic of struggle between two classes: the oppressor and the oppressed. The practical result of this has been to emphasise victimhood. If you're a woman, black, gay, etc., you're part of an oppressed group, and more so if you're a gay, black woman. And members of an oppressed group are, by definition, victims. Victims have become 'objectively progressive' (which must please several millionaires from the subcontinent and West Africa). And here's the leap of logic we still cannot get our heads around: those who in this simplistic narrative aren't victims necessarily become oppressors.

What's more, the problems or hurdles faced by victims are now always the fault of someone else – irrespective of what the problem is. The phenomenon of identity victimhood has spawned a whole industry, and the last thing the many second- – sorry – third-rate academics and 'thinkers' making money out of this business need is a solution which would involve getting off the gravy train and getting a proper job. This might prove challenging for those who peddle this nonsense. Clothed in the guise of compassion, these latter-day social justice warriors (SJWs) are like the angry mob of yesteryear. They have adopted witch-finding as sport and embraced denunciation as eagerly as any French Jacobin. Remarkably, they do this while bemoaning their own sense of victimhood.

The Labour Party has too easily fallen for this illogical narrative and behaviour, and, rightly or wrongly, this affiliation has come to define many people's views of the party in recent years. It is a sorry situation that only hinders what was once a progressive political force.

Woke strictures have removed agency from individuals, thereby helping to infantilise both individuals and groups in our society. People acquire greater moral approval to the degree that they are 'oppressed'. They cease to be agents with personal responsibility and the ability to exert control over their actions. Moreover, the deliberate blurring of groups – for instance, with acronyms that become titles, like BAME – suggests that all members of that group suffer identical or even similar problems across society. They don't. They share some, but they share others with the white community.

For example, in 2019 the UK's Office for National Statistics published figures highlighting improvements in employment rates between people from ethnic minorities and what would loosely be termed the indigenous 'white' population. Between 2004 and 2018, employment among Asians increased by 9% (among Bangladeshis and Pakistanis it increased by 13%), among the black population by 7%, and among the group defined as white British by just 2%. Indian employment rates are broadly comparable to white British, but Bangladeshi and Pakistani employment remains 19% below both. This improvement was not a surprise to those of us who lived in Newham, with its long-established diversity. But it indicated how little the real issues facing ethnic groups are understood. When Dr Tony Sewell's report for the Commission on Race and Ethnic Disparities was published in March 2021, the woke establishment wasted no time in disparaging it; not because it was factually incorrect, but because it failed to support the narrative of the new orthodoxy. The report was criticised as soon as it was published, and the criticisms were predictable. Some of the responses were petty, such as an act for which the board and council of Nottingham University should hang their heads in shame. In an act of pique they chose to withdraw an honorary degree from Dr Sewell; not because he was wrong or because his research was poor, but because they disagreed with his conclusions. Why rely on facts when prejudice works?

It is politically convenient to talk as if people are the same no matter where they are from, so long as they are part of an identifiable minority, as this deliberately overlooks the religious and ethnic divisions, attitudes, and aspirations that exist within minority communities. That approach is OK if we don't want to change anything. But suppose we want positive change to the genuine disadvantages faced by parts of what until recently we called the BAME community? In that case, we need to understand the differences between individuals; not to lump them into some amorphous group. This is not simply a question of 'Is the glass half empty or half full?' It is a matter of mindset. If this issue is raised merely to prompt angry outpourings of grievance-fuelled street violence, or demands for state-sponsored largesse to particular interest groups, then there is no point in understanding the problem. However, if it is a genuine problem to be solved – and we believe it is – then it is a question to be understood and addressed. And if it is to be understood, that may mean asking questions and establishing facts that are currently taboo. For example, relations with the police and lower-than-average entry to Russell Group universities are both problems for certain ethnic minority groups. But they are problems of a very different nature, and require different public policy and societal responses.

By defining people's needs based simply on their melanin levels, we see them in one dimension, especially if we don't differentiate between people whose families originate from wholly different parts of the world, with different cultures, histories and experiences. Intellectually, the approach of those who conveniently bundle all ethnic minorities into a single category is lazy. It is also misguided. That is, it is misguided if you want to solve problems. If your real agenda is to overthrow the 'systemically racist' society and replace it with something else, then it is pretty helpful to lump everything in together, because the last thing you want is nuance and complexity which will interfere with the narrative.

There is an alternative. The wider community can still support people who are experiencing problems, but do so on the basis that we work together to solve those problems rather than engage in communal hand-wringing or vacuous condemnations. And this is at the heart of the revitalisation of social democracy. It provides the means by which most people, most of the time, are able to achieve the life to which they aspire. For the first time in history, we live in an age when personalised solutions are possible. Powerful data companies are marching towards personalisation – towards the atomisation of our society whereby each individual can be targeted based on their revealed preferences rather than on predetermined characteristics. If this can be done to sell stuff to people, it can be done at the policy level to offer personalised support.

Personal resilience, which we defined as developing the aspirational capacity of the individual, required us to look at that individual when determining Newham's approach. It doesn't preclude challenging prejudice (far from it); nor working with groups who have things in common. But to develop personal resilience, we need to work out what motivates people – and that can be family, money, a type of work or a desire to contribute to society. Incentives drive people (and organisations), and identifying what drives somebody is the key to supporting them in developing greater resilience.

Newham has always suffered from higher levels of unemployment than the rest of the country. The stereotypical response of the Corbynite Left was that we should campaign for higher benefits, or (if they were being creative) set up state-funded job creation schemes. At Newham, we took a different view, not wholly unrelated to the slogan Christian Aid has popularised: 'Give a man a fish, and you feed him for a day. Teach a man to fish, and you feed him for a lifetime.' We are not against higher benefits, but the reality was that they were not arriving any time soon, and in the meantime people in Newham – sometimes whole families – were living in poverty. The only realistic way such people were going to get out of poverty, in our view, was by working and drawing a wage. The problem was that job centres were not terribly good at finding work for our residents.

So, we created our own jobs brokerage. When Workplace, Newham's bespoke brokerage, was established in 2007, it was evident that the first part of our vision was about to be fulfilled. Business, with associated jobs, was indeed coming to the area. We have described elsewhere how bureaucracy stifles the ability to deliver personalised solutions, as rules tie people down and flexibility is eschewed. As a result, local job centres generally do not provide the kind of service which would really make a difference. This was clearly demonstrated when we established Workplace. The head of the local job centre in Stratford went rogue and provided resources and support, and sent clients to Workplace as the best way to help them. His incentive? Wanting to help people. His reward? None, and after a while the job centre stopped providing support. So, we did it without them. A perfect example of how a bureaucracy cannot adapt to local conditions in a systemic way. However, as individuals, Graham Houghton and Derek Harvey from Stratford Job Centre can at least be confident that they had a significant impact on Newham's residents. Interestingly, some of the workers at the job centre did keep sending residents to Workplace, knowing that they were more likely to get a job there; an example of people in a bureaucracy trying (despite that bureaucracy) to do the best they can for their clients.

However, a cursory glance at Canary Wharf, the astonishing development in neighbouring Tower Hamlets, demonstrated that the new opportunities would not necessarily benefit the local population. Canary Wharf increased wealth and generated jobs, but local residents were being outcompeted by immigrants who were more likely to be prioritised by employers. And why not? They were dynamic self-starters, with precisely the qualities and skills employers were looking for. More jobs were necessary but not sufficient in themselves. We did not want to repeat the same problem. We had to help our residents to compete.

With Workplace, we found that people wanted to work, but poverty has a way of grinding the life out of you. Through research, we discovered that some long-term unemployed residents lived their whole existence within a radius of two hundred metres from their front door – and some lives were an endless downward spiral of mere day-to-day existence. Anxiety often compounded depression, and any confidence these people had possessed had evaporated. We resolved to stand alongside our residents and give them the support they needed to take their first steps back into work and, by extension, their wider community. If you believe (or are constantly told) that you are a victim or oppressed, then you cannot be expected to sort out significant issues facing you as any sense of agency is removed. Workplace sought to encourage agency and offer support to people who aspired to improve their lives. It assessed an individual's capabilities – using criteria often different to those utilised by national job centres – and then sought to match them with a job. People were supported, encouraged and trained where necessary. If they had the motivation, Workplace offered assistance.

Workplace was tasked to understand what employers were looking for and build relations with them. In some cases, staff were even embedded with employers to better understand the requirements of roles offered locally. The aim was not to force employers to choose local people; forced outcomes don't really benefit people or employers in the long run. Instead, our aim was to provide a choice of candidates of sufficient quality so that employers could appoint from those we recommended – and would return to Workplace for all their future job vacancies, knowing that they would get quality candidates who met their requirements. As part of that offer, candidates were given packages of support targeted at the jobs that were available and suited their skills. These packages could be anything from a few days to weeks of training, and included free English language lessons where necessary. Another example of support to increase candidates' job readiness was the Mayor's Guarantee Scheme. We noted early on that there existed a perception among some locals that taking up a job could result in a loss of income or welfare support – the result of the 'benefits trap'. So, Newham guaranteed that everybody who took a job would be no worse off financially, or the council would make up any financial shortfall. In practice, by focusing on in-work benefits and advice, nobody was worse off. But that wasn't clear when the guarantee was introduced. Nevertheless, our view was that if people wanted to work, disincentives created by the government had to be neutralised.

A vital element of this approach was ensuring that what was promised was delivered. This was typical of all council initiatives: work out what needs to be done, design a system to deliver it, implement it, then keep checking the results and changing the process to ensure that you get what you want. The scientific method at work in a social context.

Workplace paid dividends locally. Not immediately, because it takes time to develop relationships and understanding among residents. And we also realised that if we were to have a meaningful and long-lasting impact, our delivery would need to be at scale. So that took time. Small initiatives are loved by many politicians. They enable badly or superficially run departments to generate press releases and showcase their virtue at little cost, though with little impact. That approach wasn't for us! We decided to invest heavily in supporting residents into work, and Workplace grew into the largest jobs brokerage in the country – though at a considerable financial cost borne by the council. Initially, to control demand, the scheme was open to anybody who had been resident in Newham for at least twelve months, but later that was reduced to just three months.

The results were spectacular:

- Between 2007 and 2018, Workplace filled more than forty thousand jobs with local people.
- Almost half (45.9%) of Workplace jobs were for young people aged sixteen to twenty-four.
- Around 40% of those securing jobs were previously long-term unemployed or had never worked before.
- The ethnicity of those placed reflected Newham's working population.
- From 2009 to 2015, across the seven North-East London authorities (including Tower Hamlets, which is home to Canary Wharf) there were 43,726 job outcomes

recorded because of local authority intervention. Of these, 24,054 (55%) were filled by Newham.

- 80% of people who got a job through Workplace were still employed six months later, compared with the London average for government work programmes of 55%.

We would describe these metrics as typical measurements indicating success. But when other issues were also considered, the impact of the policy became even more apparent. Newham had the fastest-growing employment rate in the dynamic capital, moving from an unemployment rate of 4.4% higher than London's average in 2009/10 to just 0.2% higher in 2016/17; the biggest increase in employment in the country. We took it as a given that employment was the only sustainable route out of poverty for most of our residents – not necessarily as a result of the first job, but the journey needed to start somewhere. According to the Index of Multiple Deprivation, Newham experienced one of the largest decreases in deprivation in the country, moving from the third most deprived borough in 2010 to the twenty-fifth in 2015 – with rising employment being the critical factor. So, Newham exited the bottom ten for the first time in living memory. The change wasn't achieved by importing wealthy people, as had happened elsewhere in the East End. Much of the surge in employment occurred before significant increases in housebuilding across the borough. In addition, the index's map of deprivation showed substantial improvements across all wards across the borough.

Even though Workplace was posting excellent results, there was a determination to extend its scope to ensure that everybody benefited. The employment rate for people with learning disabilities in Newham was at or near the bottom of London boroughs, at 2.8%. Support was provided to locals by various organisations, but it was patchy. So, Newham introduced a supported employment team, to be based at Workplace. Initially, this involved staff experienced in supporting people with learning disabilities and mental health problems. But it quickly became clear that it was better to have people who were experts at finding people work, who were then taught about supporting residents with disabilities and mental health issues. Our focus remained on bridging the unemployment-to-work gap.

In the eighteen months before starting Workplace in September 2014, some thirty-three people were helped into work. In the thirty months after the switch to Workplace, our team supported 226 people into work. By March 2018, Newham's employment rate for this group was 11.5%; nearly twice the Inner London average of 5.9% and the second highest in Inner London (behind only Westminster, with all its advantages). Better, but still very low compared to where we wanted to end up. In fact, the figures for other boroughs often included people studying or training. Newham only included those who were still in paid work after six months. There is little point in employment-related training and study unless it leads somewhere.

It was our intention to develop a capacity at Workplace to help clients (including the council and the NHS) to redesign jobs to create more opportunities for this particular client group. This was not supported by the new administration in 2018. The Workplace approach was the antithesis of a woke approach. It was open to all residents with a time-in-borough qualification. Though largely poorer, participants were self-selecting in the sense that they had a desire to improve their lives and prospects. For the philosophically minded, the approach was closer to that of the 'dead white male' philosophers of the Enlightenment, whereby we treated people as people. It rejected the ham-fisted intersectionality that labels people according to group and undermines agency. This was resilience in practice: working with people to develop their skills so that they could improve their situation using the council's expertise to generate opportunities.

Obviously, many of the jobs were entry-level. If that was the job level people wanted, and if they were happy with it, then that was fine. Anyone who works deserves respect. But many of our Workplace users sought promotions after being in work for a while. That showed the resilience we wanted to develop. And if people wanted a new job altogether, it was far easier to apply from the position of being in work than out of it. Workplace support was not restricted to first jobs. Once a person got a job, support continued to enable them to get better jobs and improve their income. The Workplace motto was 'A job, a better job, a career.' It's not scientific evidence, but the pleasure of those who landed work through Workplace was palpable. People often said, 'Thank you for getting me a job.' Our standard reply was always, 'We didn't get you the job – you did. We just helped.' We also (usually) didn't say, 'Don't forget to vote for us.'

One of the great frustrations when doing something unusual is that it is seen one-dimensionally. Workplace is recognised as having helped people into work. However, it was also an anti-poverty programme, a health initiative, an anti-crime initiative etc. The only real long-term solution to poverty is a job, and then, ideally, a better job. As described elsewhere, handouts can be demeaning and disempowering. Work does not solve all problems, but it helps. A lot. Workplace was not set up as a public health project – but it could have been. We didn't measure applicants' physical and mental health before and after placement. In hindsight, this might have been beneficial. However, noting the work done by Professor Marmot, and the frequent and repeated unsolicited approaches from our residents, there is little doubt in our minds that Workplace led to significant improvements in the mental and physical health of many.

In crime-ridden districts of Los Angeles, California, they have a saying: 'Nothing stops a bullet like a job.' Our records show that Workplace made a difference to the chances of ex-offenders not reoffending; one of the most demanding public policy challenges facing the UK and other democracies. At one point we were asked how many ex-offenders we had helped into work. The answer was that we did not know. When people asked for help, we looked at their skills and tried to match them with an appropriate job. Whether they had served a term in prison was not necessarily relevant. 120 ex-offenders had volunteered the information so there is a baseline, but the real numbers will be much higher. Many people have been rescued from crime through work. It is not unreasonable to assume that the impact of Workplace has been greater than those of many of the anti-crime projects so beloved of the virtuous.

We kept records to monitor Workplace's performance, but only where we thought they were relevant to the task and to ensure that we were not discriminating, albeit unintentionally. Given that access to the programme was based on self-determination, the key for us was to ensure that every individual had the same opportunity. This contrasts with jobs programmes often rolled out by governments, which tend to start by assessing who should deliver the scheme, before defining a narrow range of recipients. We started with the employer – the person offering the job – and asked what we had to do to persuade them to give our people a chance. Every person who wants a job is as worthy of assistance as the next person, irrespective of their background. As we said earlier, successful job applicants reflected the ethnic mix of Newham's working population; something we checked regularly. As a result, tens of thousands of what the SJWs used to call BAME residents got jobs. The most successful anti-discrimination initiative in the country, perhaps?

One final comment on employment and skills. Newham provided an agile funding stream for these on a scale unheard of elsewhere in London. National schemes tended to focus on major qualifications, yet some employers only wanted smaller, more flexible training rather than qualifications which could take one or two years of full-time study to achieve. This was particularly true of customer service and construction, both of which were a key part of the Newham economy at the time. Smaller qualifications were more manageable for residents with family commitments and other barriers to employment. This agility – even though local government procurement is pretty bureaucratic – meant we could move much more quickly and effectively than nationally commissioned programmes. This is one of the reasons why we are unconvinced that government understands, or is capable of providing, the sort of skills offer the economy needs; and by that we mean the requirements for the jobs which our people should be accessing.

The results at Workplace were spectacular. There is nothing to stop this model from being applied elsewhere. In the following chapters, we outline the problems and issues that need to be addressed to achieve that.

Since writing this chapter we have seen an increase in discussion on the need to grow the economy and, in particular, to get millions of people currently on benefits into paid employment. Workplace was open to all, but our key objective was always to get the long-term unemployed and those who had never worked into work. It is no good only offering just this cohort to employers – they have business needs. Instead, by focusing on the needs of business and matching residents to jobs, we were able to provide a range of candidates to meet employer needs, and as a result 40% of those helped were long-term unemployed or had never previously worked.

Chapter 5

DEBT AND MONEYWORKS

There are 350 varieties of shark, not counting loan and pool.
(L. M. Boyd)

'Debt is the worst poverty'
(Thomas Fuller.)

Robin's mother was a credit traveller. Her job was to sell stuff to people that they would then pay off every week. The highlight of the year for many of her customers was the delivery of a Christmas hamper. People would experience the thrill of chomping their way through its contents during a relaxing family Christmas, and then spend the following year covering the cost of next Christmas's hamper through weekly contributions to the supplier. When he was older, Robin would accompany his mum as she delivered the hampers. Since they were heavy, he was given the role of carrying the food into the house (he was fitter then!). His abiding memory of that period is taking a hamper to a family living in a council house. There was almost nothing in the sitting room: just a settee, a coffee table and a television. The kids were barefoot, and stones and bits of coal were scattered around the floor. The kids had been off school with infections in their feet, but they could hardly contain their excitement when the festive hamper arrived. The package's contents were worth about half what the family would end up paying, and since they included at least some goods that the family were probably not that keen to have, Robin estimated that, in effect, the family paid something like £3 for every £1 spent. Mothers and fathers desperately wanted to give their kids a Christmas treat but were not equipped to understand how they were being ripped off by the supplier. It felt wrong, and was a formative experience for Newham's future Mayor.

In the UK, poverty is not simply an absence of money. Instead, it goes hand in hand with an absence of education, resilience and ambition. It is an absence of a sense that 'Things will improve tomorrow if only I do something today.' Every student who has ever been skint understands that things should be better tomorrow. At least, their education allows them to understand that things are likely to get better.

Like many people, we recognise the importance of providing affordable credit to help people who are struggling and need some financial support. On every high street, Newham's residents used to be offered what appeared to be enticing finance deals on hire purchase (HP). What these deals hid, or downplayed, was that the items being purchased were often offered at a price that was 50% or often 100% higher than that charged at other outlets. Low weekly repayments became the focus of advertising campaigns, masking the often unconscionably high interest rates being charged. This was of interest to us as elected politicians who genuinely wanted to make a difference to people's lives. If we wanted to help poorer residents to help themselves, we had to understand and provide solutions to the problems that were holding them back both practically and psychologically.

Debt can be debilitating. So, at Newham we reasoned that to support the development of personal resilience, we would need to help people resolve their debt issues. The experience of getting out of debt would both improve their confidence and remove an enormous psychological burden. It was a step towards developing personal resilience. Nobody got free handouts, but they did get the support of an organisation that was used to dealing with multimillion-pound commercial organisations, and which stood by them as they took steps out of poverty. In this, we firmly believe that the council represented the values of our community – and time and again, the community has shown that it wants to help people in difficulty. We reasoned that those who are striving deserve community and council support.

To gain a greater understanding of people's experiences of living on low incomes, Newham commissioned the London School of Economics to conduct interviews that explored the relationship between financial problems, credit, debt, and the impact of welfare changes. Not surprisingly, the LSE's findings, along with quantitative data from Newham's Household Panel Survey (the last undertaken in 2017), underlined the significant impact of financial problems and debt on local residents. When housing costs were included, just under half of households were in relative poverty, and the level of poverty increased as the number of children in the household increased.

So, in March 2016, Newham Council established MoneyWorks; a debt advice agency with an associated credit union, the London Community Credit Union (LCCU). Many good local authorities offered this fairly standard service – we wouldn't claim exclusivity over that. However, in what is thought to be a unique move, the council also set aside funds to underwrite and extend affordable credit to residents unable to secure low-cost credit, even from the credit union. That was new and different, and it again marked out Newham as going the extra mile for its residents. Our thinking was that the council knows quite a lot about people and can obtain a vast amount of information from a detailed conversation about personal circumstances; information that credit reference agencies don't have. Even Google and Facebook, the modern masters at harvesting mega-data, don't yet have all the data on residents that councils hold and protect.

In practice, many people were attracted by the offer of a council loan but were in such financial problems that additional credit was not the answer. MoneyWorks provided support to help these people begin to tackle their problems. The offer of a loan was the hook that enabled them to access help they would otherwise have avoided. From its inception to May 2018, MoneyWorks granted almost 750 loans based on roughly 2,400 applications. That's 750 families who accessed low-cost credit who otherwise would have been denied it. Work also continued with those who did not qualify for a loan to help them resolve their debt. MoneyWorks did not eradicate poverty locally, and it wasn't for everyone. But it was a step forward. It made life-changing differences to many struggling families at little net cost. People with no hope, people who were suicidal, people who were self-harming; real lives were changed as residents were helped to find a way out of the debt spiral.

MoneyWorks was also able to exercise discretion on the recovery of council debts, including council tax and housing rents. This did not encourage non-payment; rather, it was a way of seeking to give people the opportunity to resolve their debt problems with the council in a manner that was sympathetic to their circumstances. The aim, ultimately, was to have MoneyWorks involved in all council debt cases. There are sensible management reasons for creditors (in this case the council) to seek court orders for debt recovery. But it is perverse to add extra debt to the financial burdens of people who want to pay but can't.

As a result of MoneyWorks' efforts, defaults on loans were low – anecdotally, perhaps half the level that might be expected from such a high-risk group. In any event, some defaults were necessary for us to understand who repays and who does not – and why. Trial and error; the scientific method in action again. We had to take some financial risks to understand what probable repayers looked like. Armed with this information, we could then target future loans at those less likely to default on their repayments – and we could set reasonable interest rates since losses from non-payment were minimised. From the start it was expected that this radical approach would result in a one-off loss to the council until a credit scorecard was developed as a means to help us to extend affordable credit to those denied it on the high street. Not everyone, but many more people who would otherwise not have had access to low-cost credit. Not a silver bullet; just a way to help people through tough times. A whole cohort of families with access to low-cost loans for the first time. The idea was that once the behaviour of those receiving loans was better understood, low-interest credit products (including affordable 'payday loans') could be offered to those most likely to repay them. Interest rates could also be varied to allow for changing default levels, so that the effective cost of loans to the council could be set at or near zero. This system worked to the benefit of some of the hardest people to reach within our community, and made a positive difference to their lives.

There is an interesting debate to be had here, though. Why should those who repay their debt have to pay additional interest because other people who (demographically and economically) 'look like' them are more likely to default? It is convenient and (so far) unavoidable, but those who honour their commitments still end up paying for those who don't. So, one of the challenges for councils seeking to replicate schemes like MoneyWorks is to think through how to tackle that lingering problem.

One other objective of MoneyWorks was that if we could identify those people likely to repay debts and provide them with affordable credit, then we would erode – in a good way – the customer base on which the contemporary usurers prey. Take away the better payers, and the usurers' exploitative lending model becomes less sustainable.

MoneyWorks also had strong links to Workplace. It was instrumental in helping people to improve their lives through their own efforts; in essence, developing resilience. It was the kind of programme we came into politics to deliver. Sadly, with the change in administration in Newham, this vision has been lost. But there is nothing to stop other councils from taking up the gauntlet.

It is now commonplace among the woke to wring hands over the crushing problems of debt facing many across the UK. But delivering widespread change does not appear to be on the agenda. While wringing one's hands may signal one's virtuous intent or solidarity with this week's member of the oppressed, we believed that muscular action by our council would resolve some – though not all – credit issues for poorer people. And it did! We thought that this was a good result, and shared it with colleagues in the council. One younger and woker councillor turned her nose up at the scheme: 'You only help 50%; you're doing nothing about the others.' It epitomised the modern Labour Party: real action to help marginalised people was dismissed in favour of a 'virtuous' but empty gesture.

Chapter 6

EDUCATION, CHILDREN AND YOUNG PEOPLE

Education is the most powerful weapon you can use to
change the world.
(Nelson Mandela)

Helping people into work and providing the means to access affordable credit (where such access makes sense) are difficult things to do. That we managed to achieve both aims is a source of considerable pride – and was entirely consistent with our pragmatic approach to resilience. We had a goal and worked empirically to deliver the initiatives that moved us towards that goal. But our view was that, while we tried to help people deal with the circumstances in which they found themselves during their adult lives, we also had to drive up educational standards to support the next generation. This was a long-term project, but one with potentially great rewards.

When Robin was elected as Newham's leader in 1995 (before the post became that of a directly elected Mayor), the borough's schools and schoolchildren performed poorly. Every year, the children of our deprived borough languished at or near the bottom of every education performance table. The received wisdom was that this was only to be expected.

Newham was similar to neighbouring boroughs with almost identical problems, so, the argument went, it stood to 'reason' that these were poor children from poor areas, and therefore their education and achievements would be equally poor. It was the prevailing mindset. But it was also utter nonsense. Robin's elevation as Newham's leader preceded the election (to a slightly bigger role) of one Tony Blair and his stated commitment to three priorities: 'Education, education, education.' These two factors sparked a transformation that saw the performance of Newham's schools improve markedly and the life chances of local children improve exponentially. The Blairite commitment to education may have been political hyperbole, but it was hyperbole aimed at improving the life chances of children in poor neighbourhoods. It was a perfect social democratic aim.

As described elsewhere in this book, we spent the late 1990s and early part of the new millennium improving the efficiency of local services while controlling costs. The positive and negative impacts of this were apparent in the new local commissioning and management schemes developed (by Whitehall) every few years. And while it sometimes felt as if we were hopping from one government hobby horse to another, services to our residents undoubtedly improved. That was the backdrop to the development of the three components of resilience: personal resilience, financial resilience and community resilience. People (or, specifically in the case of education, children) did not exist in a vacuum. They had families and friends, were part of social networks and communities, and their parents were active in the local economy. We believed that better educational standards would improve local resilience by helping young people secure decent jobs and careers – and we saw no reason why the glass ceilings imposed by the previous prevailing mindset should hold back our local children.

Education is key to the development of resilience. It can show us different worlds and expose us to different thoughts and ideas. At its best, it opens up the world and helps people towards a more fulfilling life. Yet young people learn things in school that are not part of their lived experience. When the white middle classes take part in Black Lives Matter marches, they are not marching to the beat of their lived experience, but to that of their education. And therein lies an irony. While the woke middle classes are happy to march to support those in need and against the 'oppression' that maintains their comfortable lifestyles, they show little egalitarian fervour when it comes to fighting to get their kids into the best schools with the better academic outcomes at the expense of children with parents who are not as well versed in the navigation of quasi-governmental bureaucracies.

Our view was that we were there to improve the life chances of all children in Newham – but the challenges facing the borough were enormous. For too long before we established ourselves in office, the council had focused on the wrong things and obsessed about irrelevant matters. As Quintin Peppiatt, former Cabinet Member for Children and Young People, recalls:

> I vividly remember in my first education committee one of the crucial decisions was the ordering of toilet rolls for schools. It seemed clear to me that this was not the way to oversee the eighty schools in Newham.

In this, Newham was not significantly different from other local authorities. Successive governments moved to reduce the power of councils over education because they believed (correctly) that councils were not effective at – or even interested in – improving school standards. Though councils were rather good at distributing toilet paper!

For some time before we got going in Newham, the mantra from some reactionary head teachers and teachers (including reactionary Left-wingers) was that our children were from poor backgrounds and therefore 'difficult' to educate. Our children were oppressed by virtue of being the heirs to multiple negative indicators. This was precisely the anti-resilience mantra that prevails among the woke today: a middle-class movement with innate anti-working-class prejudices. We believed that such prejudices excused poor educational performance and infantilised the very people they purported to support.

We had an alternative. Our vision was to support youngsters in developing the tools and personal resilience to make meaningful choices in their lives, and to help those helping children. But improving school standards could not have been done just by empowering head teachers and school governing bodies. It was also necessary to look strategically at the school system and individual schools and, where there was clear underachievement, to change how a school was run. Positive interventions fuelled by clear improvement aims and plans. We supported the partnering of schools to improve performance and (where that did not work) enabled changes of leadership, or 'academisation' – the process whereby a school was removed from local authority control and run independently as an exempt charity funded by central government. The only question to be answered was: would a particular intervention improve the education of the young people concerned?

When academies were introduced, they represented a determined attempt to tackle the poor quality of education in many schools; particularly in London. For us, academisation was always a means to an end, and not an end in itself. The key was to support schools in tackling underperformance and to achieve a broad and balanced curriculum. Local solutions tailored to local education problems; not a one-size-fits-all approach. As an aside, the evidence now seems clear that the academy chains are generally no more or less effective than those schools which are described as local education authority (LEA) schools. What started as a successful intervention to drive up standards has become a centralised bureaucratic sacred cow. As always, governments end up focusing on organisation rather than delivery.

The council's determination to improve standards was aided by the many decent head teachers, teachers and school governors who shared our passion for excellence and desire to improve children's life chances. Strong support from parents also helped immeasurably. The election of the national Labour government in 1997 and its wider drive to improve standards were crucial in reducing opposition to educational improvement. With Westminster beating the drum for better standards, local authorities that rejected the past mindset felt greatly empowered too. We were committed to improving the attainment levels of our children. By necessity, these were measured by exams at various ages – and we saw local results improve dramatically.

But education is not just about exam performance, and children cannot be entirely separated from their home lives and neighbourhoods. Every day they are affected by social and emotional factors. On the macro level, these include the negative effect of the broader peer group, and the threats and inducements of violent and criminal behaviour. At the micro level, factors such as whether Dad or Mum has a job, or even whether Dad is at home, play a part in a child's attainment. It is difficult to study if you are hungry, and concentration wanders if your primary concern is the threat of violence when you leave the school gates. We are very aware of current concerns about a focus on black youths by the police. But we have yet to see a willingness from some campaigners to implement the policies that will improve the safety of young people of colour who want nothing to do with gangs. Instead, some campaign groups oppose policies which would save young black lives (see Chapter 9 on enforcement and how to disarm young people).

An additional challenge for local schools during this period was the considerable growth in demand. School places had to be increased by 40% in just twelve years. There were many challenges in Newham's schools. But there were also specific challenges in early years and post-sixteen education.

Preschool

We suspect that most of our readers (assuming that there are some) will come to this volume with an appreciation of the benefits of education, and will have internalised the value of both formal and informal education. They will have an understanding and respect for what we have come to call 'hard' and 'soft' skills. This is not a universal appreciation.

For many years we had been aware that children entering school at age five came to education with vastly different experiences, and that that coloured their life chances. In the early years sector in Newham in the mid '90s, there were relatively few local-authority-run preschool facilities and a small number of voluntary and private operations. Expanding this sector during a period of sustained population growth in London was a major challenge. The strategy we pursued was to greatly increase the provision and then drive up the quality of that provision. It was a long-term strategy in line with our underlying principle: ensure that quality is available, but how it is delivered should be left to skilled practitioners. We saw this as the council exercising its ideal role as an arbiter of standards, but not as the operational manager.

As we have already stressed many times, our role was to improve residents' lives. It wasn't to create a bureaucratic empire within the authority. Where it was appropriate, we supported the economist E. F. Schumacher's observation that 'small is beautiful'. Big organisations develop their own self-interested agendas over time. But smaller organisations can be incentivised to maintain standards. Our role was to ensure that we (or our partners) delivered. So, when it came to the education world, we had no problem with 'small'; nor with the idea of removing schools from local authority control if the outcome of doing so was likely to be better for our children. As you might expect, this approach was met with internal opposition from practitioners who preferred state bureaucracies. But our Cabinet Member for Children and Young People, Quintin Peppiatt, held his nerve. Local results justified his courage, and Quintin deserves a special mention for the major improvements in educational outcomes for our children.

Underpinning the improvements for our youngest children was the Best Start in Life programme.

Best Start in Life

After the financial crash of 2008/09, government cuts hit early years programmes across the country. We recognised the critical importance of early years provision and committed to retaining services, though not necessarily in the same form. Savings were made through rationalising accommodation, bringing council services together in one building, thus improving efficiency and reducing costs by getting rid of existing expensive accommodation, and putting the service through the small business programme.

In April 2016, Newham guaranteed:

- Fifteen hours of free eligible childcare, increasing to thirty hours as government proposals were rolled out.
- Regular 'Stay and Play' sessions in each community neighbourhood (there were ten in Newham).
- Programmes, workshops and sessions offering evidence-based advice and guidance to improve parenting capacity in each neighbourhood.

- Regular employment advice sessions in each neighbourhood (run by Workplace).
- In each neighbourhood, a range of family health and development sessions on topics including antenatal support, the transition to parenthood, the early weeks of life, perinatal well-being, breastfeeding initiation, healthy weight and nutrition, managing minor ailments, reducing accidents, and supporting speech and language developments.

Part of our guarantee was to keep services under review and provide the necessary finances to ensure that these schemes were maintained. In September 2017, Newham's offer to its people was reviewed – and the results confirmed that we were performing and delivering as promised.

We were explicit in all of our early years work that we wanted to ensure that the attainment gaps between our children and the wider community should be reduced or eradicated. This started early. According to Anne Longfield, then Children's Commissioner for England, nationally 40% of children fail to meet their attainment goals when they enter school at age five. For those receiving free school meals, that figure is 50%. Our sustained investment in early years provision meant that by 2018, Newham was the only local authority in the country with no attainment gap between disadvantaged pupils and their more affluent peers at age five. This was important because it meant that, for the first time, our poorer children entered formal schooling with something approaching equality with their middle-class peers. We saw this as a precondition to their taking full advantage of broader educational opportunities. This was not simply the creation of a narrative to meet the political prejudices of our supporters. We started from a very poor position. But in the course of Robin's mayoralty, the early years foundation stage (EYFS) in

Newham improved from 149th to seventeenth out of 150 local authorities by 2017.

The reading guarantee

If early years was a success, we recognised that our focus should continue on children just starting school. In 2011, Newham struck a deal with the Tory-led coalition government (via the impressive Schools Minister, Nick Gibb) to ensure the delivery of a phonics programme throughout local primary schools and improve reading performance across schools.

In addition to the drive on phonics, we introduced what we believe to be a unique part of the initiative. One-to-one tuition was funded directly from the borough's revenue budget for all children behind the expected reading standard in Year 1 (age five to six). Analysis indicated that around 42% of children who were behind their peers at this age caught up normally. But we wanted much more than that – and as a result of the initiative, 83% caught up. The intention was to provide one-to-one tuition if these children fell behind in future years. But further evidence showed that, once they had 'caught up', they tended to perform just as well as their peers after that. Thanks to this initiative, hundreds of local children can now read who would otherwise have struggled. To their credit, schools subsequently assumed responsibility for funding this successful initiative because they recognised its value.

It's not rocket science, but the willingness of politicians to look at problems in a new way and treat them as something that can be overcome is essential if we are to give schoolchildren a genuinely equal chance. A second necessity is for politicians to be prepared to grasp the nettle and expend both money and political capital to drive change forward. Another example of this was the introduction of free school meals.

Free school meals

According to the Trust for London, currently some 52% of children in Newham live in poverty, and while we may quibble about the way in which poverty is measured and defined, it is a standard measurement across the country, and it shows consistently that more children in Newham tend to be poorer than those in other parts of London.

Free school meals were primarily intended as a means of supporting children in their education and in making the most of their educational opportunities. But the scheme became much more and was a significant weapon in our arsenal to combat poverty. Newham was the first area in England to fund free school meals for all primary-school children, resulting in significant gains in education performance. The initial pilots of this project in Newham and Durham (jointly funded by the Labour government and the councils) were evaluated by the social research centre NatCen and the Institute for Fiscal Studies, who commented:

> [P]upils in the pilot areas [are] making between four and eight weeks' more progress than similar pupils in comparison areas. The improvements in attainment tend to be strongest amongst pupils from less affluent families.

Following the withdrawal of government funds after the pilot period, Newham continued to fund free school meals because we recognised the educational and nutritional benefits. This was done partly to improve education results, but also to support working families who saved around £437 annually per child. Had we been able to continue the small business programme and transformation initiatives, there was also an intention to extend the free school meals programme to secondary schools.

One point of interest here is that children from less affluent backgrounds were the primary beneficiaries of this innovation. Free school meals were already available to families on benefits, but this was a programme to support working parents on low incomes.

We are genuinely astonished that free school meals for all children have not been introduced at every state-funded school in the country but are pleased to see that the London Mayor, Sadiq Khan, has committed to ensuring that this initiative is spread across the capital. Our results were indisputable and, while it carried a price, the initiative did not cost the earth. What is the downside? As a society, we should ensure that all children eat well, irrespective of the quality of their parenting or the home resources available to them. There are direct benefits to educational attainment, and the benefit from investment in children's well-being is immense. Plus, it supports the 'squeezed middle' that every politician will tell you they want to help (here's a question as to why free school meals isn't national policy: do some politicians *really* want to help such people?).

The Every Child programme

We have written above about the way in which children do not simply 'exist' in schools. They are part of a family and have wider networks. We wanted to expand the horizons of our children to encourage and enable them to take advantage of opportunities on offer. Newham's Every Child programme provided free local access to a wide range of cultural and sporting opportunities including music lessons and instruments, sports lessons, theatre trips, and chess tutorials. Exposing children to various experiences was part of our thinking around the development of resilience.

After it started, and at the cost of £2 million per year, Every Child a Musician (ECaM) delivered over one million lessons, making it the largest free music scheme in the country. Tens of thousands of children were taught to play to Grade 1 standard and given their own musical instrument, e.g. violin, trumpet, keyboard etc. (Not drums! We wanted the votes of neighbours as well as parents.) Tuition was weekly and typically on a one-to-four basis, and 90% of children passed their Grade 1 assessment. Thanks to ECaM, in Newham around four thousand additional new musical instruments were being used a year. At its peak, 130 tutors delivered more than three hundred thousand lessons annually to twelve thousand children across one of the country's poorest areas. In total, fifty thousand children benefited from the scheme. Our primary justification was the importance of supporting children to develop additional skills. The argument ran: 'If it's good enough for the middle classes, then it's good enough for all our kids.' And so it was.

An awful lot of research evidence supports the idea that musical education at a young age can improve children's development outcomes. It appears to support the development of reading skills, for starters. As part of our belief in the scientific method, Newham commissioned several independent studies to assess the impact of the music scheme locally. In addition, in 2011 the New London Orchestra conducted a quasi-experimental trial in Newham of a five-month intensive music programme. Professor Graham Welch from the Institute of Education evaluated the trial in two separate cycles and found that ECaM had a positive impact on writing and maths, with a significant average improvement of 6.6 months in participants' reading development. Gains were made by all ethnic groups and levels of deprivation had little impact on learning. Indeed, such were the success and scale of the programme that, working with Professor John Howard of the University of West London and Philip Alfred, chief examiner of the London College of Music Examinations, ECaM had to develop bespoke graded examinations as most music services enter children for exams in small numbers, so when thousands need to be tested a bespoke system was required. Based on this clear evidence, we firmly believe that the government should run similar programmes across different areas and assess the benefits fully. Given our local evidence base, not to do so would seem to be a dereliction of duty.

Interestingly, there was significant opposition to this programme from middle-class woke types, who argued that only children whose parents wanted them to learn should receive the tuition. Others argued that the money should be spent on something other than taking a generation of relatively poor children and introducing them to the arts in a way that enhanced their personal skills. ECaM was closely associated with Robin so, when the council's leadership changed after 2018, the new regime chose to close the programme. It is a sad loss – not because it was associated with Robin, but because it improved children's skills and academic achievements.

ECaM was the largest element of a programme which included Every Child a Sportsperson, Theatregoer, Chess Player etc. We made significant inroads in our determination to add value to the curriculum children and young people enjoyed at our (mostly) very good and ever-improving schools. Exposure to more experiences is how you build resilience, and surely we urgently need to do something to increase the resilience of our young people today.

Post-sixteen years

Newham's educational performance at the post-sixteen level was horrible in the mid '90s. We were close to the bottom of every league table covering post-sixteen offerings, and around 50% of our sixteen-year-olds were travelling out of the borough for their education. Many of the brightest minds never returned.

The borough had set up a further education college – 'NewVIc', or the Newham Sixth (VI) Form College – but this catered only for some youngsters and could in no sense be described as a top-class offer for pupils with high academic aspirations. This is not to criticise what was on offer; it was 'acceptable to good' for the young people who attended the college. But it wasn't enough.

We determined to support a higher academic offering. We supported new schools in the borough, such as the London Academy of Excellence. This was supplemented by developing a council-inspired (but not council-run) sixth form provision: Newham Collegiate Sixth Form Centre. But sometimes our determination to see better results locally just meant getting out of the way of existing practitioners skilled in delivering more for young people; for example, the superb team behind Brampton Manor Academy, whose 2021 cohort received more Oxbridge offers than Eton's. Indeed, the Academy of Excellence, Brampton, and Newham Collegiate all appeared in 2021's top ten schools for Oxbridge candidates. In 2022 Brampton announced that 95% of its sixth-formers had earned three A or A* grades. Not bad for a poverty-riven borough with 'difficult to educate' children, eh? And a huge achievement for the leadership in those schools. It's always about the leadership in schools.

So, we hope you can see from our approach that councils don't have to deliver everything – other local experts often want improvements and can be better at delivering just that. What councils should consider is a mixed (or tailored) local support package, moral support, and the necessary political vision.

In Newham, this was a question of mindset. The council's previous 'command and control' approach had required a vast expenditure in terms of time, monitoring and management. Setting ambitious goals but leaving schools to determine how they met them released the energy and enthusiasm of local staff and head teachers. Elsewhere in this volume we rail against the command and control of large bureaucracies, and this was how we sought to reduce that locally. Our role was to achieve the best educational offering for our children and their parents. It was not to manage everything.

For all of this, it was still a work in progress. Children's services as they are currently structured are led by demand, and the demand was significant. When we left office the director of the Children and Young People's Service had only been in post for a relatively short time, but was beginning to get to grips with the service, which was 'improving' in Ofsted terms. A year later she too would be gone, and the service would be declared 'failing'.

Education results

Over a sustained period, the results of our education-related programmes in Newham were impressive (results shown here are for 2017/18):

- Comparing positions in Key Stage 2 tables, and allowing for English as a second language, Newham became the second-best education area in London (excluding the City of London) when measuring league positions for writing, GPS (grammar, punctuation and spelling), and maths.
- At Key Stage 4 some 64.6% of local pupils achieved the equivalent of a grade C in English and maths; this was up from 63.5% in 2016. Newham was ranked twenty-third in England on this measure. Against the Progress 8 measure, Newham was the tenth-best authority in England.
- Newham moved from 128th to eighth in the national league table for A level results. That's correct: Newham moved up 120 places.
- In 2020, three Newham schools were in the top fifty for Oxbridge offers. In 2021, three of our schools were in the top ten.

- Newham ranked second in the country for progress between Key Stages 1 and 2.

Other national measures also supported these findings. By 2018, when we left office, Newham had more primary schools in the top five hundred than any other council in the country. In addition, we ranked second in the country on phonics screening tests at the end of Year 1.

We believe that, had our focus on early years and the various initiatives we implemented continued, we might have seen even more improvement in education standards. But unfortunately our passion for education was not replicated in the new administration. There is a sense in which this replicates the national division in Left politics between controlling the narrative and delivering measurable change. The woke obsession with narrative is in some senses nothing new; politics has always required the ability to win the battle of ideas, and part of this means dominating the social and intellectual landscape. When we talk elsewhere about virtue-signalling, this is what we mean. Making statements that sound worthy, while failing to effect genuine improvement; change sometimes, but improvement rarely. Locally, this was seen in the rhetorical hostility to academies, which appeased those who identified themselves as being on the Left but was unaccompanied by any real effort to improve educational outcomes for the children of the borough.

As we hinted above, for us the medium was always of secondary importance when compared to the outcome. What was important was what worked.

We've seen the future and it doesn't work

The effects of Newham's determined approach to improving local education outcomes can be seen in the results achieved by the end of our administration. However, the national government trend of squeezing out local authorities from education meant that it was increasingly difficult to influence much above Key Stage 2, and our sustained improvements began to slow.

As power has become more centralised in whatever the Department for Education is currently called, the ability to monitor and challenge schools has increasingly foundered. As outlined elsewhere, large bureaucracies struggle to perform well. Yet the government has worked relentlessly to create an ever-larger centralised bureaucracy in education. In Newham, our view was that the local democratically elected organisation responsible for representing the community should have a major role in monitoring standards and taking remedial action wherever necessary. This was very much in line with the council's broad policy that, in general, we should have responsibility for setting out what was required, monitoring outcomes, and taking appropriate action in the event of poor delivery. How things were delivered should be left to skilled practitioners (head teachers in the case of schools), which is precisely the approach of the small business programme outlined elsewhere in this book. It is much easier to influence a head teacher when you have both the relationships and the tools to encourage (and coerce) than to influence a faceless bureaucracy. And this can be done at a far greater speed locally than can be achieved from the centre.

It was always our view that challenging poor performance is essential; the ability to act not just against the poorest schools (which is relatively easy), but also against coasting schools. On one occasion, Robin and Quintin approached the Schools Commissioner regarding the performance of three of the worst-performing secondary schools in the borough, with the intention of taking some action. They were told that a plan of action was not possible because the three schools were above minimum national standards. This illustrates a tension in the education sector. 'Good enough' when dealing with thousands of schools was not 'good enough' in Newham. Our ambitious local authority was hampered by the dead hand of the civil service and a national one-size-fits-all approach. Officials weren't being deliberately obstructive, but could devote neither the energy nor the attention to improving coasting schools – and nor were they willing to delegate the authority to do so to the council. Good enough for the government, but not for Newham! No wonder there is so often frustration at the national government's influence over local services. Newham had genuine ambition for improvement, but government regulation and inertia prevented it.

It is entirely appropriate that the government should also be concerned with standards and monitor the performance of local authorities and schools. We must not return to the broken systems that betrayed generations of children (for example, the shocking Inner London Education Authority). But not all councils are prepared to do what is necessary to ensure that their young people get a decent education. In such cases, intervention by the national government is to be welcomed. However, the tools for dealing with failing schools are different to those needed to improve mid-ranked or coasting schools. There needs to be flexibility, and we believe that decisions regarding what form that flexible approach takes should be made by local leaders. Grandiose centralised systems cost more and, sooner or later, change the focus of their work from children's education to the maintenance of the organisation.

Chapter 7

HEALTH

The care of the public health is the first duty of the statesman.
(Benjamin Disraeli)

Others before us have noted that, while we have an NHS, it is less a health service and more of a treatment service. The greater part of what happens to affect health takes place outside of the NHS. We also know that those who are poorest have the worst health. A widely quoted observation is that you lose a year of life expectancy for each stop along the Jubilee Tube Line from Westminster to Stratford. It is not precisely accurate, but it is true enough: life expectancy certainly declines as you move east from Westminster. But this is true of all areas of urban and rural deprivation.

In his 2010 review *Fair Society, Healthy Lives*, Sir Michael Marmot explained the problems and what needed to be addressed. Yet England has seen little progress since that groundbreaking study. In 2020, the Institute of Health Equity published a follow-up report entitled *Health Equity in England: The Marmot Review 10 Years On*. The follow-up (also written by Sir Michael) noted that little had changed and that, as in 2010, reducing health inequalities required action on six policy objectives:

- *Give every child the best start in life.*
- *Enable all children, young people and adults to maximise their capabilities and have control of their lives.*
- *Create fair employment and good work for all.*
- *Ensure a healthy standard of living for all.*
- *Create and develop healthy and sustainable places and communities.*
- *Strengthen the role and impact of ill health prevention.*

The approach to health policy we adopted in Newham reflected these objectives. Resilience, controlling your life and environment, education and employment; much of the groundbreaking work and success described in previous chapters, we found, could be applied to health issues.

For now, it is sufficient to understand that when we pigeonhole something like health by referring to the NHS, we are discussing how we deal with people who are ill, rather than stopping people from falling ill in the first place.

Clive was a champion of tackling health inequalities over many years. But he also had the task of engaging with the local NHS to develop partnerships for change. An observation. Partnership is often included in the objectives of a service – especially the NHS – which demonstrates obeisance to process rather than results. If you are focused on delivery, partnership is a means to an end; it is not the end itself. And it is usually more honoured in the breach than in observance.

For us in the Labour bastion that is Newham, it was a given that everything the Tories say and do is wrong. Except when it isn't! In the early years of the Conservative-led coalition government, the 'blue' wing encouraged collaboration between different public services at a local level. Under the 2012 Health and Social Care Act, from 2013 this was formalised in the shape of health and well-being boards.

Relationships and trust

Health and well-being boards (HWBBs) are formal committees of the council that bring together the council, the local clinical commissioning group, and other stakeholders, to improve the health of local communities. For the uninitiated, CCGs commissioned health services and (alongside the council) social care services locally. They were largely coterminous with councils until 2018 when, in the first of three organisational restructures taking place over four years, another round of reorganisation merged neighbouring CCGs. Is this seriously any way to run a service?!

But back to our main point. In theory, what the 2013 reforms did was bring together health, care and council decision makers in one committee designed to coordinate local health services and do things better.

The formal functions of HWBBs are pretty limited – to agree a joint strategic needs assessment (JSNA) and a joint health and well-being strategy for the locality – and there is a danger that they will become merely a forum for rubber-stamping policies developed elsewhere. At Newham, we saw HWBBs as a genuine opportunity to develop relationships to ensure that the organisations worked better together. We wanted results and (as we explain elsewhere in this book) it is in the boundaries between organisations, or between different parts of the same organisation, where the greatest potential for failure exists.

Across the country relationships between health and care authorities and local councils have sometimes been strained, and that had certainly been the case in Newham for some time. So, it was a stated objective of our council leadership that relationships with clinicians and health administrators had to be improved. In the early days of the brave new HWBB venture, both authors expended considerable time and effort in meeting with key players in the primary care community; a task central to Clive's ongoing work.

Newham's JSNA varied little from one year to the next so, with better relationships, it was possible to agree a long-term set of objectives to address critical health priorities:

- Promote healthy behaviours.
- Tackle mental health barriers to employment.
- Tackle long-term conditions.
- Build child health and well-being.

Of course, everybody in the public sector talks about 'partnership working'. It is a catch-all buzz phrase that reflects a necessary outcome of mixed service provision. But partnerships should be able to evidence benefits. It was the outcomes for patients that were important; the 'partnering' was merely a means to that end. For us, effective partnerships meant exhibiting benefits in terms of hard cash or better services – and preferably both. And the way we delivered this locally was through integrated planning.

Even before the Better Care Fund (BCF), a funding programme introduced in 2013 to promote the integration of health and care via local government and the NHS, Newham operated a virtual pooled budget between our CCG and adult social care. When the BCF became operational, we quickly agreed to one of England's largest BCF budgets at £125 million per year. We also eliminated cost-shunting, whereby one party within the HWBB sought to save money by shunting costs to another. By focusing on tightly defined outcomes, it was possible to spend according to joint priorities rather than haggle over who paid for what (a toxic situation that blighted some other councils and CCGs). This was particularly true with regard to adult social care, and specifically when it was that someone ceased to be a patient and became a resident in need of support. As we were able to focus on the needs of that individual, it became gradually less important whose budget paid for a service.

As another example of integrated planning, we looked at ways to work more closely together, recognising that it is often in the interaction between two groups where mistakes are made and money wasted. A good example of this was when the CCG was looking to move. Around 2015, the lease for the local CCG's administration building expired. But because all parts of the HWBB worked increasingly closely together, particularly across adult social care, it seemed sensible that our adult services (what residents would generally think of as 'social services') should be located close to the CCG, or vice versa. The council had acquired a large new building, which realised savings in property costs and through consolidating staff at a single site. The new HQ also made us money through rents, because almost half the office space was leased to outside organisations. So, we offered a floor within one wing of the building to our local CCG, at a very affordable rent. This would have meant that both our adult and children's departments were only minutes away from the CCG. That would have made it a lot easier to achieve the desired integrated working between council departments and the local NHS, and it seemed like an ideal and pragmatic solution.

There was just one problem: our generous offer was not received with the enthusiasm we had hoped for. For some reason, the CCG's board members did not want it to be seen, however erroneously, as just another department within the council. So, they found a new suite of offices in the north of the borough; some distance from council staff with whom they were supposed to 'integrate' and work. This was a blow, but we thought on our feet. Rather than lose the benefits of staff working closely together, we undertook to move our adult social care department into the same building as the CCG, and they are now located on the floor below. We did this despite the additional cost because we cared about improving health outcomes through integrated working.

It would have been easy for us to dig in our heels and refuse to move our adult care staff. But accepting what had happened and coming up with a Plan B was the correct decision. The revised arrangement still allowed for quick and easy meetings between all health and care staff, including those 'water cooler moments' that allow for the cross-fertilisation of ideas. 'If the mountain won't come to Mohammed...'

In 2016, the local CCG published their estates plan. Newham was unusual in its general practitioner (GP) profile. With a bigger population than some neighbouring boroughs, we had fewer GPs, though they were spread across a larger number of surgeries. More than sixty GP practices were sustained by an ageing workforce, with (too) many single- and two-handed practices. These nonetheless carried patient lists which were 30% above the recommended level. Single-handed practices could not provide the extended hours and services that modern medicine demands. Additionally, newer and younger GPs seemed to want a different working model to the one offered by our cohort of retiring GPs. For reasons best known to themselves, they appeared to want a better work-life balance and to spend some time with their partners and children! They also wanted to practise medicine and were not enraptured by the prospect of staff management, payroll services and estate maintenance (or mortgage debt).

NHS Newham (the CCG) had for some years sought to rationalise provision as individual GPs retired. To many councils, the dual problems of GP recruitment and the primary care estate would have been solely the province of the CCG. But we interpreted our responsibilities under the 2012 Act more broadly. Additionally, we discussed with the CCG the place of non-medical interventions in the provision of primary care. The oft-quoted example is the elderly lady who attends the surgery every Tuesday morning for an appointment to discuss non-specific aches and pains, depression or anxiety; all of which are real in that she feels them, but which may not be the result of chemical imbalances or injury. More often, this occurs because the surgery staff are the only people this elderly lady talks to from one week to the next. Appointments become her way of socialising and tackling loneliness. It would, of course, be far better to offer her opportunities to meet people, do some simple 'keep fit' exercises as part of a group, or something else that would help her to meet with, and enjoy the company of, other people.

We wanted the new generation of GP surgeries to offer a range of services and activities to improve people's physical and mental health, but which would not necessarily be 'medical' solutions. The theory was that part of the surgery would be exclusively for 'medical' work, but part would also offer broader community health services. Spaces where residents could do yoga or keep fit were obvious. But we also wanted coffee bars in which a knitting group could meet, room for localised benefits support services, access to employment via a more relaxed and comfortable Workplace setting, or actually any activity that grabbed people's attention and gave them an interest and a way of feeling part of the community, but with clear health benefits, be they physical or mental.

In the north of the borough, two surgeries employed a practice nurse who viewed her role more broadly. A church member in the area, she conducted keep fit classes for groups of women in a church hall and saw dozens of women from every ethnicity each week. This remarkable woman must have saved the NHS thousands of pounds in time and prescribed medication, and in doing so immeasurably improved the lives of the women who attended her sessions. Supporting the CCG in this way became an important priority for the council, and our initiatives traversed the borough. In Manor Park in the northeast of Newham, the CCG wanted to amalgamate several smaller GP practices. Drawing on his knowledge of the local area, Clive identified a struggling community centre (the Froud Centre) and helped to bring the two services together to deliver the desired outcome of more joined-up GP services. A new health centre has recently opened its doors as an integrated part of the community centre. In Beckton in the south of Newham, an enterprising team of GPs wanted to rebuild their premises but, for reasons best known to the London Docklands Development Corporation planners, the site sat on a small island surrounded by roads on four sides! Again, using his local knowledge, Clive was able to bring together the GPs with a community centre operated by the local diocese and a library/resource centre operated by the council. By adding a small unused plot of land owned by the council, a new primary care facility and much-needed housing were made possible. These are currently at the planning stage. Interestingly, and probably helped by the fact that the area dean (church leader) has extensive knowledge and understanding of local government, those involved in the project have proposed almshouses instead of housing association properties. One of the blights of urban housing has been the extension of Right to Buy from council houses to housing association properties. Owner-occupancy is a positive thing. The trouble is that increasing numbers of publicly funded homes are being sold at a discount, and within a few years (or even months), they are sold on or passed to children for whom they become simply a secondary source of income. The number of affordable properties available to local people on low incomes has thereby been reduced. The reintroduction of almshouses, which cannot be bought under Right to Buy schemes, offers an interesting solution to the challenge of providing social housing that will not become subsidised investment properties.

The projects described above were ad hoc initiatives that used community intelligence and the ability to exercise influence on council departments. Such good work goes on in many other councils. However, it became clear that an ad hoc or piecemeal approach was not the answer to delivering twenty-first-century primary care services across the whole of Newham.

In the years when the CCG luxuriated in zero annual budget growth, the local authority made significant savings. By this point in time, the loss of central government grants within Newham amounted to around £137 million a year. Elsewhere we discuss the approach Newham adopted in respect of making savings and transforming operations but, with the loss of income in mind, senior councillors and directors understood that they were expected to find ways of saving money and generating revenue. This approach was not without political risk. There is a section of the Labour Party for whom spending other people's money is the defining core of socialism. This attitude was, and still is, present across parts of Newham. Any policy programme that was not 'tax and spend' was simply alien and anathema to such members, and saving cash was considered a Right-wing deviation.

Clive and Grainne Siggins (Newham's director of adult social care) regularly discussed Newham's wider health and well-being strategy. As the issues faced by the CCG were explored, it became clear that there was a chance to make a generational change for both the council and the CCG – but we faced several challenges. For the CCG, the key problems have already been outlined above: an ageing cohort of GPs, younger GPs not wanting to run businesses, too many small practices unable to provide modern facilities including non-medical services, and attracting new medics and health professionals since general practice was less fashionable and the London cost of living prohibitively high. For the local authority, there were a number of additional challenges:

- We were fans of Lord Ara Darzi's recommendations to improve London's NHS services. Though the peer's various studies seemed by 2010 to have fallen out of favour with the Conservative-led coalition, their content provided a serious framework around which primary care should be designed, including the use of 'polyclinics' in which primary care, some secondary care and community services could be co-located. Newham had some larger practices, but nothing one would describe as a polyclinic. Indeed, one of the larger GP sites had three practices in the same building, each with its own entrance and supporting its own admin team. Additionally, these larger centres were not spread equitably around the borough.[4]

- Good primary care would result in better health outcomes for our residents, particularly if married to services that addressed the social factors behind ill health.
- We were short of housing and looking to utilise land that we owned for development.

If addressed in a coordinated way, we realised, overcoming these two sets of challenges could generate significant benefits to the health of Newham's residents.

The potential synergies included providing the CCG and GPs with a much better understanding of the planning aims of the local authority, enabling them to structure planning

---

4   Lord Darzi's five key principles seemed to us to be a sensible way in which to plan local healthcare:
1)   Services should be focused on individual needs and choices.
2)   Services should be localised where possible, or regionalised where that improves the quality of care.
3)   There should be joined-up care and partnership working.
4)   Prevention is better than cure: social factors might be addressed on-site but might equally be addressed within the provision of the local authority.
5)   There should be a focus on reducing difficulties in accessing healthcare, which for us meant a reasonable geographical spread of primary care services and access to centralised services on major public transport routes.

applications to align with the council's policy approach. This promised the delivery of new or expanded sites better equipped to deliver health improvements. Steve Gilvin, the CCG's chief operating officer, commented, 'We had experienced great difficulties in finding sites for facilities to rehouse surgeries in existing communities, and working together with the borough to identify suitable sites – for example, sites that might not be on the market but could be available and would have planning support – was an important synergy.' The borough had land. GPs who wanted to retire had land. We quickly realised that these sites could be made available for redevelopment for housing and consolidated primary care facilities – and, if necessary, funded by loans guaranteed by the public sector. Other potential synergies included better working conditions for staff at new, well-equipped sites, and the offer of 'homes for rent' to medical key workers which might encourage new health professionals to come to the borough. In fact, the more we discussed this approach, the more it all made sense. But there was much work to be done, and we needed to fund reforms. So, the key to this particular Gordian knot – or perhaps the sword with which to cut it – was Newham's access to capital at historically low levels of interest. With that in mind, the council determined to fund a major transformation of the primary care estate.

To the credit of the CCG, the benefits were immediately recognised, and they became strong advocates for Health and Care Space Newham; a joint venture owned fifty-fifty by Newham Council and the local NHS. This provided the opportunity for the CCG to plan for expanded primary care across the borough, including in areas of development where provision had traditionally lagged behind housing development. The CCG was also gifted the chance to consolidate GP practices. Older GPs were bought out when they wanted to retire, and their land was put into a development pot for housing or new medical facilities. Today the expectation is that over a decade some twelve new surgeries will be developed across Newham, housing integrated health and care services primarily wrapped around GP services. Four or five of these will be large facilities closer to Lord Darzi's polyclinic model.

And they will be in the public sector. That was important to us, because there are some things the public sector does better than alternative providers. Too many government initiatives simply remove risk from the private sector by way of state subsidy, and may well distort the market as they do so. We see value in the state underwriting necessary infrastructure development, as this has both economic and societal value to the whole community. But we see no virtue in the public sector taking the risk to provide a private operator with a risk-free profit. And there will be profits – from rents on up to 250 new housing units, and from new GP surgeries – but all of this will be ploughed back into local health and social care services. Moreover, it will increase the capital estate of the local NHS and council by roughly £200 million. For us, this was a virtuous circle. It was a pragmatic response to local health challenges that enabled significant improvements to be made, but one that remained true to our philosophical roots while not being encumbered by prescriptions of what was (or was not) truly socialist. The benefits that can flow from muscular local government working with a supportive local health service should not be underestimated.

Health challenges: understanding and rethinking problems

We have all been in meetings in which a problem is raised and, instinctively, a standard and often poor response is given.

When tackling health inequalities, we discovered an issue at the maternity department of Newham General Hospital. Almost a third of women were first coutacting antenatal services later than the target date. This was not simply an admin problem: it meant that we had one of the highest perinatal mortality rates in the country. It was an urgent issue, and it required redress.

The problem was discussed at our local strategic partnership (non-statutory meeting of public, private and voluntary sector bodies), and the automatic suggestion was made to produce leaflets to tell people what to do and distribute them at GP surgeries. Problem raised; action taken; move to next bit of business. Right? We demurred. Historically speaking, it seemed that it didn't matter too much what stakeholders suggested at local meetings about services, as long as it seemed reasonable, and somebody could say that the issue raised had been addressed. But action taken did not necessarily mean that the problem was resolved. This box-ticking approach did not fit our public service model. We prefer results that improve lives and generate resilience. We wanted to find out *why* women presented late before we determined an appropriate course of action. The cost of producing a leaflet was a pittance, so it was not about price. This was about cause.

After analysing the problem, we discovered that half of the 30% of women presenting late had gone to their GP on time, but the GPs were still sending paper results to the local hospital by post, meaning that there was a subsequent delay in the hospital contacting patients. The tardy communication between GPs and hospital was fixed by the introduction of new IT, and half of the problem disappeared without the need for leaflets. Half of the remaining women presenting late had conceived while out of the country. No matter what we did, we could not affect the choices of women we knew little about, and who were often five thousand miles away. The figures would continue to show that our health staff had failed to meet the required antenatal appointment targets. But there was no way of mitigating that fact, given that some of these expectant mothers had not yet registered with a GP in the UK because they were on a different continent. The trust would still be castigated by the NHS, but not by us. We had at least reduced the problem by 50% simply through a better understanding of the problem.

This brings us to rethinking problems. Again, let's use a real example of what we mean. Over the past two decades, London has experienced a significant problem with tuberculosis (TB); a serious and contagious bacterial infection. Newham and Brent shared the worst figures in the country. In 2015, the *Tackling TB in London* report published by the Greater London Authority's (GLA) health committee said:

> *The people who are most at risk of developing active TB disease are people whose immune systems have been weakened. This makes it difficult for the body to fight off the infection or keep the bacteria in a latent state. People with chronic poor health due to lifestyle factors are more likely to suffer from weakened immune systems. These factors include smoking, poor nutrition, stress, and drug or alcohol abuse. Many people in high-risk groups, such as rough sleepers, have a number of co-existing health problems which make them particularly susceptible to TB. TB is strongly linked with deprivation. Overcrowded and poorly ventilated living conditions make it easier for TB to spread in the air. This can affect people who live in crowded or sub-standard accommodation, as well as prison populations and people who sleep rough or in hostels.*

This was the received wisdom; an analysis you would find anywhere in the world. But in terms of those susceptible to TB in London, it entirely missed the point.

The GLA health committee suggested a policy direction and consequent financial commitment to 'outreach services which work with vulnerable groups [which] should be prioritised'. This formed the basis of their first recommendation to London's

Mayor. But two years before their report, Dr Ajit Lalvani, chair of infectious diseases at Imperial College London, said, 'Seventy per cent of people with latent TB who arrive in Britain are missed. They aren't currently infectious, but... the TB bacteria could sicken them in the future and cause them to infect others. There is a vast reservoir of TB that comes into this country silently.' The GLA health committee appeared to be aware of the issue, as its report went on to state:

> While more than 80 per cent of London TB cases occur in people who were born abroad, it is unlikely they brought active (infectious) TB into the country: people from high incidence countries must be free of active TB to get a visa to enter the UK. We do not know, however, how many people are coming to London with latent TB. It is not feasible or cost-effective to screen for this, and those with latent TB do not present an immediate public health risk.

There is some significant linguistic artistry in the above paragraph. But suffice to say that, even when they had the information in front of them, the health committee continued to make a fundamental error. They recognised that 80% of TB in London occurs in people from abroad. They then stated that 'it is unlikely they brought active (infectious) TB into the country'. Not only was it unlikely, but the Home Office screening programme made it virtually impossible. The point which the committee sidestepped, for reasons about which we can only speculate, was that people with TB latent in their systems could still come in because they would be missed in the screening. This was precisely the point that had been made by Dr Lalvani two years before. So far as we know, Dr Lalvani was not invited to submit evidence to the GLA committee.

The implications were twofold. Firstly, because latent TB was not considered an imminent threat, it could be ignored. Secondly, for reasons that are not obvious, screening for latent TB was not regarded as cost-effective. Quite how the committee came to either conclusion is not obvious. In a sense, the committee absolved itself of responsibility by declaring that there was little that it could do, at one point claiming, 'infectious diseases like TB cannot be addressed in isolation by one city or one country'. GLA members simply restated guidelines issued by the UK's National Institute for Health and Care Excellence (NICE) and the World Health Organisation (WHO), which aimed to disrupt the transmission of TB among high-risk groups.

Thus, we come to one of the implicit tensions in policymaking: that between informed opinion, which becomes the new orthodoxy; and new ideas. In truth, we like informed opinion. We like the idea that people who advise policymakers actually know what they are talking about. But any advice needs proper scrutiny. When the orthodox view does not actually solve the problem, then it might be time to seek an alternative solution. In this case, when you know what the problem is – a high incidence of pulmonary TB linked to latent TB – why would you not try to address it, or at least put a cost figure on it? The answer, of course, is that the GLA was desperate to avoid blaming immigrants. But to achieve this, they were also (unforgivably) prepared to ignore logic. Their approach would allow people to continue developing TB – and for some to die – rather than address a problem that had political ramifications. That was not our way.

In 2013, responsibility for local public health departments was returned to local authorities from the NHS. Newham's new-found responsibility arrived just as national headlines declared that our borough was the TB 'capital' of Europe. At one point there were some 119 cases of TB per hundred thousand of the population, making Newham the most extreme case in the European Union. The NHS, NICE and WHO had identified those they considered most vulnerable to contracting TB. These included the destitute and homeless, those living in overcrowded accommodation, former prisoners, and those living with HIV. All correct; those are all risk factors. Unfortunately, across London we had been spending hundreds of thousands of pounds a year on these groups without making a dent in the TB figures. In fact, cases increased while London spent huge sums on trying to find those 'at risk'. Nationally, the Home Office screening programme had reduced the number of people entering the UK with active TB, but the effect of this was marginal to the overall figures. The NHS guidance urged public bodies to 'provide targeted outreach interventions, informed by proven models such as "Find and Treat" in London'. Locally, Newham had previously X-rayed high-risk individuals at centres across the borough but saw no more than three hundred individuals a year. In terms of identifying people with TB, this approach was a costly way of failing. It identified TB in about 0.5% of all people examined. Local teams went to the most vulnerable groups (as defined by the NHS), and found TB in approximately one in every two hundred people they examined. With 119 active cases per hundred thousand people, we could have spent the entire public health budget on desperately trying to find new cases – and still not succeeded, because we did not really know where to find what we were looking for. What was required was not a new team, new drugs, or new equipment. It was a new way of thinking; a new approach. Something radical and Newham-like.

Our first job was to establish a single narrative about TB locally, rather than competing messages delivered by well-meaning specialists from different sectors (housing, homelessness, health etc). The second was to ensure that we had the evidence available to support that shared narrative. We had no shortage of experts locally, but they were experts in their specific policy areas. So, in developing a central pool of information, we also benefited from the enormous well of information and analysis available from Public Health England.

Some politicians like to think that they have power when in post. In truth, we are more likely to have influence; particularly when seeking to change the ways in which external bodies operate. Necessity demanded that Newham's TB issue was a shared problem, and finding a solution would be something we did together or not at all. We had the benefit of the kudos of the health and well-being board, which Clive co-chaired, and the expertise of the public health department. Thus, Clive convened a summit of health professionals, practitioners, and those interested in acute services, primary care, public health, the local authority and the voluntary sector. A map of the borough was commissioned, showing the dispersal of TB cases geographically. To anyone familiar with Newham, it immediately became apparent that the areas with the highest incidence of TB cases were home to greater concentrations of our South Asian population. In some super output areas (SOAs), the infection rate ran to over 150 cases per hundred thousand people. In contrast, areas in the south and west of the borough – those with the lowest levels of immigration – were almost entirely free of TB. So, the countries of origin of cases were investigated. The rates of TB were 250, 150 and 120 per hundred thousand for residents of Indian, Pakistani and Bangladeshi origin respectively, compared to about ten per hundred thousand within the 'white British' population. A picture was beginning to emerge. Further review of social risk factors (homelessness, former prisoners, and drug and alcohol users) found that only 10% of those with TB actually had those risk factors. This meant that 90% did not! This information was available from Public Health England and had been referred to by a leading London health academic. The GLA health committee had been aware of it but chose to ignore it!

Our medical analysis showed that there were several strains of TB linked to particular geographical areas. It also seemed certain that it was primarily male migrants arriving with strains of latent TB, endemic in their home countries, which became active in around 15% of cases after two to nine years in the UK. This group provided the reservoir for nine in ten local cases. But all of our early identification and prevention services had been focused on the 10%. We had been doing *nothing* to prevent the onset of TB in 90% of our cases. Yet, Newham was doing the right thing as far as the NHS was concerned. In reality, this meant that large amounts of money were being spent extremely inefficiently and there was absolutely no impact on the number of people with TB.

We soon discovered that this situation had been replicated across the country. Trends that were true for Newham were also especially true for the rest of London. It is reasonable to assume (but it is only an assumption) that stress, poverty and poor housing had all contributed to the spread of TB in the capital, but none of them was the cause. While the specific trigger factors could not be absolutely confirmed, the population most affected could. Newham's summit made it clear to everyone: to tackle active TB figures, the issue of latent TB in men who had recently arrived in the UK from one of a small number of countries had to be addressed. Of course, this was a sensitive issue. Some experts have branded country-specific screening as racist and divisive, discriminatory or stigmatising. In one newspaper article, the author went so far as to suggest that any link between active TB and immigration is a myth created by anti-immigrant and neo-fascist parties. In the GLA report, the authors went to great pains to avoid asserting a link between immigration and TB. They contended that they were unable to find out:

We do not know, however, how many people are coming to London with latent TB. It is not feasible or cost-effective to screen for this, and those with latent TB do not present an immediate public health risk.

As we demonstrated, they did know how many people were arriving in this country with latent TB. Or they should have known. The consequence of GLA-style thinking is that people self-censor and avoid addressing the key problem, preferring instead to address a problem of their own creation. Such an approach might be more palatable politically, but it is ineffective and serves only to worsen health outcomes.

After analysing our data, the position was clear: we could say with a very high degree of certainty that the levels of TB in London were linked directly to immigration from a relatively small number of countries. TB was also overwhelmingly found in the male population aged twenty to fifty-five. If we could so easily identify the relatively small number of likely carriers, it seemed to us perverse and a little irresponsible not to do so.

One argument for avoiding identifying sections of the population who carried latent TB was, of course, to prevent certain minorities from being stigmatised or targeted. But upon examination, this argument did not stand up on a social (let alone a medical) level. Not least because unchallenged myths about how TB numbers got so high led some to point the finger at groups of immigrants who were *not* responsible – which only served to stigmatise those groups. If you need evidence of this, just read this response in the comment section following a *Daily Mail* article about the issue:

> *Of course we now have more cases of TB... we are having more people from the Eastern and Middle Eastern area where TB is rife.*

Identifying and targeting the wrong demographic served only to stigmatise others and draw attention away from an effective plan of action focused on those most at risk. So, locally, a plan to address the main causes of active TB, by preventing its activation in the first place, was developed. We did not need a new and expensive TB unit because we knew that:

- TB was latent in significant numbers of people from a small number of countries.
- It would take between two and nine years (with the biggest hike between two and four years) before latent TB became active in roughly 15% of new arrivals who carried the bacillus.
- We have a very well-developed primary care system, and almost everyone registered with a GP when they moved into the borough.

We determined to use those strengths and target resources on a solution. Within months of the summit, the CCG had ensured that every GP in Newham offered a TB swab to screen young men aged eighteen to fifty from five high-risk countries. Unlike the high-risk group screening, which identified 0.5% as positive, the latent TB screening identified more than 40% of those screened as carrying the TB bacillus. They were offered antibiotic treatment, and within a few years the borough experienced the most dramatic drop in TB numbers in the country. Newham's model was so successful that the NHS adopted it across other London boroughs. In September 2018, the NHS declared that TB was at its lowest level since 1990. Across Newham, we reduced local TB figures annually and moved from 119 cases per hundred thousand residents, to forty-seven per hundred thousand by 2018.

This example has been described at some length because it demonstrates clearly three of the themes outlined elsewhere in this book:

1. The scientific method works. Analyse problems before coming up with solutions.

2. Failure to discuss the actual facts surrounding an issue because they are sensitive will lead to errors – in this case, snowballing TB rates and the squandering of scarce public health resources.

3. Open and free speech, unencumbered by political correctness, is essential to address and solve many of the problems facing us.

Influence

The number of people diagnosed with Type 2 diabetes (T2D) in the UK has roughly doubled in twenty years. If the research published in *Diabetologia* in late 2022 is correct, there are some 250,000 people living in the UK with undiagnosed T2D.

Studies in genetics and observation of the increased prevalence of T2D in diverse communities suggest a genetic predisposition making people from some ethnic groups more susceptible to the condition. Diabetes UK reports that South Asians are six times more likely to develop T2D, and Africans three times more likely, than Europeans. Locally, this meant that roughly 50% of our population was at elevated risk. Thanks to the work of our GPs and researchers at Newham University Hospital, we knew that locally more than twenty thousand people were diagnosed with T2D. Their research further suggested that there were probably some ten thousand people undiagnosed and living with diabetes, and a further seventy thousand at risk of developing the disease in the next five years.

When responsibility for public health issues came back into the purview of local government, one of the areas Clive looked at, along with TB, was the incidence of T2D and how well it was being managed locally. He discovered that there was often poor patient compliance with the treatment prescribed by GPs. Patient compliance at the very best practices peaked at just above 50%. Those at the poorest performing practices managed just 10%. To clarify, at the cost of roughly £3,500 per person per year for medication, up to 90% of the drugs prescribed by some practices were being wasted, left unused, or taken irregularly, undermining their medical effectiveness. In purely financial terms, for one hundred patients receiving medication at an annual cost of £350,000, some £315,000 of this was wasted! (We had twenty thousand patients on diabetes medication.) That is obviously the worst case, but the best practices only managed to get half of their patients to take their drugs correctly. Millions were being spent annually, and most of it was having no effect. We could have built a bonfire and burnt the money for all the good it was doing! In terms of human cost, three quarters of patients with diabetes were at increased risk of developing complications including blindness, kidney disease, heart disease, strokes or amputations.

This realisation led to discussions with leading GPs in Newham, and the apparent acceptance of the status quo led to one of the few hostile altercations Clive had with medics. The result of this brutish intervention by a politician was a change in the community elements of the service. Working with the diabetes team in the acute trust, joint local research was commissioned which provided more accurate data to determine the number of people living with T2D locally. We were also able to obtain data for those with prediabetes, a reversible condition which predicts the number of people who will progress to T2D.

T2D in Newham is endemic and intergenerational. Parents and grandparents had it, and children were at high risk of developing it. The borough has some of the highest incidences of diabetes in pregnant women, too. But if T2D is managed well, the risk of complications is low and patients have a good quality of life.

The first step to improvement was to get patients to follow the treatment programme advised by their GP. Under the auspices of the HWBB we convened a local summit, rather like the TB summit described above. We inquired about the support and information given to patients at the point of diagnosis. It turned out that there was an information session offered to patients and, though we cannot remember the details, let's say it was one session offered at 3pm every Monday. What was obvious was that we needed to increase the number, geographical spread and timing of these sessions, so that there would be some in the morning, some in the evening and some at weekends. This simple act increased both attendance and understanding among newly diagnosed patients. The expertise on offer also made patients far more likely to take medicine as prescribed, rather than hoard it in a bathroom cupboard. GPs were aware of the problem, and a renewed focus on diabetes and incentivised funding ensured that the identification and treatment of T2D were improved. The most recent figures show that GPs in Newham are now among the best performing in the UK for the identification of T2D, and their treatment compliance rates are also among the best. This change took about six years to complete, but it was worth it!

Research has also shown that the effects of T2D are reversible. We should explain a little. T2D results from relative insulin insufficiency. The amount of insulin produced by the body is insufficient for its needs, or the body is resistant to the insulin produced. Weight gain and/or increased body fat contribute significantly to the onset of diabetes. Exercise and physical activity improve the body's sensitivity to the insulin produced. Researchers in Newcastle showed that if a person can lose a significant amount of weight (close to fifteen kilos) soon after diagnosis, T2D is potentially reversible. The patient then does not require medication, and remains in remission if they can maintain the weight loss. While many people find it difficult to lose large amounts of weight, studies have shown that even a slight weight loss can help the insulin produced by the body to work better, improve blood glucose control, and reduce complications. In short, losing weight is the answer to much of the problem. However, in Western societies, and increasingly in affluent areas of the developing world, losing weight is not easy. Affluence brings access to the high-protein, high-sugar and high-fat diets that evolution has primed us to enjoy. Lentils and vegetables lose out to McDonald's, beef steak and chocolate.

So, how to tackle this problem? One approach was to increase activity and make changes to people's lifestyles. We ran several sports-based programmes aimed at changing the lifestyles of people with T2D, the most recent being the 150 Club. This encouraged people with (and at risk of developing) T2D to maintain 150 minutes of physical activity a week; the recommended activity level for a healthy life. This approach works well with some people, but it only reaches around a hundred people per year. You have seen the numbers. If we were to reverse the trend in T2D, we needed to massively increase the numbers and target five hundred people per year.

We made significant progress against T2D, but we were keen to improve further. Before leaving Newham, Clive was working on another summit. It was not aimed at improving the treatment of T2D, but at reversing its snowballing prevalence. The cost of treatment for T2D is such that, with the projected increase in numbers, it could bankrupt primary care in our inner cities. There has therefore been an emphasis on diabetes reversal, based on several recent trials. The work of medical researchers in Newcastle and Glasgow, referred to above, has shown that significant and sustained weight loss through a low-calorie diet, with weight management support, could lead to a reversal of diabetes. Other programmes – including altering a patient's gut bacteria, bariatric surgery, and use of insulin-stimulating drugs – can also help significantly. But few people know which treatments work best for different people and groups; nor whether cultural or genetic factors affect the efficacy of different approaches. With Newham's extraordinarily diverse population, this is an area in which progressive leaders, councillors and officials could measure the effect of different approaches with different groups – with the potential for groundbreaking progress that could influence treatments across the globe.

The promise of change is still there. But, in our absence, it remains merely a promise until a new generation adopts our approach and is willing to take on this challenge.

Chapter 8

MAKING 'PLACE' AND COMMUNITY WORK: HOUSING

A decent home for all at a price within their means.
(The Hills review)

Housing is a difficult area made more complex through incessant government tinkering. Yet it's not rocket science. Most people want a decent, suitably sized, affordable place to live; ideally in a 'nice' area. If, as a nation, we believe that everybody should have access to this sort of housing, then there are implications. Our ambition should surely be to provide the necessary funding to ensure that all people live in decent housing. Start with that ambition and then work back to determine how to achieve it.

We reflect here upon Newham's approach to housing at a local level, but most of the problems we faced were the result of national issues. In twenty years the population of the UK increased by 9.7 million, but in the same period fewer than 2.8 million new homes were built. Added to this, more of us are living in smaller household units; often a single person in a property which in previous decades would have housed between two and four people. And we all seem to want to do this in the south-east. Little wonder that there is price inflation and high demand.

The fundamental cause of the problem is that there are, in effect, two housing markets. One is a developer's market in which developers will build housing if they can make a profit. There are risks involved in this activity, and unless they make profits they will not build. Generally, housebuilders and developers act in a commercial manner. The second market is a demand market in which a number of households want accommodation at a price they can afford. But the key problem is that demand outstrips supply; something that makes sense for developers but not for society. Households needing housing, but unable to afford the type of housing they would like, settle for a reduction in quality and size. One of the revelations of the private sector licensing scheme (see below) was that we found families and individuals living in frankly disgusting conditions.

The number of new homes provided with some form of subsidised rent is determined by the level of capital subsidy invested in each new home. You can think of it as the state paying for a bit of the property on which rent is not then charged. The money for this comes from a number of sources including taxes on development, government subsidies, the use of public assets, and cross-subsidy from housing association sales.

There are effectively two taxes levelled on land development: the community infrastructure levy (CIL) and Section 106 agreements. The CIL was introduced in 2008 and is a direct charge placed by local authorities on new developments. It pays for infrastructure (including health, education, roads etc.) which can sit outside the immediate development area. It cannot be used to provide 'affordable' housing. Section 106 agreements are used for infrastructure within a development and, crucially, to support the provision of housing at 'affordable rents'. Developers will only develop where they can make a profit, and unreasonable taxes can make schemes unaffordable or produce unintended consequences, such as reducing the size of rooms in houses to squeeze more properties onto a development site (something which Newham opposed vigorously). Equally, low levels of taxation mean that developers effectively enjoy windfall profits. The public tends to be rather critical of such easy pickings, and rightly so. Setting the right level of local taxes on development is a difficult balance to strike. Nonetheless, most councils try hard to get it right.

The second area of income is government subsidy. Government funding (channelled in Newham's case through the Mayor of London) has a major impact on the number of affordable properties that can be created. If central government effectively subsidises more affordable accommodation, that is a good thing – but it's hardly something for regional government or local councils to crow about (it doesn't stop many of them, though!).

There is a further potential source of subsidy. If the land being developed is already in public ownership (and there is a lot of land in public ownership), then the value of that land can be used to subsidise the cost of development and, thereby, the cost of finance. As an aside, many and various proposals are dreamed up to provide affordable housing without spending cash. The housing press is full of them. They nearly always involve taking something of value (such as public land) and inserting it into their proposal, and then pretending that their scheme is cost-free. The casual way in which people treat public assets never ceases to amaze us. One of our proudest boasts is that, in Newham, we massively increased the level of our net assets – i.e., we did not sell the family silver. Leaving more for the next generation than we received seems to us something which is morally required of government. However, spending wealth created by others is attractive to many politicians.

Government does not like to subsidise affordable housing directly; it is expensive. They tend to prefer to concentrate on encouraging developers to build more housing, which will usually include some affordable housing (though sometimes developers pay a cash sum to subsidise affordable housing elsewhere). And in this they come up against the planning system; a bureaucratic system of micromanagement which manages to obstruct much of what we want. Endless tinkering with the planning laws has failed to deliver a system fit for purpose. Indeed, it is our contention that the scariest words in the English language are 'Hello, I'm a politician and I am here to simplify the planning system.' It always ends up worse, for reasons described elsewhere in this book. There is much we could say about the planning system, but rather than go into great detail about how it could be reformed – which would take a book in itself; one that would start with the words 'Let us sweep away every part of the current system and start again' – we will confine ourselves to a couple of observations, since it is not the main point we wish to stress. (To reduce the suspense of wondering what that point is, feel free to jump ahead and avoid planning.)

Elsewhere we have stressed the importance of incentives. What would you do to create a system of incentives that would enable us to build more desirable housing of suitable size? (By 'desirable' we mean beautiful housing in a nice environment with decent infrastructure.)

Development is currently frequently opposed by NIMBYs. There is much criticism of such opposition, but change imposed from outside is rarely welcome, and when the inherent threats of such change include a reduction in land values or a change to the nature of the local environment, opposition is a perfectly rational response for the individuals concerned. Politicians, ever mindful of votes, are incentivised to support the NIMBYs who can and will vote, rather than the people who will move into the new housing unaware of and ungrateful to those politicians for the risks they have taken to provide that housing. The answer, we suggest, is to give local people, through their council, the ability to create local plans for new developments, but then remove politicians completely from the decision-making process when a developer wants to build. Local people should have control over deciding the nature of development in their area, but the current system provides existing residents with something approaching a veto.

The planning process today demands housing that is carbon neutral, but this costs money and so increases the cost of the housing. We would encourage thinking in a new way. For example, if solar panels or domestic wind generators are viable means by which to generate electricity, they should be integrated at the design stage. We propose that the government pays for the additional costs of installation by way of a direct grant, which would be spread across the whole development. Then, over the next ten years (or whatever the appropriate time is), 50% of the income produced by generation goes to the homeowner and 50% to the government via an additional charge by the power company until the cost is repaid. Thereafter, the panels become an asset that attaches to the home.

As an aside, in this book we have not really discussed the environmental challenges facing the world. The way in which we have sought to incentivise behaviours (as above) seems to us to be a way in which 'green' initiatives might be funded. For example, for established properties we could fund the retrofitting of home insulation in the same way as suggested for energy efficiency measures in new homes. This might even give pause to those who believe that only they have been granted unique insight into the challenge of global warming, and that this gives them the right to inconvenience everyone else. By the way, when we say that the government should provide the money, we are not against private investors (e.g. pension funds) providing the money with a government guarantee which will reduce the level of interest charged because the level of risk is reduced.

There is a serious problem whereby planning permission is given to develop a piece of land which can result in significant increase in value, providing a windfall for the owner which is paid for through an increase in the cost of the resultant housing. It seems to us that there should be a limit to the profit landowners can make through simple redesignation of land; after all, they have done nothing to increase the value of that land. The downside is that limiting profit will make it less likely that landowners will want to develop land. So we should perhaps consider giving councils greater power to use Compulsory Purchasing Orders (CPOs) to enable the councils to purchase land to drive more development. Landowners should still make a profit – just not an obscene one. This would provide additional subsidy for affordability.

If we really do want to do something about improving the planning system, we need to remove the huge (and increasing) level of complexity and focus on what we think is important: beautiful housing of a reasonable size in an attractive neighbourhood. Which brings us nicely to the most important way in which we could bridge the gap between current developers and demand. Get councils to do what they have done historically: build houses. When Thatcher effectively removed councils from housebuilding, the housing associations were supposed to take the strain. There is a debate to be had (though not in these pages) as to how well they have risen to the challenge, but what is not up for debate is that they have not been able to deliver the amount of affordable housing that is needed (though, given the rapid population rise and the concentration in the south-east, we wonder if this is actually achievable). Historically, under both Labour and Tory governments, when councils built housing we built the housing we needed. Having said that, some council housebuilding was awful, so, while we discuss how to get councils building, it is essential that quality is maintained. Housing should be beautiful; not simply a succession of units slung up to be knocked down a few years later.

Housing delivery and affordability

In Newham, on our watch, we realised that the subsidised housing likely to be built would fall well short of the amount we required – particularly that of affordable housing. We knew that waiting for central government to provide the support necessary to tackle the housebuilding crisis would be like waiting for West Ham United to win the Premier League: it will happen, though unfortunately we might not still be around to witness it.

Between 2013 and 2016 Newham delivered more than five thousand homes – the second-highest total in London. In addition, from 2002 Newham delivered the third-highest number of affordable homes in the capital and the second-highest number of new homes for social rent. All of this was achieved even though our task was made more challenging by the creation of the London Legacy Development Corporation (LLDC), formed by London's broader mayoral authority in 2012. The LLDC took control of planning and land around the giant Queen Elizabeth Olympic Park in Stratford, which had hosted the 2012 Olympic Games, and formed part of Britain's 'legacy' plan for the post-Games period. The Park and its surrounding area became the premier housing development site in Newham – thanks, in no small measure, to us (or so we like to think). Unfortunately, we believe that the LLDC proceeded to develop land with fewer affordable properties than might have been achieved.

Since the changes wrought in the housing market by Thatcher, homebuilding has been the preserve of the private sector and housing associations, with councils limited to seeking to facilitate development. Recently, though, there has been a welcome and long-overdue increase in direct council housebuilding.

The absolute level of new homes built is important but, we believe, not fully appreciated on the Left. The focus on the Left is for 'affordable' housing, or sometimes 'social housing'. But the simple truth is that if many homes are built, house prices and rent increases will slow, stop or fall. This is the law of supply and demand. Given that most people do not live in 'affordable' homes, this means that the simple act of building by the private sector can impact most of the population. In addition, if more housing is built that includes an element of affordable housing, we increase that supply as well.

We realised that if we were to impact on housing need, it was necessary for councils to build. So, we determined to build houses ourselves. Newham established a housing company, Red Door Ventures (RDV), a wholly council-owned company with an independent board and management team. The aim initially was to provide RDV with around £2 billion and a quantity of development land owned by Newham that was significant enough to make real inroads into housebuilding in East London. By the end of the administration, we were building – or in the process of building – more than eight hundred properties, with a further 1,800 earmarked in a detailed business plan. For the biggest developments, our plan was to have a large organisation handle the development side of things while RDV retained many of the rental properties – providing a significant council income to subsidise more housebuilding.

The aim was not to build and sell everything, as many councils and housing associations do. Rather, it was to build and rent – both at market and sub-market rents – with just a few sales made to support mixed tenure in particular areas (we did not want to create so-called social housing ghettos). With market rents subsidising sub-market rents, we envisaged substantial investment with significant growth over several years. And because we wanted to invest billions, this was potentially a real game changer for housing in Newham.

Because we took a view that spanned decades rather than years, as the loans were paid off the council would have a welcome new problem. With unencumbered capital assets in the form of housing, the council of the future could choose to rent at market levels and take an income, or offer tenancies at subsidised rates. We don't know what the political priorities will be in fifty years' time, but this would give a future council options. We also took the view that the sale of properties (without subsidy) to sitting tenants would be encouraged, provided that we reinvested the receipts in housing, and that we could buy back the property (at market price) to ensure that properties did not end up privately rented.

Unfortunately, all of this required long-term political commitment. Properly run and financed, RDV would have changed the nature of housing not just in Newham, but across East London. Unfortunately, that level of ambition has not continued since we left office. The mantle has now been picked up by neighbouring Barking and Dagenham Council, which is trying (with considerable success) to build housing in difficult areas by making use of cheaper land values. In Newham, the past few years have been a missed opportunity. If there had ever been a time to invest in revenue-generating opportunities, then that period of historically low interest rates was it.

When council finances were squeezed after 2010, most recognised the sense in investing in commercial property, until ministers moved to prevent it (thank you, Spelthorne Council!). However, as an investment class, housing not only provides an income stream but is well understood by councils, and is intrinsically a less risky investment when viewed in the long term. Magically, at the same time, it provides a place for people to live, it provides jobs, and it provides tax revenues. We reasoned that building housing for market rent would provide Newham with a long-term source of funds. Making rents more affordable requires capital subsidy, but if we invested in market rent housing the profit would generate a surplus which could be used to subsidise affordability or fund more development. This was particularly true if we built on land owned by Newham, which would make the housing cheaper. It is always open to councils to build on their land and use the capital value of that land to invest in affordability. Once spent, however, there is no more subsidy from the land value. Invest it for the future and you can create more affordability over a period. Otherwise, you are at the mercy of government subsidy – a situation in which you do not want to be.

So far we have used the word 'affordable' casually, but it is a highly charged word in politics and has many meanings. 'Affordable' incorporates social rent, intermediate rent, and for-sale products. In 2020 the Affordable Housing Commission concluded that many of these products were unaffordable to those on middle to lower incomes. The response of politicians and campaigners has been to co-opt the word 'genuinely' to create a tautology: 'genuinely affordable'; a term that has also now lost its meaning. Perhaps we need a new phrase: 'really, honestly, genuinely affordable'?! If this sounds a little cynical, it is. Obfuscation in politics has been developed as art across the housing sector. As we explain in the regeneration section of this book, it is difficult to compare performances when discussing housebuilding achievements. When it comes to 'affordable' there is a bewildering number of different affordability points covering both rental and purchase. In truth we use the term 'affordable' and apply it to a property – to the bricks and mortar – irrespective of the tenant. An alternative to this opaque nomenclature might be to compare a rent level to the disposable income of the tenant to determine whether it is 'genuinely affordable'.

This was something we intended to do with RDV properties. We intended to flex rents annually to reflect household income: increase rent as income increased (up to market rates) and use the saved subsidy to support other families. Setting one 'forever low' rent benefits one household and effectively means that taxpayers (some of whom are poorer than the tenant) are subsidising the rent of a family who could easily afford to pay a higher rent. Subsidised tenancies, particularly council tenancies, have become a long-term tax-free grant. The model we proposed would have contributed to the benefit of a larger number of residents and been more closely aligned with the ability to pay. Higher subsidy levels in a few properties result in only a few households benefiting, while smaller subsidies over a larger number of properties will help more families with 'genuinely affordable' rents.

This disconcerting confusion (not to mention unintended outcomes) is par for the course once the inevitable virtue-signalling of modern politics becomes the norm. The confusion suits both the woke and the statists, as they carve out a little niche of virtue that does not involve the messy business of building homes for rent that are 'really, genuinely, honestly affordable'. Across the housing arena people virtue-signal in spades, rather than encourage the spades in the ground that are needed to actually build homes and address problems.

This virtue signalling is not restricted to affordability, either. It affects the whole issue of housing construction. There are several classic positions adopted by the woke and the statists, each of them a complete myth:

- *The only worthwhile affordable housing is, of course, council housing. Anything else is not really affordable.* Yet the reality is that council housing tends to have the lowest rent, and hence requires greater subsidy than other 'affordable' schemes. This, in turn, means that fewer households benefit from lower rents as the same level of subsidy is spread across fewer households.
- *The only worthwhile development is where X%[5] of the development is affordable – and we will set rules to*

---

5   30%, 35%, 50% – take your pick depending on how woke you want to be.

ensure that only such developments are built. Targets for affordability are not bad things, but each development is different. Slavish adherence to a figure may mean that a development is not viable. This means that the planned housing, including an element of affordable properties, will not be built.

- *Developers are intrinsically evil because they want a profit from their development. So, when developing council assets, there should be no joint ventures with evil developers.* This tends to be the view of the statist Left. Yet developers are usually people who know how to build things, and without profit they will have no capital – so nothing will get built. This reflects the hard Left/woke approach to almost any attempt to improve people's lives; preferring the demonstration of socialist credentials and rejecting any and all developments that involve working with people who do not share the purity of socialist/ woke thought. This, of course, is at the expense of people who would benefit from such initiatives. As an aside, after leaving office Robin had the pleasure of meeting a regeneration 'expert' from a leading university – and was promptly informed that development should only be for social good. Profit, the academic said, should not be allowed. This is precisely the unswerving attitude that stops housing from being built in the first place. And this person was actually teaching students!

- *No development should occur where there is opposition from residents.* This comes in two forms. Opposition, generally in rural areas, occurs where residents who have benefited from previous development want to stop any further development. Fearful of losing their seats amid local public anger, politicians are often too willing to support such views. The Conservative Party, for example, is currently running scared on just this issue. But to be fair, this can be a wider party political problem (see Canning Town and Custom House below). As one developer put it, 'The fight for new rural housing is the fight to bring in the next group of objectors to further development.' Alternatively, in inner-city areas, brownfield sites need to be developed to provide homes – particularly when the area's transport links are good. Statists/Trots will support the few people left in the (often poor-quality) homes on brownfield sites in opposing development, and hence deprive more people of new and better homes – including the very people who currently live there. There is often limited electoral downside to this, since many of the residents affected will be decanted to other areas and their political opposition dissipated. However, if the development is large enough and spread over enough time, there can be consequences. As Niccolò Machiavelli, the Italian political thinker, put it:

It ought to be remembered that there is nothing more difficult to take in hand, more perilous to conduct, or more uncertain in its success, than to take the lead in the introduction of a new order of things. Because the innovator has for enemies all those who have done well under the old conditions, and lukewarm defenders in those who may do well under the new. This coolness arises partly from fear of the opponents, who have the laws on their side, and partly from the incredulity of men, who do not readily believe in new things until they have had a long experience of them.

So, when we wanted to develop the Carpenters Estate, a substantial area of twenty-three acres next to the Queen Elizabeth Olympic Park, the Trots, the statists and their supine fellow travellers were out in force to prevent the development of thousands of homes. We repeat again: it suits the Trots and the statists to prevent good things from happening, as this enables them to criticise 'the system' and endlessly argue for a revolution.

Councils must keep council housing money separate from their general fund (money obtained from government, business rates, parking, council tax etc.) in a housing revenue account (HRA). Most councils uphold this commitment, though few are those that do not craftily bleed at least some cash from their HRA into their general fund to cover the cost of other services. This separation was a Thatcher-era initiative and there is no doubt that, before the change, councils often used housing money to heavily subsidise other services. However, while the change has worked to protect cash earmarked for housing, it has had the additional effect of focusing local political attention almost exclusively on the HRA as opposed to the possibility of using the general fund for housing.

As we have explained, our position on affordability is that subsidy/support should be tailored to the individual household. Unfortunately, this is not possible for HRA-funded properties since the government controls rent increases. One reason, we believed, for building properties separate from the HRA funding pot was to provide this flexibility. Central government initially capped the amount that councils could borrow to fund HRA housing developments, but has recently relaxed the rules. Nationally, local government argued for this relaxation. But in Newham we took the view that, while we were happy enough to build some homes using HRA money, we wanted to concentrate on building using general fund borrowing, which meant that we'd build homes that were not covered by Right to Buy programmes and were generally free from other government diktats.

We are somewhat bemused by the obsession with building houses using HRA capital. Why do Labour councils follow

Thatcher's rules when they simply don't have to? If government were serious about devolution, they would free councils to build homes and establish rent schemes that benefit residents rather than conform to government bias. We recognise that there might be benefit implications which would need to be considered. But the ability to flex rents according to individual circumstance would be a powerful tool which could provide 'genuinely affordable' housing to more working households.

Given that elsewhere we argue for resilience and appropriate incentives to support people, it is hardly surprising that we believe that encouraging homeownership helps to raise the standard of both the property and the local environment, if and when its primary purpose is to provide a home. Our proposals meant that people would have been able to purchase the homes in which they lived, if that was what they wanted to do. All we would have required was the ability to repurchase the home – at a market rate – if the owner later chose to sell. The idea that people should be able to buy their council home is a good one, providing a replacement affordable home is built or purchased and that the person lives in the property rather than lets it out. Entire estates have turned into ghettos through the private renting of former council housing, with the loss of large numbers of social rented properties. As we have said, increasing the level of assets to bequeath to future generations is morally right. Had politicians taken this to heart, our housing situation would be so much better than it is. But you, dear reader, voted them in.

We would argue that if the government incentivised councils to build housing (through guarantees, cheap credit via the Public Works Loan Board, allowing long-term rentals to generate ongoing profits, allowing some profit to be recycled to develop more housing etc.), this could go a long way towards resolving the housing crisis. And in the longer term, we would expect it to realise a profit.

Housing will not be fixed in a single Parliament, or even two. Even if the government decided to start investing seriously, or created an environment in which councils could do so, plans take time and supply chains need to be built up. Businesses need to know that it is worth their while to invest over a long period, and nothing damages confidence more than government policies constantly switching back and forth. When governments change political hue, the incoming government often feels that it has to prove that everything done by the last lot was worthless, and so the policy changes begin again. Repeat, mistake, repeat.

We cannot understand why successive governments have not grasped this nettle. (Actually, we can, and elsewhere we show why they are incapable of carrying out tasks for which they are responsible.) But you get the point? Government hands are currently being wrung over the fact that the next generation will be disadvantaged, in housing terms, compared to 'baby boomers'. But actually, it isn't true. The future is not set in stone and our actions can change it. The only reason things will be worse in the future is because we allow our virtue-signalling politicians to continue to determine it. If we can (quite rightly) spend billions fighting a pandemic, we can spend billions fighting a housing crisis, particularly as the historic evidence indicates that we will get the money back.

Future housing plans

An example of what could be done is the housing plan developed by Newham to deliver affordability using its own land and resources, and by working through Red Door Ventures. Plans were in place for the following developments between 2018 and 2023 (this is a bit detailed/boring – jump over the bullet points if you find yourself falling asleep!):

- We identified several small sites on which around 1,400 properties could be built. Since all of the land was owned by the council, and the plan was to use modern construction methods, all would have been available at social rents.
- The Carpenters Estate development has sat more or less becalmed for the past four years. Had this been carried forward with determination, it would by now have contributed 1,500 homes, of which 525 were due to be affordable and 260 social. And because the council was due to retain a number of the properties, rents on the market properties would have produced profits for reinvestment in further housing.
- The Canning Town/Custom House development is already producing new housing, and we estimated that, if adequately supported, it could deliver around five thousand homes, with 1,230 affordable and 550 at social rent.
- RDV was expected to deliver three thousand homes, with one thousand affordable and five hundred at social rent. Again, from the market rental a profit was expected, and that was earmarked to support more developments.
- The giant Olympic Stadium/Park development made possible several housing development sites. As part of the agreements on these with the Mayor of London, £40 million was to be made available to support the provision of affordable homes.

So, over five years, Newham expected to have completed or started building more than five thousand affordable homes, of which around three thousand would have been available at social rents. In addition, with Newham's clear desire to work with developers to produce more affordable housing, we thought we could probably double these figures. But you are always at the mercy of the market. By taking firm control of the housing programme up to 2018, Newham had been well set to produce enough affordable housing for our residents and perhaps others.

Of course, it's easy to talk about plans, but plans also need to be delivered. However, at this point in our narrative, we believe we have demonstrated that delivering on plans was one of our strengths.

Private sector rented housing

We illustrate our approach to 'enforcement' elsewhere in this volume, as well as our successful attempts to improve the environment in a deprived urban area. It's important because without the commitment carry through one's plans, the plans are just so much wishful thinking.

Newham's drive to improve the local environment, and simultaneously housing quality, reached its apogee with the introduction of the first borough-wide private sector licensing schemes in the country. Before this, Newham had one of the country's largest private sector housing enforcement operations, but there was only limited benefit from the service. While it acted against some properties causing a blight, the overall effect was minimal. It was not making a difference to the borough's look and feel, and the costs were considerable. Yet there was strong evidence linking antisocial behaviour with the private rented sector. Following legislation by the national Labour government, Newham determined on a borough-wide licensing scheme to drive up housing standards and challenge criminal landlords across the private rented sector.

In March 2010, Newham started a pilot covering 257 properties in the Little Ilford ward in the borough's north-east. Several lessons were learned; primarily to keep the fee structure simple and focus on the landlords who breached the scheme. A light-touch approach was sufficient for most decent landlords.

Overall, there were thirty prosecutions within the pilot area (nearly one in every eight properties in the scheme). So even from these small numbers, it was clear that there was a systemic problem. The pilot provided a clear rationale for a borough-wide private rented sector licensing scheme.

It was also clear from the pilot that enforcement would be key if we wanted to change behaviours. There was an argument, articulated by the landlords and their associations, that a compulsory borough-wide licensing scheme was not necessary. Instead, they argued that the council should run a voluntary licensing regime. But when we did run a free accreditation scheme, a risible 5% of landlords joined. To make the licensing scheme work, it was necessary to find some way to identify landlords who had not registered (the group most likely to include rogue or criminal landlords). Considerable work had produced a data warehouse bringing together information from the council's various systems. A tenure intelligence model was developed using predictive analytics, which identified 7,500 unlicensed properties. But identifying is not the same as enforcing. Newham had worked over time to develop an effective integrated enforcement team covering various disciplines – trading standards, environmental health, planning etc. In addition, we were paying for forty Met Police officers, with the ability to deploy them on the council's priorities.

Richard Lambert, CEO of the National Landlords Association (not exactly a fan of the licensing scheme), said:

> *Personally, I think Newham's real success, and the aspect of their approach which is most frequently overlooked, is the way in which they have restructured and re-prioritised the council budget to enable them to ramp up the scale of enforcement action. I can't help thinking that in pushing the benefits of licensing rather than enforcement, Newham are actually underselling their real success.*

We would partly agree. The licensing scheme made it possible to identify potential rogue or criminal landlords. However, without effective enforcement the scheme would have no effect. We talk elsewhere about the importance of praxis, and this is an outstanding example of the need to ensure that the practical aspects of policy are fully understood and engaged. The choice between a virtue-signalling council keen to make a profit from the fee paid by landlords and a council determined to make a difference locally is the difference between those who want to improve the lot of residents in poor areas and those who think residents exist as a tax base to fund their personal political hobby horses.

Broader evidence seems to suggest that tackling criminal landlords is not a high priority for many councils, with about three quarters of authorities issuing fewer than five civil penalty notices over three years, and some issuing none.

The results of the licensing scheme were spectacular. Antisocial behaviour had been a major reason for implementing the scheme, with significantly more incidents recorded in private rented properties compared with council and owner-occupied property. The licensing scheme led to a significant reduction in antisocial behaviour: from around 1,600 reported incidents per year before the scheme was implemented, to just over four hundred. By January 2018, more than 1,200 landlords had been prosecuted and 750 people arrested. This was not about a failure to comply with a bothersome bureaucracy. These prosecutions were brought where informal approaches failed and where landlords put the lives of their tenants at risk. At the scheme's peak, half of the landlord prosecutions in England were pursued by Newham Council.

The London Fire Brigade borough commander for Newham said:

Whilst we cannot put numbers on it, there is no doubt in my mind that the property licensing scheme in Newham has saved lives.

When asked, 89% of residents agreed (33% strongly) that continuing the licensing scheme would improve conditions and management of private rented properties. So, the experience of the scheme had clearly been viewed positively by our residents.

However, we were aware that the scheme breached the 'polluter pays' principle that we tended to favour. Why should *all* landlords pay £150 to £750 (for a five-year licence) when the system is designed to target criminals? It is perhaps OK to charge a low fee and ensure that a level of service is provided to help some of the more amateur landlords, but in the end it is unfair to penalise good landlords for the actions of a smaller group of bad ones. Devoid of other choices, though, we felt it was the right thing to do because it improved the housing sector locally. We believe the system could be amended to levy much bigger fines on rogue landlords who have behaved appallingly. Why shouldn't someone who is happy to pack twenty people into a three-bedroom house full of dangers pay a substantial penalty?

Judging by comments received from Her Majesty's Revenue and Customs (HMRC), we understand that around half the borough's landlords were unknown to HMRC before registration – and therefore were unlikely to have been paying tax on their earnings from their properties. We estimated the loss to the Exchequer across the country because of landlord tax evasion at £180 million a year. There was an immediate financial benefit to the council of £3.5 million in unpaid council tax as well. A sensible government would agree with local councils to provide part of the tax gain to ensure enforcement continues and that we can generate income from these tax dodgers. It could even be funded by fining criminal landlords for tax evasion. Councils can be motivated to do the right thing if the correct incentives are in place, particularly when it is also a win for the Exchequer. HMRC ignorance was reflected in the ignorance of Newham Council when the scheme started. Initially, we thought there were about five thousand landlords in the borough. The eventual number identified was twenty-eight thousand. The granular detail of what was going on in the borough was simply unknown.

This is a lesson that bears repeating. Local and national government do not know what is going on in many cities and towns. Doncaster, Rotherham, minimum wage, the Leicester rag trade, miscalculated local Eastern European populations – the list goes on. Even when a well-intentioned politician quotes what they think is a reliable statistic – say, from the Office for National Statistics – the question should always be 'How do we know it is accurate?' It is certainly true that, throughout the 1990s and noughties, we were convinced that the ONS population estimates for Newham were wildly inaccurate. This mattered because it affected our funding allocations. We spent a considerable amount of time working through the various estimates and challenging the ONS's figures. As an example, we discovered that to work out the number of people coming into the country, the ONS counted incomers at Heathrow. That makes some sense. However, we also discovered that the researchers packed up early in the evening. Unfortunately, as flights from the Indian subcontinent arrived later in the evening, that meant that more incomers were missed, and so the population in question was rather underestimated. Still, at least the civil servants got home in time for dinner…

Social housing

There was a time when social housing was seen as aspirational, and residents were expected to look after their properties inside and out. However, successive governments have followed a policy of supporting the very poorest in a 'devil take the hindmost' manner. In most places today, if you cannot prove your 'need' in terms dictated by the bien-pensants you don't exist. People trying to build a life through hard work are excluded from the state's largesse. This is not a policy to which the epithet 'For the many, not the few' can be ascribed. Instead, it might better be expressed as 'For those who do, nothing; for those who do nothing, something.'

This is a refrain throughout this book. Political attention is focused on the neediest rather than on the 'squeezed middle'. People who work hard to give their family a decent life are disregarded other than rhetorically. If this were not true, we would see some sort of reaction from progressives against council tax and its regressive nature. Instead, increasing council tax becomes a sign of virtue on the Left, probably because the middle class who comprise the self-proclaimed woke Left earn enough not to be overly bothered by council tax.

As the late John Hills, an expert at the London School of Economics, commented in his report on social housing in 2007:

Over the last quarter century, the role of social housing has changed. The sector has become much smaller as a proportion of the total, although nearly 4 million households still live within it. While post-War provision was aimed at households on a range of incomes, since the 1980s provision has become more tightly constrained and new lettings focussed on those in greatest need. As a result, the composition of tenants has changed, with tenants much more likely to have low incomes and not to be in employment than in the past or than those in the other tenures. Seventy per cent of social tenants have incomes within the poorest two-fifths of the overall income distribution, and the proportion of social tenant householders in paid employment fell from 47 to 32 per cent between 1981 and 2006. Tenants have high rates of disability, are more likely than others to be lone parents or single people, and to be aged over 60. More than a quarter (27 per cent) of all black or minority ethnic householders are social tenants (including around half of Bangladeshi and 43 per cent of black Caribbean and black African householders), compared to 17 per cent of white householders. Looking at today's social housing stock, 93 per cent of it was already within the sector nine years ago (although 750,000 dwellings were transferred between local authority and housing association ownership...). For tenants, there is much less movement between dwellings than within the private rented sector, and more than 80 per cent of those living in social housing today were also within the sector ten years ago (if born by then).

It is worth pausing here. Hills told us, with great clarity, that after spending hundreds of billions (at current prices) on social housing, we have ended up with ghettos of deprivation. And what has our response been? To double down on allocations based on need. He told us, in essence, that social housing was changing from aspirational housing to social services housing. Not what the radicals who developed the housing originally would have wanted, we suspect.

A more general question might be: given the vast sums of money poured into anti-poverty schemes, charities etc., how do we know that spending on various initiatives is working? Tax credits worked to reduce child poverty. Free school meals in Newham had an impact on child poverty locally. Both put money directly into the pockets of working people; a direct cash subsidy to people's income. We are unconvinced that many existing anti-poverty schemes do more than perpetuate the poverty they are meant to reduce. But we could be persuaded if there was a proper objective review of the efficacy of programmes. Without that, what can we believe?

Interestingly, even as people argue that Britain contains institutionally racist organisations, access to state-funded (taxpayer-funded) social housing is greater for every ethnic group (other than Indian, Chinese and 'white other') than white UK. This represents a massive economic transfer to all such ethnic groups. Institutional anti-racism?

Following on from the Hills report, Newham prepared a document, *Race to the Bottom*, which described how, by prioritising 'need' over many years, social housing has come to be the housing of last resort and ghettos of poverty have been created. This runs directly counter to the philosophy of resilience. We will not develop resilience if people firstly need to prove how needy they are, and then those who win that competition are all housed together. Since 'need' is ever-changing, this meant that people would sit on the housing waiting list for years while those who could demonstrate greater 'need' jumped ahead of them in the queue. As a means of creating disharmony within a community, it is hard to imagine a more effective policy. As we have explained elsewhere in this book, when local people (of different ethnicities) accused Newham of 'putting immigrants ahead of us', it was somewhat true in practice – even if that was not the policy's intention.

Newham adopted policies to reverse this ghettoising trend in social housing. The largest concentration of social housing was in Canning Town, which was an unpopular choice for those qualifying for it. Newham launched what was to become the fifth-largest regeneration scheme in the country to mix the housing, but it was seldom mentioned because it took place just as the Olympics were about to kick off in nearby Stratford. The scheme introduced high-quality private rented properties while maintaining the existing quantum of social housing. Although challenging in the early years because of low land prices, this scheme has now led to Canning Town being viewed as desirable.

Newham's allocations policy was changed to minimise, as far as allowed by the government, the role of 'need' in allocating housing. It was a crafty move, but it worked. By classifying as many people as possible as being 'in need', it was possible to effectively implement a 'wait your turn' system, though necessarily we retained the ability to make a small number of urgent allocations (e.g. for those fleeing domestic violence), and to satisfy statutory obligations. In addition, Newham determined to prioritise people in work when it came to accessing social housing. Interestingly, even with this priority, there was a lower percentage of people in work accessing social housing than there were such people in the community – but it certainly helped to provide a more level playing field.

Difficult decisions in the short term can lead to improvements in the long term. Newham was clear. We would not support the continuation of social housing as ghettos. Of course, the activity of Workplace contributed to helping with housing. Once people had a job, it was easier to afford higher rents (though not *that* much higher), and this provided opportunities to improve the quality of housing chosen by families. This is one reason why policy needs to be understood as complex. When we examined the maps from the Index of Multiple Deprivation, what became clear was that although the whole borough was improving, the areas where this improvement was slowest were those where there was a concentration of social housing. The result of the policy of placing people in greatest need in social housing over many years was clearly shown. Families and lives were destroyed by people who wanted to show how caring they were for poor 'unfortunates' by placing them together in ghettos. They didn't care enough to make the hard decisions that could help to improve and change lives.

Our needs-based changes were just one approach Newham adopted to improve housing outcomes. Another was to look at the quality of local estates. Every year in Newham, in line with our view of how you best find out what people think, we conducted an independent survey of tenants who returned decent (but not impressive) satisfaction levels. We felt that the estates were not 'loved'. We looked at the excellent example of

Poplar HARCA, a local housing association just over the border in Tower Hamlets, which builds relationships with tenants and where the estate has a feeling of being cared for. Until the introduction of the small business programme, we had no real way of improving the quality of our estates. Delivery by large private companies was as inefficient as in-house models. So, we settled for in-house delivery and tried to improve and control standards. This worked, after a fashion, but didn't provide the kind of estate we thought people would be proud to live on.

Given the powerful impact of the small business programme, we began to make preparations to create a similar type of business to manage and maintain council properties. We anticipated significant gains in satisfaction by applying the principles we outline elsewhere. Unfortunately, the incoming administration stopped the process for ideological (Corbynite) reasons. However, by developing a business that would be closer to the residents and incentivised to improve tenant satisfaction, we are confident that the results would have been as impressive as those we achieved in other areas of public policy.

Statutory homelessness: local space

The confusion throughout government housing policy is well exemplified by homelessness legislation. To be clear, we are not discussing people living on the street. 'Homeless' families are those to whom the local authority has a statutory duty to assist with housing (that is, if they can prove that they have sufficient need as defined by the government). In general, the problem of homelessness is primarily a London problem, though some other metropolitan areas also have a significant number of 'homeless' households.

Government diktat says that councils must give priority to homeless and overcrowded families. In other words, councils must prioritise 'need', which disincentivises resilience. The allocations policy followed by Newham meant that some families who presented as homeless were housed in the private sector, while others were offered social housing (very few, given the paucity of supply). Of course, the total sum of housing remained the same. Such an allocations policy does not increase supply. If you take one family from the private sector, you create a vacancy in the private sector. Choosing which family to allocate a scarce resource to merely determines which family will benefit from low social rents. Overall, there is no change in private or public sector housing numbers. However, government funding regimes meant that there was a cost to be borne by the council, since the accommodation offered to the 'homeless' family had to be affordable, which meant a council subsidy was necessary. It was a price we were willing to pay to remove ghettos from our borough.

Across the country, we have implemented a policy of creating ghettos of people who are most needy, and thereby created ever more problems for the individual families and society in general. When David Cameron pursued his 'troubled families' initiative, he might have started by looking at the housing in which we were dumping these families. But then, joined-up government appears to be beyond our political masters.

However, we also took other action. In 2006, Newham established Local Space, a housing association created to buy private sector properties in and around Newham for 'homeless' families. Local Space initially borrowed £250 million against a council rent guarantee; using the power of the council covenant to intervene in the market on behalf of residents. By 2018, Local Space had more than 2,100 properties, which was predicted to increase to 2,600 following a further agreement with the council. Many other councils have attempted to follow Newham's lead, but only one or two have succeeded in purchasing more than a few hundred units (the most we have seen elsewhere is around four hundred). This seems to be for reasons described in the section on small businesses and the problems associated with bureaucracies. Otherwise, the experience seems to be that attempts to purchase properties are slow and generally limited in scale.

The standard of Local Space accommodation is, as you would expect, well above that for most homeless properties in the private sector. Yet the council has realised considerable reductions in homelessness costs, and benefited from a share of the Local Space surplus (nearly £14 million from 2008 to 2017). Meanwhile, by 2018 Local Space had net assets of more than £180 million. In fact, even though the accommodation is classed as 'temporary', most people do not want to move from Local Space properties, and so turnover is low. In reality, thousands of families have been permanently housed in decent, affordable and secure accommodation entirely due to our council's initiative. And we did it at a time when interest rates were much higher.

Chapter 9

CRIME, ENVIRONMENT AND ENFORCEMENT

If you have laws that you don't enforce, then you don't have laws.
(Donald J. Trump)

Just because Donald Trump says something doesn't automatically make it wrong. The question here, as it is so often, is: why won't the Left apply the common sense that most of our voters prefer?

If the difference between working-class Somewheres and woke Anywheres is evident in their attitude to benefits and work, it is equally apparent when assessing crime and the environment. By 'environment', we don't mean issues like global warming. In this book, and for our policy purposes, this term means the places where people live.

In her excellent assessment of Labour's crushing 2019 general election defeat, *Beyond the Red Wall*, the political strategist Deborah Mattinson writes, 'Place means more when you live, work and socialise nearby.' Quite. Mattinson's book also describes the views of working-class residents she talked to in the 'Red Wall' seats (former Labour strongholds of Northern England lost to the Conservatives), whose votes did so much to deliver Boris Johnson's majority. Explaining these voters' attitudes towards crime, she observed:

A lot of the talk focused less on serious crime and more on frequent, irritating anti-social behaviour, which people tended to blame on kids not having enough to do. People told me about intimidating groups of teenagers hanging about on street corners, about litter and graffiti, and about damage to local buildings.

Interestingly, one of the early acts of our administration was to disburse a one-off fund to the (then) ten community forum areas. So, we asked people what they would like to do with the cash. In every single area, one of their three top priorities was to provide activities for young people so that they had something to do. We thought that said a lot about the people of Newham.

As in the north, so also in East London! Lazy political and media clichés often divide England into north versus south or London versus the rest of the country – usually based on a flawed understanding of the south in general and London in particular. But, according to a 2019 report by the Institute for Fiscal Studies, 'London has the highest rate of poverty across all poverty measures' in the UK. What's more, the greatest concentration of poverty is found in East London, with the worst three boroughs being Tower Hamlets, Hackney and Newham. The annual residents survey we conducted at Newham placed crime and antisocial behaviour in the top three issues of concern to residents each year, usually at number one.

Antisocial behaviour and the state of local environments are essentially working-class issues. Poorer areas look and feel worse, and street and personal crime are more prevalent in working-class neighbourhoods for reasons which are pretty obvious to most people. As a result, the working-class Somewheres who live in these areas are much more supportive of tough enforcement measures than Anywheres, who tend to be more middle class and live in better neighbourhoods. While the latter are repelled by robust actions to constrain criminals and criticise those who believe that there needs to be determined enforcement, the former are happy to lock 'em up and throw away the key – for some crimes, at least. It is perhaps another example of woke culture that the sensibilities and foibles of middle-class Anywheres often carry more social weight than the views of those who live in areas of high street crime, and who generally don't have the option of moving.

Living in poor housing, in areas riddled with crime and antisocial behaviour, and in streets full of rubbish and litter does not encourage resilience and aspiration unless you know it will change at some point. To promote resilience and aspiration, there must be a sense of hope and a sense of worth, and for us in Newham this was about improving where we lived. We wanted hope that our neighbourhoods would get better, not that aspirational residents would bank on being able to move out. The Newham view was that, even as we helped people improve their circumstances (Workplace, MoneyWorks, education, community activities etc.), we also had to enforce against people who did not want to contribute and who were happy to make areas and the lives of their neighbours worse. In poorer areas, most people try to live decently. A small minority who do not care often make areas unpleasant for the majority.

So, the key to tackling the problem is enforcement. Yes, in the long run, education might provide answers – but we have been waiting a long time for education to solve this problem. In the meantime, we felt we should still use other means to divert young people away from crime. Creating jobs, for example, was a powerful way to attack the causes of crime, and in that, Newham excelled. But enforcement mattered. Those who disregard society need to be made aware that there are penalties for blighting decent people's lives. The key to enforcement is to join up the disparate parts of any council that needs to take action against wrongdoers and align their activity with local policing. That's not to say that we bombarded local police with thousands of minor requests; more that we worked to ensure that they were aware of our plans to improve local environments through stricter enforcement, and knew which activities to keep an eye on.

When we started this initiative, the boundaries of the Metropolitan Police Service's (MPS) Newham Division were coterminous with those of the borough, and, while local police were under pressure to meet the targets and priorities of MPS leaders, the London Mayor and the Home Secretary, it was at least possible to have a conversation about jointly tackling our priorities. During our time we were lucky to have two or three MPS borough commanders who shared the council's vision and no-nonsense approach. When that happened, we found opportunities to attack problems from two sides: tackling crime and some of its underlying social and environmental issues.

When the borough commanders did not share Newham's concerns, it was very difficult to get anything done to tackle issues that may not have been policing priorities, but that mattered to local people. Local government simply does not have the power to tackle many problems encountered in areas where too many people do not care about the consequences of their actions. Yet it is local government, through the local ballot box, that often gets accused of failing to address problems.

We find it interesting that, due to the need to make 'savings' during the austerity years, the Met no longer has a borough commander covering just Newham. So, many of the benefits gleaned by police and council officials working closely together in recent years, and becoming more effective on the ground, have been swept away in pursuit of efficiency and lower costs. A case of knowing the cost, but not the value of something? Incidentally, in the early noughties there was a similar attempt by the Mayor of London to implement such a change. It was defeated by London councils (the collective body of all London councils – then called the Association of London Government), where Robin was the chair – perhaps the only time Ken Livingstone listened?

Much local enforcement activity is undertaken by council officers. But even within a council, joining up work across different departments is complicated – and much of Newham's success in improving enforcement only followed once joint working had been imposed upon officers and embedded within working cultures. A further hurdle we had to overcome was the attitude of the Home Office, which often failed to understand the work done by local government enforcement officers in tackling low-level crime. Mind you, the general view of the civil service (outside the department responsible for local government) is that councils are inconvenient pests.

But back to the local picture in Newham. When analysing crime, antisocial behaviour and enforcement as policy areas, we quickly realised that consistent feedback from residents showing high levels of concern did not necessarily mean that local crime rates were high. In reality, some types of crime were common locally and others were not. But a highly publicised stabbing in a street near a resident's home is inclined to weigh more heavily on their mind than any number of reassurances from ourselves or the Met. The bigger issue, we discovered, was that with demand on wider police time soaring each year, including the time and resources it now takes to investigate the most serious crimes (for example, rape), petty vandalism and low-level drug-dealing fall to the bottom of the policing priority list. Yet we found that these more common 'smaller' issues blight the daily lives of residents – and so they appear regularly in residents' concerns during feedback.

To be fair, even with a fair wind and the sort of system we advocate, antisocial behaviour is a notoriously difficult issue to combat. The published measures for doing so are poor, and they frequently change, which makes it difficult to quantify how successful any council is over time in combating antisocial behaviour. Police areas are judged by their results on an annual basis, which are then pored over by politicians and the media. This often leads to a culture of 'initiativitis', whereby an issue (say, moped gangs) becomes a matter of public concern, resources are deployed, actions are taken to deal with the upsurge, and then, as the issue fades from public view, those interventions are halted or reduced – leading to another upturn in the future. And so we get a never-ending Sisyphean cycle of recurring problems that are never fully resolved. Initiatives are necessary, but they only have real value if they lead to long-term improvements.

Much of the antisocial behaviour that blights the lives of residents is not stuff that the police would engage with. If the council didn't take action, no one would. What follows are some examples of how we approached various issues, both alone and with the police.

Dumped cars

The first major initiative launched by the Newham mayoral administration to improve the environment was to tackle the epidemic of dumped cars. Following a decline in the scrap value of cars around the turn of the millennium, the number of abandoned vehicles soared. It was a big issue. In 2001/02, thousands of vehicles were dumped across London (with Newham being the area most affected), and almost a fifth of Londoners soon reported that dumped cars were among their top three concerns.

Newham responded by dealing with abandoned vehicles as quickly as possible; an expensive and chronic task. Residents remained unhappy with the impact on the local environment. Yet we were spending good money trying to hold back a tsunami. So – you guessed it – we applied the scientific method and assessed the data. On investigation, we discovered (unsurprisingly) that the overwhelming majority of dumped cars had no road tax.

Worse, we also learned that around 20% of *all* vehicles on the road in Newham were not taxed. One in five! This hinted at a novel approach to proactively tackle the problem 'upstream'. If we were to remove cars with no road tax, regardless of where we found them, then owners could either pay the fine and tax to get the car back, or simply let the council dispose of it. This still involved cost, but it also attracted income through fines. Cars of no value were scrapped, but the fines raised were sufficient to pay for the entire operation. Of course, if a taxed car was dumped, the owner could be traced. This was reported in 2004, in *Protecting the City Environment* by the environment committee of the London Assembly:

> *In 2000 the council (Newham) approached the Driver and Vehicle Licensing Agency (DVLA), asking to be given the same powers of removal as the DVLA in a borough pilot... Newham now claims the quickest abandoned and untaxed car removal rate in the country.*

The result was spectacular. The number of untaxed cars on Newham roads dropped to below 5%. More importantly for residents, the number of dumped cars collapsed – the most significant reduction in London by a considerable margin. Indeed, in November 2002, Michael Meacher, then a minister in the Department for Environment, Food and Rural Affairs, acknowledged that Newham had seen a 'vast reduction in the number of dumped cars'.

This was an excellent example of analysing a problem and then tackling it imaginatively and innovatively. The lessons were not lost on us. One additional attraction was that those breaking the law by not taxing their cars paid to clear up the problem. Instead of taxpayers paying to remove dumped cars, those responsible paid the price. A lot was learned from this initiative, and it aided us when we moved on to another area in which we were performing poorly compared to other London boroughs.

Trade waste

If you live in an urban area, you might be familiar with the problem. Not organised dumping, but the miraculous appearance of heaps of rubbish bags, often during the hours of darkness and without any obvious sign as to who is responsible.

Every trader must have a commercial waste agreement with the council or with a private waste disposal organisation, or provide evidence that they are getting rid of their waste correctly. When Newham examined this, it became clear that large numbers of local traders were not complying with those rules – and random tips scattered around the borough's wastelands indicated this. So, we decided to enforce the requirement that traders needed to prove what was happening to their waste.

To do this effectively, several council departments had to work together. In the first instance, businesses were visited and warned that if they did not have a trade waste agreement, they should get one. Failure to comply led to fines. Enforcement officers investigated to ensure that businesses obtained an appropriate agreement (i.e., they paid for the correct quantity of waste to be disposed of). A considerable amount of time was invested in ramping up effective enforcement activity.

The result was that the number of businesses without waste agreements fell from more than 20% to just 3%. Since many traders then took out agreements with the council, this enforcement resulted in a financial gain for the authority. Those who still didn't have an agreement suffered penalties in the form of hefty fines. Thus, the social and political incentive to enforce was matched by a financial incentive which covered enforcement costs. Again, this was an example of those breaking the rules paying the cost of enforcement: the 'polluter pays' principle we favoured.

Our response was no different from what many good councils around the UK do; at least in theory. But we used it to develop an approach to enforcement that wasn't just window dressing; it was effective. Looking good didn't matter to us – getting results did.

Knife crime

Before Covid-19, there was an epidemic of knife crime across the UK, particularly in London. There was a spike in knife attacks across London in the mid noughties, and Newham had the worst record.

In response, the excellent new borough commander, Nick Bracken, agreed to implement a substantial stop-and-search policy, on the proviso that the council supported it politically. We backed the initiative because we were concerned about the lives of our young people. In simple terms, we wanted to help save young lives.

In more recent years, it appears that the fashion on the Left has swung back towards denigration of the police as an oppressive occupation force that is damned when it tries to prevent violent crime and damned when it does not. The police initiative in Newham targeted all young people, irrespective of ethnicity. It stressed the need to treat people with respect. In addition, it was explained to youngsters that while we were inconveniencing them, we were trying to disarm Newham's population. Correctly done and managed, the result was a two-thirds reduction in knife crime across the borough without any increase in complaints. Interestingly, the very people in Britain who condemn America for its quantity of guns in circulation and argue for disarmament across The Pond are unwilling to relieve young British people of the weapons that kill or maim their peers. This confused stance made us wonder whether such critics – who included some politicians and activists – actually cared about young lives lost. In some instances, it is our view that they didn't! We are happy to be proved wrong, but are uninterested in virtue-signalling protestations.

Instead, let's see what those in positions of power have done and whether it has reduced knife crime. We now know that the 'progressive' experiment in the USA of defunding and reducing the police presence in many urban areas has been a complete disaster resulting in the additional violent deaths of many thousands of predominantly young black men. Our approach, which was one of supporting local police and communicating why, worked. The Newham programme received recognition nationally, and not just from our political party. In October 2008, Chris Huhne, the Liberal Democrat Home Affairs Spokesman at the time, even told the BBC's *Question Time*, 'Robin Wales has led the field in gripping the crime agenda in Newham.' It was kind of him to personalise the issue. But our local success was the product of many people working together to deliver a safer environment. In particular, it took a borough commander willing to abjure the politically correct agenda to save youngsters.

Today, police have body cameras which should make stop-and-search programmes much less problematic if the police are properly led. Studies show that police wearing body cams receive far fewer complaints (up to 93% fewer, according to some research) about their handling of stop and search. But of course, disarming people in our community requires action, and the woke would rather virtue-signal. As a result, kids (usually poor black kids) are dying on our streets – and people wonder why we are so angry at those who have foisted their woke agenda upon us. Interestingly, when body cameras became available, the Met took years to provide them to all police officers. Newham made them available to all people involved in local enforcement as quickly as possible. It made sense to add an evidence-gathering tool. We were also conscious of their role in managing good behaviour in our own staff and minimising vexatious complaints from members of the public.

When the opportunity arose (thanks to Stephen Greenhalgh, then Deputy Mayor for Policing and Crime in London), Newham undertook to pay the costs of forty police officers tasked to work in the areas and on issues that mattered to local people. This approach became particularly effective when the former borough commander who had organised the stop-and-search initiative joined Newham Council, bringing with him area expertise and knowledge of police cultures. He was tasked to run a joined-up approach to enforcement and keep the focus on issues of importance to local people. Interestingly, Nick's comment was that he wished he had held the local authority job before the borough commander role. It was only when he saw both sides of enforcement activity that he realised what could be done by joining everything up. Is there, we wonder, something in this observation that might be of relevance in the training of senior police officers across the country?

Prostitution and Trading Standards

Whatever your view on prostitution – and in recent years there has been a shift towards targeting those controlling the industry, rather than the (mostly) female sex workers – the presence of brothels still tends to be unpopular with residents.

We took a slightly unusual approach to tackling the issue. Think Al Capone and tax evasion! Newham Council closed more brothels than the Met's Central Team (which worked across the whole of London), through the simple act of classifying brothels or 'massage parlours' in private residences as businesses – and then using existing planning powers to close them down. As described by one police officer, Newham Council officers (plus police) would turn up at a brothel only to be assured that it was a massage parlour. To which a council officer would reply, 'Well, that's a business and you can't conduct business in a residential building, so I am closing you down.'

Trading Standards teams have extremely wide remits. We used this in our efforts to extend protection to young people. The primary focus of our teams was changed to identify the sale of illegal products to underage people. Knives, alcohol, tobacco and explosives (fireworks) – reducing the quantities of these in the hands of youngsters seemed quite a good idea. As a result, underage checks increased massively and there was a corresponding increase in compliance by shopkeepers. Comparison with other authorities is not easy, but we believe Newham undertook the largest number of checks in London by a considerable margin.

And the deterrent effect was significant. It may be apocryphal, but a story is told of one underaged youngster working with the Trading Standards team as a secret shopper. He asked for fireworks in a major supermarket. The assistant told him to wait and assured him that she would bring the fireworks to him. He waited and nothing came. After twenty minutes, he approached the woman who had served him and asked where his fireworks were. Her reply was, 'If you wait there until you're eighteen, I'll bring them to you.' We desperately wanted to believe that it was true!

While this approach to Trading Standards and underage checks massively reduced the incidence of illegal sales, Newham was obviously spending more to protect our young people than other councils. We funded it because we believed that we had a moral duty to protect our young people.

Fly-tipping

Significant investment in information technology ensured that our resources could be more effectively deployed. In-cab IT in the vehicles charged with picking up fly-tips meant that we could accurately measure the level of fly-tipping in the borough rather than rely on a manual reporting system.

This resulted in a recorded increase in fly-tips from 28,443 to 70,192. Lazy critics reported this as a 'massive hike' in fly-tipping locally. And counting accurately made no difference to the views of residents – they based their view on the reality they faced every day. But we needed a more accurate measure of the problem. It was in line with our belief that you cannot tackle problems effectively unless you fully understand them. We can take the criticism, even if it was misplaced; doing the right thing can be difficult sometimes!

A campaign against fly-tipping, waste in front gardens, and other 'enviro-crimes' had a significant impact across the borough. There was a considerable reduction in incidences of fly-tipping (remember, it was being monitored electronically, so the figures were accurate). In 2017/18 fly-tips fell from over seventy thousand to fifteen thousand. Impacting the local environment in poorer areas is not easy but it can be done. The results were dramatic and showed in residents' satisfaction levels. Sadly, the number of fly-tipping incidents increased to more than thirty-seven thousand in 2019/20, under an administration with different priorities.

Private sector landlord licensing

Perhaps the biggest success of our approach to local crime and environment was achieved when we introduced a borough-wide landlord licensing scheme. This was covered in Chapter 8, but the fantastic success of the approach was due entirely to the joined-up organisation we had laboured to create.

The above list covers our successes, but there were some areas in which we failed:

Phone use while driving, and seat belts in cars

Parliament had long decreed that the use of handheld mobile phones while driving is forbidden, and that seat belts should be worn by passengers in the back seats of cars. But both laws were and are widely ignored, encouraging increased disrespect for other laws and poorer road safety. The police, with other things on their minds, do not commit resources to deal with these infringements.

Realising that incentives work, and with the success of our initiative against untaxed vehicles fresh in our minds, the council approached ministers over mobile phone and seat belt use in cars. We suggested that if we were given the authority to enforce these laws, working with the police, fines obtained from enforcement could be retained by the council and the cash used to provide overtime for police officers. This would lead to better enforcement and save lives at zero extra cost to the police. We were confident that, once word got out, people would stop acting illegally (as with driving in bus lanes, which happens very infrequently because of the certainty of a fine from the local council). Our proposals would also have avoided concerns about the police being incentivised to enforce, since the process would be led by the council. We were confident that both programmes would have been successful.

But the government rejected our proposals. We could not even test the hypotheses. What would have been so bad about running a pilot? The civil service's unwillingness to engage means drivers continue to flout these laws. People continue to die because idiots use their mobile phones while driving and passengers refuse to wear seat belts. It was incumbent on the government to consider our proposals seriously, and truly sad that ministers and officials did not.

Minimum wage enforcement

This is another policy area in which, for many years, the scale of the problem locally went unnoticed. We began to receive anecdotal reports that there was a problem with some local employers not paying the minimum wage – a legal requirement. Initially, we didn't know if these reports were accurate, and we certainly did not understand how many employers were involved. But our concern was sufficient to look into the matter in more detail.

Newham commissioned a study that revealed that around 20% of people working in the borough did not receive the minimum wage. We were gobsmacked; the minimum wage had been a centrepiece of the national Labour government's policy reform upon taking office. Throughout this book, we have repeatedly returned to the practice of virtue-signalling among the political woke at the expense of actually helping those on low incomes. And here we were, staring at figures which indicated that, while key national government legislation had been enacted (and we were and are firm supporters of the minimum wage and the absolute necessity to increase it significantly to ensure that work pays), widespread non-compliance went unchallenged. Worse, we discovered that in many circumstances the local means to enforce such important legislation – and possibly local will to do so – did not exist. Take, for example, this 2019 parliamentary statement from Conservative MP Kelly Tolhurst, in response to a question from Labour MP Jo Stevens about the number of prosecutions under the minimum wage legislation:

The government is committed to enforcement of the minimum wage. We have increased HMRC's annual minimum wage enforcement budget to £26.3 million, up from £13.2 million in 2015/16. In 2017/18, HMRC took action against more than 1,000 businesses, identifying

£15.6 million of pay arrears for workers and levying financial penalties of £14 million. Since the beginning of 2010 there have been a total of seven prosecutions for breaches of national minimum wage law.

That's right: there had been just seven prosecutions over nine years. That was the extent of the Conservative-led government's commitment throughout the period. They had almost doubled the enforcement budget, and for this, they forced just one thousand businesses to ditch unlawful practices. Newham alone could have achieved a significant percentage of that number in one year! And for a lot less money.

We initially approached the last Labour government and asked to run a pilot scheme designed to enforce the minimum wage. We explained that the scheme would be implemented at no cost to the national government. Ensuring that residents were paid the lawful wage was something *we* wanted to prioritise; our incentive wasn't financial, but moral. The idea was to identify the extent of the problem and then develop a solution to ensure that bosses who cheated workers could be held to account. A secondary aim was to get the government to engage with us as we tested a potential solution. We felt that this would help to increase knowledge of how local labour markets interact with minimum wage legislation across deprived areas in our major cities. With an operation of sufficient scale, we believed the benefits of enhanced knowledge for all parties would be considerable.

As with the private sector licensing scheme, until operations were conducted on the ground, we could not know what we did not know (hat-tip to Donald Rumsfeld!). With the development of our data warehouse (see Chapter 8 on housing and the enforcement of a borough-wide licensing scheme in the private rented sector), Newham was particularly well placed to develop a predictive model to identify rogue and criminal employers.

Linking the data warehouse to a comprehensive enforcement section gave us the capacity to carry out a large-scale pilot. In addition, it is a near certainty (though we can't know for sure) that those who do not pay the minimum wage also dodge tax. So, as with private sector housing, we were confident that the government could generate significant tax revenues from effective minimum wage enforcement because employers would be forced to pay and report their earnings truthfully.

Unfortunately, successive governments refused to allow enforcement by Newham. The dog days of the national Labour government were beset with problems, and the idea was ignored. After that, successive Conservative-led governments failed to see the revenue-raising potential even as austerity gripped Britain. Meanwhile, all governments demonstrated their inability to deliver effective enforcement of the law. In 2021, the lid on this was lifted with the exposure of sweatshops in Leicester paying less than the minimum wage. Our inquiries locally suggested that bosses who do not pay the minimum wage are also pretty likely to ignore health and safety legislation.

If we are serious about ending unlawful low pay, it must be embedded in enforcement work. 'Parachuting in' investigators for limited periods across the country will expose some bad practice, but is unlikely to generate the necessary changes in employer behaviour in cases where lower-than-legal wages are part of their business model, because the risk of getting caught remains so low. Criminal employers build any likely costs into their business model, to which the only effective answer is systemic enforcement at a local level. Even if caught out, bad employers often simply declare bankruptcy and disappear for a short period, only to reappear elsewhere under a different guise (different 'owners' and directors declared at Companies House etc.). Enforcement needs to be far stronger, much more regular, and consistent to make illegal business models uneconomic.

Most – dare we say all? – local authorities do not know the extent of the underpayment of minimum wage across their area. This is not a criticism; hitherto, it has not been a requirement of their job. Central government certainly doesn't know – otherwise, it would have prosecuted more than seven employers in nine years. Newham only became aware of the extent of non-compliance because we commissioned a specific piece of research on the subject and took a potential solution to Whitehall. We firmly believe that central government should earmark some of their enforcement spending and commission similar research across several rural and urban areas, to get a better idea of the scope of the problem and likely locations upon which to focus enforcement action.

Our contention is that enforcement should be done in conjunction with local authorities, because they are the only bodies with the incentive to ensure continued monitoring and action on behalf of their residents. Newham would have been far more aggressive than a reluctant central government in pursuing cases to court. A slap on the wrist might act as a minor deterrent under the current lackadaisical approach. But the threat of significant fines, or worse, would be a considerable incentive to change business models at firms hell-bent on not paying their staff a fair wage.

We sincerely hope that central government acts on this blight soon. It's not as if they haven't been warned. But that is the story of this chapter. People have complained for years about low-level crime and antisocial behaviour across local areas of the UK. Little has been done about it, although the Blair government did make some headway and provide some additional powers to local authorities.

In Newham, we are proud of our record. We addressed several problems that scarred our area; not by passing resolutions or by making public statements about our virtuous feelings, but by utilising existing legislation to encourage changes in behaviour. And the primary tool for this was enforcement. Newham Council funded these activities because that was what our residents wanted – and a crucial part of any council's job is to listen to residents.

We believe more could be done across the UK to fund enforcement activity through fines against those who commit acts that despoil our neighbourhoods. These fines should be of sufficient weight to help fund enforcement activity across a more comprehensive range of activities. The authors of this book differ on where the line should be drawn and quite how draconian enforcement should be. For example, should a person running a business based on criminality (e.g. dumping rubbish by the side of the road) risk losing just the business (Clive's view) or his home as well (Robin's view)? Whatever the answer, this is a debate that needs to be had at a national level, and we need to remind our legislators that antisocial behaviour blights the lives of millions of our citizens.

Chapter 10

COMMUNITY

Community (noun): The people living in one particular area or people who are considered as a unit because of their common interests, social group, or nationality.
(Cambridge Dictionary)

As early as 1955, WA Hillery identified ninety-four different definitions of the word 'community' – and there are doubtless many more now. With the possible exception of 'socialism', there is more nonsense talked about the community than any other word in the political lexicon. Everybody now 'listens to the community', 'works with the community', 'blah-blah-blahs with the community'. There are serious brownie points to be made virtue-signalling about the community. People regularly seek to assert moral authority for a proposition they favour because they represent the community. Quite how legitimate these claims to representation are is often debatable. But the word 'community' disguises a vast range of unspecified allegiances.

It might mean that a speaker expresses the desires of a religious or ethnic group, or indeed a sect or tendency within that group. But rarely do those asserting moral authority acknowledge that. Instead, they almost always claim to be from the wider community. Likewise, community representations might emanate from one street or block. The motivations of such representatives might stand in stark contrast to those of other residents of their area, such as when low-traffic policies are implemented and change traffic flows, with some winners and some losers. Community members might approach the press to oppose a development that would boost local housing stock and provide homes for those on the housing waiting list. But because those on the housing list haven't arrived in the area yet, their community has no voice. Instead, it is the incumbent media-friendly voice who states with absolute certainty that their view represents that of the community. Politicians often acquiesce to such soft lobbying at the expense of providing leadership in local government. Likewise, a community voice might be the senior officer at a local charity (and, as such, the highest-paid person in the neighbourhood!) seeking to get increased funding for their project. Yet they claim to represent the community and rarely address meetings by stating that they are a lobbyist for their organisation seeking greater influence and financial support for their salary... oops, our mistake – their organisation!

You get the point? Almost everybody interested in local or national politics says that they are from and represent the community. And institutions such as local media help to reinforce the elastic use of the term, often giving a disproportionate voice to individuals with a political axe to grind, or a barely concealed agenda, because they speak as a 'community expert' or 'community leader'. There is nothing wrong with these people speaking to the media. But when journalists choose not to challenge the material they provide and don't even clarify that their contacts have a personal interest, their opinions or assertions are presented as fact rather than as contestable ideas. (We don't often agree with Guido Fawkes, but to be fair the website has for some time rightly demanded that the BBC identify the political allegiance or interests of people they interview.)

The traditional political view of community participation is one of some sort of structured monthly or quarterly meeting or forum at which residents are invited to discuss issues. Such gatherings are the backbone of democracy, we're told. But the cold, hard truth is that they are often a sham, substituting a flawed process for real engagement; virtue-signalling, if you will. A large part of the problem is that there is no natural way to measure genuine community participation.

At Newham, we sought to do something different. We were determined to support the development of personal resilience to enable individuals to create a more fulfilling life. However, people are not islands and their interplay with others in society is critical. Philosophically, we took the view that it is the family unit (of which there are many models) that is the basic building block of society. Our insight was that, instead of inviting the community to events that fit the council's agenda, we should provide opportunities that fit residents' agendas. You put local citizens at the heart of everything you do only if you recognise where they are and work with their aspirations, rather than project your prejudices and desires onto them. The development of trade unions required an understanding of the importance of solidarity; recognition that, by acting in concert, people could obtain more than by acting individually. The challenge for the union organisers was to persuade people that collective action was the way forward. The aim was to organise to achieve an outcome – better conditions for all workers achieved through the power of collective action – and this played to workers' aspirations. The aim wasn't to get people to come to meetings (have you ever been to a trade union meeting?). Involvement was not the end in itself. It was a means to achieving a greater goal.

Being on the Left, we stand squarely behind the rights of the individual but also recognise that, when we act in concert, we increase our strength. If we wish to support people to control their own environment (and thereby increase their resilience), we must recognise that sometimes that control can be exercised only through working with others. Hence, community is an essential part of supporting people to develop a better life. Solidarity is a powerful force that can improve the lot of individuals – and indeed many individuals, when properly harnessed.

Community resilience is also a key element in supporting the development of personal and economic resilience. In *Quid Pro Quo* (the document in which we first set out our approach to resilience), we stated:

> *Politicians often talk about a 'culture of worklessness' where there are pockets of geographically concentrated, intergenerational unemployment. People in such areas face multiple disadvantages but a significant part of the problem they face is to do with the networks they belong to, the social expectations they are exposed to and the resources at their disposal. People looking for work in more affluent areas are able to seek advice from other working people. They understand the expectations of the workplace because they regularly see people participate in it... These people are benefiting from community resilience...*
>
> *We know that people copy behaviour that they commonly see, so a resilient community is a well-networked one, but also one where there are positive social norms and challenges to destructive behaviour. The communities we live in, the relationships and networks we are part of, are all important features of resilience.*
>
> *Personal and community resilience are intertwined. For relationships and networks to be truly beneficial to our residents the people in them need to be resilient too – so that the knowledge shared, and support offered, is as valuable to people as possible. At the same time, the creation of those networks requires personal resilience: the confidence to meet new people, or the belief that you*

can make a difference that triggers involvement in a community group. Of course, economic resilience is also vital.

Alongside the close bonds with friends and family that we all need for full and happy lives broad, looser networks are also important... Broader social networks expose us to different social norms and expectations, for example expectations around work or our responsibilities to the community.

Essential to building a resilient community is understanding the power of networks in spreading positive behaviours, knowledge and social norms. Behavioural science is offering new insights into the impact of the behaviours we see around us. We mimic what we see others do and in this way our social networks influence our ideas, emotions, health, relationships and so on. However, that means that for a resilient community we cannot be neutral about the norms and behaviours that are spreading – destructive behaviours such as anti-social behaviour, obesity and truancy can be spread this way too. Again, the importance of resilient individuals within local networks is vital.

We saw community engagement as a tool by which to build community resilience. A resident helping at a scout group or learning first aid contributed to the wider area's resilience. Community was understood as something organic that people develop themselves, and we believe the task of the state is to provide the infrastructure and encouragement to help people develop ties with others in their community as they see fit.

Unfortunately, politicians too often want to define community engagement only on their own terms. That is to say, they tend to see engagement as attending a meeting or signing a petition. Because of this, they too often see community as consisting of the same few people attending meetings to interminably discuss the same issues. But the truth is that most people have better things to do and generally have little interest in the detailed deliberations of councils. In addition, those who regularly attend meetings are often those for whom attendance operates as a kind of therapy; those representing organisations, who are often paid staff and have particular organisational or personal interests to represent; and those who are not elected councillors but think they should be.

If residents are to be active and involved, then it must be on their terms. Parents will support the school their children attend. People will attend exercise classes if they are interested in exercise. The Covid-19 crisis showed that people respond to help neighbours in need. They volunteer at homeless shelters or run football clubs when others can't. But the activity is always their choice. People can be engaged through actions, but only on their terms.

For example, during the Covid-19 emergency, many people on low incomes in Newham struggled despite the government's expensive support schemes (80% of little is even less), and there were relatively large numbers of people in the borough without access to public funds. Lakmini Shah, a progressive and active Newham councillor, used her network of community contacts during the first lockdown to organise and deliver forty food parcels every day and provide one thousand hot meals per day at weekends. Just one example, like many others across the country, of community resilience; a genuine community leader exploiting her network at a time when the community was in difficulty. Shah's food parcels were a lifeline for many families during tough times – and her entire initiative was carried out without imposing on scarce council resources during those troubled months.

Provide the right opportunities and infrastructure, and the community will develop links locally. These do not have to be controlled by the council – and indeed cannot be if the full depth of community is to be plumbed, as it is in many areas of the country (particularly outside cities). The council can act as a catalyst, but much of this community activity takes on a life independent of the local authority.

Pursuing this line of thought, in Newham we invested heavily in our community forum areas. Despite austerity, we upgraded community facilities, opening several new community hubs and improving existing facilities. We didn't close a single library, but often integrated libraries into community hubs. In practice, because the libraries already had buildings in place, we expanded their role. We also increased officer support to organise community events and support community-organised events. More than five hundred events took place every week, and these were key to our other priorities, such as maintaining an active life for the elderly and reducing loneliness.

One of the great ironies of modern city life is that you can live alongside your neighbours for years without ever getting to know them. The council could not create community, but it could support neighbours who wanted to build a community within their neighbourhood. By way of example, we encouraged street parties with a grant of £250 to anyone who wanted to organise a gathering – particularly during the Olympics and the Queen's Diamond Jubilee. This included paying a grant to one street party billed as 'Not the Jubilee'! We did not mind the punkish approach; encouraging people to get to know their neighbours, however it was spun, seemed a good way of building real community resilience. The grants meant that people could organise an event without any financial risk, and we would take care of road closure orders etc. Hundreds of parties took place.

An additional challenge to building community in Newham was that it is, ethnically speaking, hugely diverse – the most diverse place of its size in the world. But people get on well together. During the Queen's Jubilee, Robin visited several street parties.

He went to one gathering that was swimming in booze. Although invited to stay, he had one more party to visit and sadly took his leave without a drink… to go to a party with not a drop of alcohol in sight! Yet at both parties, everybody was having a great time and there were people from different backgrounds and cultures. People respected each other's views and values and celebrated differences. And they got to know their neighbours. For months afterwards, we received reports about how neighbours who had never met before had forged new friendships and supported previously isolated people in their street.

The objective in Newham was to provide opportunities for people to come together in as many ways as possible to build the links organically which would lead to a genuinely resilient community. The community consists of a disparate group of individuals and, by encouraging people to do things together, we felt we could promote and facilitate community participation. The reasoning was that if people came together to do the things they wanted to do, rather than the things the council wanted them to do, it would strengthen community links. Common purpose and common choices. The council should act as a facilitator and provide the infrastructure. But when the council acts as organiser and controller, it reduces resilience.

However, if the purpose of community activity was to develop links across our community and improve resilience, a key question followed: how could we then go on to understand the views of our community, such that we could deliver what it wanted? To answer this, we developed a consultation strategy separate from our community-building activity. There were various levels of engagement:

- Mass public consultations on general issues. For example, we published our spending plans for neighbourhood renewal funding and engaged large numbers of residents who gave feedback on crucial proposals.

- More detailed feedback from people affected by specific proposals. This included questionnaires (paper, online or through facilitators) limited to those directly affected. This is how we gathered opinions about managing the decant of tenants from housing renewal programmes.
- Focus groups or interviews when we wanted an in-depth understanding of how people responded to specific changes.

To understand the views of the whole community, or large groups within it, we commissioned independent surveys. As we have described previously, there were several regular surveys. These included an annual poll to identify residents' views on the council, local services and neighbourhoods, including what they wanted to improve. Another was the regular household panel; a longitudinal survey – we think the only one in the country run by a council – which told us much about the borough: poverty, skills, migration etc. We didn't just want to talk about basing decisions on evidence; we actively sought out evidence to inform our decisions. Conducting regular surveys did not mean that we slavishly followed the latest idea that had found favour with the public. Plenty of politicians lead by uncritically following the latest political fad or zeitgeist. In contrast, we sought a longer-term understanding of what our residents wanted, and then to deliver related outcomes. We didn't ask how to do things; instead we asked what people wanted fixing, what they were most bothered about, and what their priorities were. By actively responding to surveys, we demonstrated that we were listening to residents, which drove up support for the council. At the end of 2017, 81% of residents were satisfied with the council; double the figure from twenty years previously.

Depending on the objective, there was a place for other types of survey, meeting or drop-in session. But these were held to gather information and promote understanding. At large council events (see below) we also took the opportunity to obtain as much valuable and relevant intelligence as possible. Large community meetings were sometimes necessary. If we had a proposal to make, we felt it should be shared with all people who would be affected. That meant some major proposals invited large gatherings. Some produced more heat than light, and little came from them. Residents must be given the chance to respond to the bright ideas of politicians; the politicians owe it to their voters to try to understand what their concerns are; that does not mean always doing precisely what they want. But if you aren't going to do what residents want, you should explain why. You owe them that.

Newham's diversity meant we also had to consider issues of community cohesion. But by defining community as we did, we encouraged participation and joint working among people from vastly different backgrounds. Newham's approach to building social integration (or community cohesion, as the buzz term became) was to build common ground, bring people together, and act fairly. No particular social group was favoured, ignored or isolated. Consequently, a substantial programme of large-scale free events brought our diverse population together. These included a weekend town show at which attendance grew from five thousand people to more than fifty thousand. Another initiative was a series of free music concerts, attended by up to forty thousand people and featuring music from many backgrounds, culminating in a Last Night of the Proms-style event with the Royal Philharmonic Orchestra and a diverse audience singing 'Land of Hope and Glory'! It can still be seen on YouTube.

As an aside, a constant refrain at the council was that whatever we did should focus on quality. If we were inviting residents to events, we believed we should demonstrate, through the quality of that event, that those attending were respected. Half-baked, amateurish or ill-considered local events demonstrate a lack of respect for attendees.

To send a clear message, the Union flag was often flown at these events. In addition, on the appropriate national day (including those of the Home Nations) we flew the flag of the community involved alongside the Union flag. That sent the message that diverse communities from within our population were valued as part of a whole.

The English language is crucial for building a shared national identity and enabling everyone to participate in their communities. Despite entirely stupid government cuts to English language tuition funding, Newham continued to offer free English tuition to all residents. Partly because of this, a local survey showed that 89% of people agreed that, in the most diverse community in the world, people from different backgrounds got on well together – a score considerably above Britain's national average.

We believe that people are better when we work together with our neighbours, irrespective of religious, ethnic or political differences. We believe that we should share, learn from and enjoy our different experiences and cultures. But we came together in one borough as part of a single nation. The concept of cultural appropriation must be among the stupidest ideas ever thought up. If we are not going to share with and learn from our neighbours (and ultimately assimilate aspects of their culture), why invite different people into our neighbourhoods? Those who argue for an immigration policy that does not allow a two-way sharing of experiences seem determined to build walls between people rather than break down barriers and build communities. We must always emphasise our unity as we learn from diversity; a unity built upon shared values. Societies that do not do this will always fail. In our view, the experience of the Balkans following the dissolution of Yugoslavia demonstrated – if any demonstration was still necessary – that ethnic and communal differences can become major 'fault lines' if they are not nurtured and celebrated.

But on this point, we also have a concern about the paradox of some Black Lives Matter supporters seeking to view almost every issue in ways that isolate the black community, even if it is ostensibly for the purpose of celebration. By treating black people (or Asians, or whites) as somehow distinct when assessing every issue, such proponents purposefully exacerbate and exploit differences. And in those circumstances, disharmony too often follows. This is a worrying part of the current woke culture. We see some on the contemporary Left adopting an approach that is purposefully designed to create ethnic, religious and philosophical ghettos. Extremes observed in the USA suggest a desire (among some) for a 'progressive apartheid' wherein people of different races are separated from those who might 'pollute' them; wherein black nationalists echo white separatists in demanding living space separate from people of a different hue. It is an approach that, regardless of ethnicity, necessarily sees the 'other' as the embodiment of evil and 'ourselves' as the sole repository of what is correct.

For most people, living in harmony with our neighbours, irrespective of their skin colour or religion, is a goal to which we aspire. It is not about assimilation into the 'Borg Collective'. It is about identifying with some core values. Not necessarily support of the England cricket team(!), but the values that have been incorporated into Western society since the Enlightenment. To be a progressive is to believe in these values. On the Left, it feels like we are pushing water uphill in arguing for them. Large swathes of those who claim to be Left wing have forgotten what was fought for over centuries. They have abandoned principles that should lie at the heart of progressive politics, and embraced some very unpleasant tenets of identity politics.

Ultimately, community is about people: what makes life better for individuals, families and neighbours. Ensuring that the environment is clean and attractive, that children are educated, and that the area is a safe place in which teenagers can wander are all roles in which the state – in the shape of the council – plays a part. But we are aware of the atomisation of urban societies: neighbourhoods where those living next door to each other never meet; where elderly people live alone and rarely meet another human being. This realisation led us, when thinking of community resilience, to look at ways in which Newham Council might provide the infrastructure to assist neighbours to build their own communities and (in a psychological sense) give people permission to care for one another. Providing a safe and clean environment was a part of this. But so were the small grants for street parties and the regular activities in our libraries and resource centres. We could provide the infrastructure and even a little help to get something started, but we sought to support people in doing things rather than to be the provider of all things.

Community is what community does. It is bottom-up. Councils can help by providing infrastructure and encouraging and supporting people. But community is not determined by the council.

Chapter 11

REGENERATION

A place to live, work and stay.
(Newham's maxim)

Throughout this book, we have argued that in order to deliver effective services, measurement is crucial. It is very difficult to do this with regeneration. Regeneration varies considerably across the country. It's a local issue, and one size doesn't fit all. How can you compare London with rural England? Newham with, say, Kensington? Washurst, East Sussex (the best place to live in the UK in 2023) with Aylesbury (the worst place to live in England in 2022 according to *The Sun*)? Each area's circumstances and opportunities are so different that there is little to be gained from comparing one with another.

Level of investment is often used to demonstrate successful activity, but the work of the London Docklands Development Corporation showed how misleading this can be. With the regeneration of the dockland areas of East London, Tower Hamlets and Southwark (home to Canary Wharf and Borough Market respectively) were massively changed, but the impact on nearby Newham was very limited. Developers just did not see Newham as an attractive investment at that time, even though we housed one of the largest disused dock areas in Europe: the Royal Docks (which is, in fact, three large former docks: the

Victoria, the Albert and the King George V). When the market changed and developers recognised the Royal Docks as a viable opportunity, the pace of regeneration accelerated swiftly.

The role of the public sector may be to pump-prime; it may be to set the strategic goals and ensure that the infrastructure plans are in place; it may be to market and sell a vision for the area, but major regeneration requires the input of the private sector. Unfortunately, statists resist any developments, complaining that the private sector wants to make a profit. This can put pressure on councils not to develop. The result is that development does not take place and homes and jobs are not forthcoming. While it is anecdotal, we have heard a number of developers in London complain that development is much more difficult now than in the past. Of course there are some exceptions, such as Barking and Dagenham in East London, but the environment remains difficult.

Housing numbers are also often compared to justify council performance, though this is equally invalid, depending as it does on local circumstance. But in a world where winning the battle of the narrative is often more important than what is delivered on the ground, you will repeatedly hear politicians claiming to be more virtuous than their counterparts – often by promising to provide more affordable homes or spend more on the NHS without explaining the expected benefits. When a property developer progresses a scheme, part of the price of development will be a contribution to the local council through the community infrastructure levy and a Section 106 agreement – and that cuts into profit. Developers are shrewd and know what level of profit they require for the risk they will take, and there is a risk associated with any development proposal. The developer will not develop the area if the council asks for too much. And there's the rub. If they don't develop, then infrastructure is not delivered, the level of additional affordable (or council) housing is zero, and people in desperate need of decent, affordable housing have to wait longer. So, politicians demand ever-higher levels of affordable housing in an approach which will block development. But Left-wing credentials have been burnished by people who give not a whit for the real needs of residents. Another example of virtue-signalling at the cost of delivering meaningful change for working people.

Our approach to providing affordable housing was to negotiate the best deal we could get from developers and look to get as much public subsidy as possible from the Mayor of London and central government. This is what any good council does, though obviously outside London the Mayor of London is not the best route to public subsidy. Recognising that this would not be enough, we launched several initiatives to develop affordable housing ourselves (see Chapter 8). It's no good waiting for cavalry that never comes. We believe in muscular local government that tackles problems using all the tools at its disposal – which are considerable.

If regeneration is to be worthwhile, it must change people's lives. Most regeneration focuses on the physical, and when it is about developing housing, that can and often does make a difference. But when a development is concentrated on creating job opportunities, the issue becomes: how can this benefit local people? It is here where development often fails. For example, Canary Wharf has generated wealth and contributed to the British economy – but it has not significantly changed the life chances of local residents in that part of Tower Hamlets. Instead, hard-up locals stare out of their windows at the giant skyscrapers and are forced to look from a distance at the wealth of international bankers.

Regeneration does not solve the problems of poverty. But it can allow you to reduce them – and you can measure the impact on the poorest when it comes to increasing employment. These days, investment is often automatically taken as a proxy for improvement. It shouldn't be – how much you spend is less important than the results of that spending, such as a positive impact on more people's lives. It's easy to spend £1 million on ten people (£100,000 each). You will make that small group very happy indeed, and you may even feel that you've regenerated a tiny street. But try spending £1 million on a programme to improve the lives of a thousand people (£1,000 per person), and it is a lot harder to demonstrate a positive improvement.

Many good council leaders across the UK are prepared to expend political capital to make their area a better place and improve the lives of their residents, while cowardly leaders run from confrontation and ignore pressing needs. While regeneration is a policy area in which good things are done all over the UK to create jobs and housing, ensuring that these benefit residents is where schemes often fall short.

Our approach to regeneration was to evaluate performance by looking at the narrative and then to measure the impact on people's lives. Does the story sound reasonable, and as regeneration proceeds, is it delivering what was originally promised? Did that promise include social benefit? If not, what's the point? That, at least, you can do. Elsewhere in this book we discuss our successes (and some failures). To regenerate an area, you need to tell a story that people both inside and outside the area can understand, and each area has a different story. This is the narrative that attracts attention and the vision that excites. This is Newham's story (the short version).

In 1995, when Robin became Newham's leader, the council was considered a bit of a 'basket case'. The previous leader (now East Ham MP), Stephen Timms, had struggled with a Labour group that did not see the people of Newham as its priority. However, Stephen had succeeded in signing up the council to a campaign to have High Speed One (HS1) run through Stratford, with an international train station – and the associated investment it brought – as the prize. The physical legacy included swathes of derelict old rail land in Stratford housing scrap metal merchants, concrete crushers and a dilapidated railway station; large tracts of social housing in Canning Town and Custom House that nobody wanted to occupy; and dormant docklands with which the London Docklands Development Corporation (LDDC) (soon to depart) had done little.

We needed to change the view of Newham from a place where nobody wanted to go, to one of excitement and opportunity. One of our first acts, following the appointment of an excellent new chief executive, Wendy Thomson, was to agree on a vision for the borough:

That by 2010, Newham will be a major business location and a place people choose to live and work.

Elsewhere, we describe how this was the precursor to a more explicit commitment to resilience. However, in the context of regeneration, making Newham an important business location meant ensuring that people understood that Newham was open for business.

The battle to have HS1 (the line to Paris) come through Stratford, and to have a station there, was a long one, and Newham expended considerable amounts of time and effort in the attempt. In the event, we were successful – but Eurostar then decided that they would not stop international trains there! What was the difference between France and the UK? In France the government told those involved where to stop the trains, whereas in the UK it was left to market forces! In fact, it was a Labour government that left it to market forces. The decision actually fell into the lap of Labour's good old Left-wing Deputy Leader, John Prescott. And, unsurprisingly, 'market forces' took the commercial decision that suited them best. Incidentally, Michael Heseltine, Prescott's experienced counterpart in the Conservative Party, said at a meeting we organised to discuss some of the issues that he would have ordered the train to stop in Stratford. Funny old world!

The market is the best way to deliver goods and services. It is the only mechanism we know that can reveal consumers' preferences and incentivise the production of goods and services that people actually want. However, the right incentives need to be in place to ensure that wider society benefits, and that disbenefits are avoided. In the case of HS1, the incentive should have been that no stopping trains equals no trains. To be fair, the 'international' (though still only domestic) station has improved connectivity at Stratford, and we still believe that, one day, international trains will stop there. Mind you, we are only predicting that on faith. We cannot say that we have applied the scientific method to the problem. It seems like common sense, so maybe we're wrong. However, while this has been a setback for Newham, campaigning for a station demonstrated that the council was open for business. The station enhanced Stratford's domestic connectivity, as did the Jubilee Line extension to the town. It became the busiest station in the UK, with something like fourteen million passengers in 2020/21. To be fair, this was during Covid-19 – but Stratford is certainly one of the ten busiest stations in the country. Indeed, the development of the connectivity of Stratford Station was a catalyst in attracting Westfield, the International Quarter and the 2012 Olympic Games.

In addition, the benefits of investing in Newham were sold assiduously. For example, Newham attended MIPIM, the annual developers' junket in Cannes, against the wishes of the hard Left on the grounds that if we could attract development, we could improve residents' lives. Later, with initiatives like the Arc of Opportunity (an area of land stretching from the Queen Elizabeth Olympic Park via the Royal Docks to the Barking border), the idea of Newham as a place with land and transport waiting to be developed was sold to anyone who would listen. When developers were interested, they were welcomed, though not at any price. And we just kept campaigning. And then there were the actions that demonstrated intent – and here we offer some examples in transport, housing and education:

- When Transport for London wanted to improve the station at Stratford, we realised that, as usual, ambition for East London was lacking. So, Newham volunteered to put £12 million into the development in return for a better station.
- In December 2000, the council introduced plans to transform the unpopular estate at Canning Town and Custom House. This area housed 7,500 people, of whom 85% lived in socially rented properties. We minimised the disbenefits for residents with what we thought was the most generous regeneration package in the UK (a right of return, a right to social rented property, a right to maintain the same number of bedrooms, a financial gain etc.) to provide more housing for people who did not yet live in the area. There was great difficulty getting the programme off the ground and we paid a political price through the loss of council seats – though we won some back when people saw what we were doing. Today, the fifth-largest regeneration programme in the country will deliver between six thousand and eight thousand new homes. These are in addition to the many existing homes in the area unaffected by the rebuilding. The area is now desirable and, since this is pushing up land values (most of the land is owned by Newham Council), the possibility of increasing the level of good-quality, attractive and more affordable homes is rising. So, the programme is now delivering exactly what we planned when it first started.
- When Birkbeck College (part of the University of London) decided they would like a presence in Stratford, they approached the council about an area in

Stratford town centre where they could jointly develop an educational offer with the Newham-based University of East London. The chance of drawing an iconic educational institution like Birkbeck to Newham, with all the benefits that flow from educational aspiration, was seized upon and a plot of land was provided at less than market price. The presence of recognised and respected institutions of higher education would, we felt, influence the choices of the children of our residents (and some of the adults), so that higher education was something to which they would aspire.

- We also tried to persuade University College London to move to the Carpenters Estate, but they chose to move into the Queen Elizabeth Olympic Park instead. This is described in more detail below.

People were starting to look at Newham as a potential site for development – and then the biggest opportunity of all arose: the 2012 Olympic Games.

Newham was the first council to support the daft idea of holding the Olympic Games in East London, which was being promoted by a chap called Richard Sumray (who has never been adequately recognised for his work; indeed, the many local people who made the Olympics such a success have also not been properly recognised for their contribution). Even if we didn't win with our bid, the reasoning went, the publicity for East London in general, and Newham in particular, would greatly benefit us when seeking inward investment.

So, Newham was a firm advocate of the East London Olympics and – as the plan was developed and sold with great skill by Seb Coe, Keith Mills, Craig Reedie and others – we were proselytisers. Indeed, when the International Olympic Committee (IOC) evaluation committee came to London in 2004, the view of Stratford from Holden Point (a Newham tower block upon which we had placed a viewing cabin) was one of the highlights of the trip. The acres of undeveloped land and the many trains running close to the site presented a knockout image. We had the land the IOC sought and the means to get sports fans into the area.

Yet when London won the bid in 2005, it was just the start of the work. The IOC may talk the talk when it comes to legacy, but they most certainly do not walk the walk. It is fair to say that they consider local legacy to be of considerably less importance than what outfits to wear to their various dinners. As an organisation, their contempt for local legacy is surely only matched by FIFA. Well, it is probably surpassed by FIFA – but FIFA hasn't been to Newham!

Interestingly, on a post-Olympics visit to Glasgow to look at their planning for the Commonwealth Games, Robin was treated to a description of the accommodation and facilities by Gordon Matheson, then leader of Glasgow City Council, who knew exactly what each facility was going to be used for in legacy. It was in their DNA. The purpose of the Commonwealth Games from Glasgow's point of view was to leave a legacy (part of which was learned from Manchester) rather than just stage a Games. It may surprise some readers but, despite national politicians' obsessive repetition of the word 'legacy' in relation to the 2012 Games, this was most emphatically *not* the case with the Olympics.

Let us explain. In terms of physical legacy, the 2012 Olympics is best understood as a turbocharge to what was already going on locally. Newham was already selling Stratford hard, but the Olympics 'put Stratford on the map', attracting the attention that could help to provide jobs and housing. This would be facilitated by the infrastructure development necessary for the Olympics. As a result, public cash poured into the area quickly, along with private money and brand recognition to die for. Though, to stress again, to us this was only important if it changed the life opportunities of residents. Much of the direct Olympics investment did not.

There was one immediate and unintended legacy benefit. For some time before the Games, Newham had been trying to get development going in Stratford, and Westfield had decided to build a new shopping centre (Stratford City) there. Given the train lines running into Stratford, to local people it seemed an obvious decision – but perhaps it did not to people living outside the borough. So, Westfield's decision to build in Stratford required some vision. After the financial crash of 2008, continuing with the plan also required courage because the economy was troubled. Westfield deserves enormous credit for continuing because, at the time, the future was a little uncertain (massive understatement), and you didn't get to read much about their courage in the papers. Instead, the national and media focus remained on Newham as the home of the forthcoming Olympics, and developments such as Westfield's centre were often mistakenly reported as merely part of that. In reality, by the time the Olympic planning came around, many of the local development relationships were symbiotic. The Olympics often boosted existing plans, since many of the infrastructure initiatives required by Stratford City (the shopping centre) were also needed for the Olympics.

That's not how most readers will understand the Olympic development. Many casual observers believe that the huge redevelopment in Stratford and its neighbouring areas was all about the 2012 Games. But that wasn't the case. Remember, there are *always* things going on behind the scenes that you don't get to read about. Newham always believed that Stratford City was more important than the Olympics. The jobs it brought were to change thousands of lives because of the opportunities seized by residents through Workplace, and Westfield continued to provide jobs long after the Olympics circus left town. Despite the eye-watering sums spent on the Olympic Games in different cities down the years, there had seldom, if ever, been a legacy for poorer communities adjacent to big sports-related developments.

We think it important to recognise the work of partners who went the extra mile to help us on this point. One of the reasons we were so successful was the active cooperation we got from John Burton, head of development at Westfield, who seemed to be almost keener to get people into jobs than we were. Almost!

We wanted to change the Olympics' dire reputation for post-Games legacies, but had to fight hard. Newham's ambitions were not limited to infrastructure gains. The key objective was to raise aspirations and ambition in the local population. As described elsewhere, Canary Wharf had had little positive impact on local communities. There was a determination that that would not happen in Newham. So, even as development proceeded on the Olympics, Workplace was busily ensuring that jobs and opportunities would go to Newham residents.

Since the key was to use the Olympics to inspire people, Robin was appointed to the board of the London Organising Committee of the Olympic and Paralympic Games (LOCOG), the organisation charged with running the Games. This is not to say that we walked away from the physical benefits but, by and large, we believed that the Olympic Delivery Authority (ODA; the organisation charged with building the Olympics) would deliver these, as indeed they did. Newham engaged constructively with the ODA to ensure that whatever was built as part of the Queen Elizabeth Olympic Park complemented the local area. What we anticipated, correctly, was a significant improvement to infrastructure.

We soon found out that the Olympics extravaganza would have much greater resonance with local people than many had anticipated. A 'Big Sunday' event was organised in the ExCeL centre at Newham's Royal Docks, with entertainment, information, and the opportunity to talk to residents about what they wanted from the Games. Some thirty-five thousand people turned up to the event (nearly ten times the number who attended community events), and they swamped the computer systems. But the excitement and ambition from that event were used to drive more community activity and to inspire people.

While LOCOG was not averse to the idea of a legacy, its focus was so firmly on ensuring that the Games ran well that there was little bandwidth for actual lasting benefits. The five Olympic boroughs quickly realised that, if a legacy worth the name was to be secured and maximised, we would have to fight for it – and with one voice. Any disagreements between the host boroughs would be amplified by those with no interest in legacy issues (a surprisingly large group). So, in 2006 the Host Boroughs Partnership (chaired by Robin) was created and determined to extract from the Games the maximum benefit possible for areas that contained the highest poverty levels in the country.

Interestingly, Newham invited to a seminar several local authorities that had been adjacent to Olympic developments in the past, and asked them to identify the legacy benefits of local Olympics so that we could learn from them. We discovered that there had been precious few benefits before London 2012. It is true that some cities saw infrastructure and business development (Barcelona and Atlanta, for example). But others experienced little positive impact (Athens, Sydney and more recently Rio de Janeiro), and local people had rarely been among the beneficiaries when the Olympics juggernaut rolled through town. We would say 'never', but although we don't have the evidence from every Olympic city, we doubt that there has ever been a successful *local* legacy arising from the Games.

In the first instance, the boroughs fought for a genuine legacy; a fight that later gained traction when Hazel Blears – a Local Government Secretary of State who understood that it wasn't just about sporting facilities – established the Olympic Park Legacy Company (OPLC) under the redoubtable Baroness Margaret Ford. The OPLC was tasked with creating a legacy at both a physical and a 'people' level – and the importance of the concept finally moved up the political agenda. The boroughs at last had an ally – but it wasn't to last. With the election of Boris Johnson as Mayor of London in 2008, the OPLC was replaced by the London Legacy Development Corporation (LLDC), and Ford was removed for no good reason that we could see. It was an action that certainly had a detrimental effect. There was still an Olympics legacy – simply because we, and other local leaders, fought so hard for one. But had Margaret been in post throughout, we feel confident that more would have been achieved, particularly in the housing sector.

Newham saw Stratford as an area where jobs and business would flourish, giving local people employment opportunities. A place to attract firms and institutions with global brands that could contribute ambition and aspiration to the people of Newham. So, when UCL started to look at building student accommodation in Stratford on the Carpenters Estate (a twenty-three-acre site next to Stratford Station and the Queen Elizabeth Olympic Park), Newham's response was to offer the area at a very competitive price (cheap!), provided UCL brought research and teaching departments with them. It seemed to us that bringing one of the world's best universities to Newham would be a win for our population, providing jobs, educational opportunities and aspirations. Sadly, despite the best efforts of Malcolm Grant (then UCL's president and provost) and the LLDC, academics resisted the teaching move. Time moves on, though, and UCL realised that a considerable presence in Stratford still had merit. They have now developed plans for the site that go well beyond our original expectations – and it won't just be student accommodation. The scale of their footprint in Stratford will, we believe, soon be equivalent to 38% of their footprint in Bloomsbury. Indeed, UCL will be the premier university in East London.

Carpenters is an excellent example of the difficulties of regeneration. It comprises low-level housing and three tower blocks which have, as they say, seen better days. After the full UCL proposal fell through, our aspiration for the area was to build a significant quantity of much-needed housing, including a sizeable affordable provision – but with market rent properties also generating a profit that could be ploughed back into further housing. We also intended to build biotech labs 'on spec', because we could see that the UK, as a world leader, was short of such facilities. This was not a whim, but the result of our contacts with leaders in the biotech sector. New UK industry will not be in metal-bashing; it will be in highly skilled technical fields. Our vision was to create a significant tech hub. Given the events of the past few years – the outbreak of Covid-19 and the extraordinary response to it – we might observe that that was reasonably far-sighted.

In 2009, the Host Boroughs Partnership produced a *Strategic Regeneration Framework* with a vision for convergence:

> *Our vision for an Olympic legacy is that within 20 years the residents who will host the world's biggest event will enjoy the same social and economic chances as their neighbours across London.*

The idea was that the East London boroughs should, over a period of years, converge on the national average in terms of jobs, education, skills, housing, health etc. This idea proved very powerful and was one that Boris, as Mayor of London, supported. Key to this vision was a set of indicators covering those areas which detailed how far the host boroughs were from the UK average and what was to be done to close the gap. This was followed by action plans for 2011–15 and 2015–18. East London is home to the country's largest number of people living in poverty. If the north of England has been left behind (and it has), then so has the eastern side of the capital. Our initiative was all about 'levelling up' long before the concept was co-opted by the Tories in 2019 to challenge Labour in its heartlands. In London it was known as 'convergence'.

The Host Boroughs Partnership also commissioned Oxford Economics to produce a model which demonstrated that, with a reasonable approach, East London could generate £6.5 billion in additional gross domestic product, and £4.5 billion for the public finances, by 2030. The aim was to demonstrate that, with the right support, East London could become a net contributor to the country rather than continue as a recipient of perpetual aid like Northern Ireland and Scotland. We are somewhat sceptical of detailed economic predictions since the environment changes in response to actions and events. However, we were and are confident that investment in East London (or indeed most poorer areas) which effectively supports local people to gain capacity from that investment would provide a significant financial return to the state and increase personal resilience.

The Host Boroughs Partnership morphed into the London Growth Boroughs after the Olympics, and later still became Local London. Both were chaired by Robin, and the latter expanded to include Enfield, Havering and Bexley (though without Hackney and Tower Hamlets), to broaden the campaign for justice for East London and to continue the battle for convergence.

Even as the benefits of Stratford slowly began to dawn on UCL, Boris was pushing the idea of Olympicopolis, now called East Bank (because we can't have a name thought up by a political opponent). Using the idea of convergence to sell the government on the plans (and hence extract financial support), UCL, the London College of Fashion, the Victoria and Albert Museum, Sadler's Wells (the world-famous dance organisation), and BBC Music are all moving into the Park. Would they have come if the boroughs had not campaigned for a proper legacy for the post-Olympic period and laid the ground for UCL, the BBC and others? If Hazel Blears had not recognised the importance of legacy? If Boris had not had a 'big idea'? And, in particular, if the boroughs had not come together to campaign for a degree of justice in the form of convergence? Other businesses have been attracted to the area, too: Cancer Research UK, the British Council and the Financial Conduct Authority, to name just three. Additionally, companies working in growth areas of the economy such as smart mobility, e-sports, cyber security and digital media technology have come on board. They are welcome. In the last budget we prepared in Newham, a significant sum was put aside to work with the various organisations moving into Stratford (and more widely into Newham and the surrounding boroughs including the hugely impressive Here East run by Gavin Poole) to identify potential synergies, educational opportunities, apprenticeships, and other employment and skills opportunities for Newham's residents. Sadly, this plan was ditched by the new administration after 2018 and the opportunity to fully benefit from developments in Stratford is, we believe, slowly being lost. It's not too late, though. A reversal of policy could still deliver significant gains.

As to whether the LLDC has been successful, the physical development of the Queen Elizabeth Olympic Park deserves proper recognition. If properly used, the East Bank could transform opportunities for local people, and there is some good work going on (led by the executive director Paul Brickell, who, as an executive member in Newham, did much to flesh out the vision for regeneration and the Olympics) which will support local people in accessing jobs and skills. But as we have outlined elsewhere, opportunities need to be grasped and organisations made to deliver for people. History suggests that rhetoric outstrips benefits. In the case of the opportunities presented by the Olympics and then the LLDC, without Workplace to ensure that the benefits were used to improve the lot of local people, the results would have been much poorer; more akin to Canary Wharf and the Olympic Games in other parts of the world.

But if the LLDC has a good story to tell regarding business and jobs legacies, the vital issue of housing must be viewed as an exception. And not a particularly positive one, either. The development of the Olympic Village provided some decent accommodation, with half of the properties defined as 'affordable' (see the housing chapter to understand the corruption of this word). This was achieved through considerable government investment. Following the Olympics, the LLDC had significant land holdings around the Park. Through a policy of selling land, rather than retaining an interest and hence a revenue stream to potentially support housing and affordability into the future, the assets have been squandered. The deals struck misunderstood both the nature of Stratford and the increase in land values which were evident us on the ground. The percentage of the LLDC's affordable homes under Boris was 30–35%; not terrible, but not nearly as good as it should have been given the available public land. The failure to deliver more affordable housing in the area, and/or sums of money that could be invested in providing affordable family housing elsewhere in the borough, is a national scandal. But those primarily responsible have moved on – as is often the case in the public sector. Having written all of this criticism, we must accept that 30–35% of affordable homes is better than the sweet nothing achieved when all development is opposed. So, we are not ungrateful – just cheesed off that the initiative could have achieved more.

Of course, the so-called 'sexy' part of the Olympic development was always going to be the sporting venues in general, and the giant centrepiece stadium in particular. Before the eighty-thousand-seater stadium plans were finalised, a delegation led by Robin and consisting of Newham Council, West Ham United and local MPs had a meeting with a group representing LOCOG, the London Mayor Ken Livingstone, and the government (represented by Tessa Jowell). The then-chairman of West Ham United, Terry Brown, offered to contribute £100 million if the stadium was built for football and athletics, but his offer was rejected. To put it mildly, that irked the Minister for Sport Richard Caborn, who (like us) understood that for the post-Games stadium to work financially, Premier League football had to be part of the solution. Instead, a deplorable decision was made to build a major, iconic stadium for the Olympics and then reduce it to a twenty-five-thousand-seater venue primarily to be used by UK Athletics, who, outside of major events, struggle to fill a telephone box. Belatedly, it dawned on the powers that be that Britain couldn't simply 'lose' a a few major stadium on which it had spent so much money. So, a hugely expensive retrofit was undertaken, and thus hundreds of millions of pounds of public funds were poured down the drain by politicians and officials who made the original decision and have never had to answer for their stupidity.

To rescue the situation, Newham put together a bid to run the stadium jointly with West Ham United and other partners. Our basic idea was to let the private sector (West Ham United) run the stadium and pay for its upkeep, while we took the profit from out-of-season activities such as concerts. The deal would have generated money for the public purse while transferring risk to West Ham United, who would have had a direct interest in keeping the asset in good condition. Incentives, when properly aligned, work! Other bids were also entertained at this point, including one from West Ham's rivals, Tottenham Hotspur FC.

We are fortunate that there has been a review of the Olympic Stadium's short and woeful history, commissioned by current London Mayor Sadiq Khan to rubbish the performance of the man who took over from Livingstone: Boris Johnson. Political opponents can always be relied upon to dig out the failures of previous administrations – if there are any. The review said of the Newham Council/West Ham bid:

Based on the legacy objectives established, and comparison of the respective bids against these, we can understand why preferred bidder status was conferred on West Ham United–London Borough of Newham.

*The decision clearly underwent a rigorous evaluation
process with the respective merits and demerits of each
bid outlined in detail, and with a broad assessment of key
risks. Whilst one can debate what would have been the
better offer, the WHU–LBN commitments to retain the
athletics track were more aligned to fulfilling the legacy
objectives than the Tottenham Hotspur FC offer. Further,
the WHU–LBN bid appeared to offer greater benefits for
the local community, largely based on the involvement
of LBN because LBN's involvement was predicated on
'significant, direct, community benefit for the residents
of its Borough'. We consider that the arrangement would
have represented a good deal for the taxpayer in which
risks were substantially transferred from the public sector
to WHU.*

Unfortunately, it only took a whiff of grapeshot – in the form
of threats about alleged state aid – to scare the Greater London
Authority into running a fresh bid process that gave the officers
and politicians what they really wanted: personal control of the
stadium. As anybody who has followed this sorry tale since
West Ham moved in as renting tenants would know, the cost of
maintaining the stadium has since fallen on taxpayers – and the
bills run into tens of millions a year. West Ham United signed
a ninety-nine-year lease on the stadium from 2016. At current
rates, if this continues, the taxpayer could end up footing a bill
for the stadium running into hundreds of millions. Imagine
how many local homes could be subsidised with that. Instead,
an unholy alliance of the media; Left-wing, anti-privatisation
statists; and poor political judgement combined to cost the
taxpayer a fortune.

Newham invested £40 million in the initial stadium proposal
to ensure that the project went ahead, because we recognised
the need to retain a world-class stadium in the Olympic Park

to ensure further regeneration. We were always clear that the investment supported regeneration, but we hoped to obtain some profit. But in the end, the concession contracts were drawn up mainly by the GLA because:

LBN was to have no ability to decide or influence the outcome of the Stadium concession competition.

The contracts negotiated were inept, and the result was a stadium that continues to lose vast sums of money each year. The one thing Newham insisted on was that, if anything went wrong, the GLA had ultimate responsibility and Newham could withdraw. We got what we wanted in the end: a stadium and a Park which look great. But the whole deal could have been so much better. Ultimately, Newham pulled out of the stadium deal and Sadiq Khan agreed to provide the borough with a £40 million additional housing grant to balance the investment we had lost. It is instructive to think that, where a council was in charge of a major stadium project (as was the case with Manchester's Commonwealth Games), the authority made money from the stadium. It could have been the same in Newham.

Press critics and political opportunists are prone to looking at problems while wearing blinkers, oblivious to nuance and wider factors. As a result of Newham's action to ensure that the stadium was not lost, sites were freed up elsewhere in the borough (for example, the Boleyn Ground, West Ham's former home, became a major housing development), potentially generating around £80 million for the council and a considerable number of new homes. The benefits of the developments in Stratford enabled by the Park and stadium are generating millions of pounds in council tax. Finally, the gain in value of the land owned by Newham which borders on the Park (primarily Carpenters Estate) has been worth hundreds of millions of pounds. Could the stadium planning and deal have been better? Of course. But the legacy benefits have been significant, and Newham has benefited with an increase of hundreds of millions of pounds in its assets – with more to come when the opportunities created by us are realised. It is disappointing that these opportunities, and the associated homes, have not been prioritised. To enable a proper public discussion, some of these figures and arguments were published in *The Newham Mag* (the council's fortnightly publication). For some reason, all copies of *The Mag* predating May 2018 have been removed from the council's website. However, the excellent Issuu website has retained the information the current council did not want to share. Open government at its finest!

There are two other sporting buildings left within what was the Queen Elizabeth Olympic Park:

1. The Aquatics Centre. Newham never considered investing in the swimming and diving centre, though it was suggested by some, and we did consider financing a deal for permanently lower charges for residents. However, as an iconic building constructed with little thought of maintenance, we predict it will become a white elephant over the next decade or so. If it doesn't, we'll apologise – but we don't think we'll have to. Political hubris on a grand scale bequeathed East Londoners a structure built for show rather than for people.

2. The Velodrome, however, was built following proper and extensive discussion with the cycling lobby. It is, in our opinion, the most beautiful building in the Park, combining form and style. It will fulfil its purpose to provide excellent cycling facilities for keen amateurs and gold-medallist Olympians alike.

People often ask us, 'Was the Olympics "worth it"?'

The Games aided development in parts of Stratford and (to an extent) the wider borough including Canning Town and Custom House. Amazing businesses and institutions have been attracted to Newham and, through the council's efforts, we ensured that this benefited local people. It massively increased employment and incomes for poorer families. Affordable housing was generated, which was welcome. There is now a park in Stratford which looks more attractive each year.

In Newham, we aimed higher than any other Olympic Games location across the world, and as a result we achieved immensely more for our residents. Credit must also go to our partners, the other boroughs, and the LLDC which, while flawed, also bought into the idea that the Games might, for once in their history, do something for local people. Through our combined efforts we overcame some of the political hubris that surrounds the Olympics. London 2012 provided more local benefits than any Games before or since, which is something of which we are proud.

Chapter 12

TRANSFORMING ADULT AND CHILDREN'S SOCIAL CARE

We will learn lessons.
(Inevitable quote from every future review into child abuse)

Section 1: adult social care

One way to make good things happen in public service is to employ excellent staff. In this respect, we were fortunate to have Grainne Siggins as our head of adult social care. Grainne combined a genuine concern for residents and council staff with a determination to improve services and manage costs.

In 2010/11, Newham's budget for all adult social care services was just shy of £98 million; a significant sum. But after the 2008/09 financial crash, Britain's incoming coalition government made it abundantly clear that a period of austerity would mean substantial reductions in financial support to local government – and it seemed likely that the lion's share of the cuts would fall on urban Labour authorities. So, Newham's adult care spending went from £98 million in 2010/11 to £63 million in 2013/14. In subsequent years, though, demand increased such that the annual spend in our last year of office (2017/18) was roughly

£71 million. To compound Newham's challenge, Robin issued a mayoral edict that we could not cut any services. Change was fine; indeed, it was desired. But there would be no service cuts unless it was agreed politically that particular services were of no value to residents. One of Newham's strengths during our period was an executive full of people who shared our outlook. The members saw themselves as representing the community rather than their department or service. This brought us into the realm of 'doing more with less'; one of those aphorisms that sound good to management consultants but drain the lifeblood from those who have to put the giant cliché into practice. Nonetheless, that was what we were charged with doing, even if many felt that this particular circle would never be squared.

Cuts in public sector budgets are often referred to as 'salami-slicing'. In practice, this means that if the authority must save 5% on its annual budget, each department aims to save 5%. Such an approach is easy, at least for the accountants, and delivers the required savings, after a fashion. What salami-slicing doesn't do, however, is ensure the continued delivery of a coherent service that meets the needs of local residents. Taking 5% off some departmental costs is easy. But with other services, removing 5% from the budget can make provision unsustainable. So, with Robin's edict in mind, we had to find ways to remove unproductive costs and radically change how services were delivered, without dumping those services. Salami-slicing would not do. What was required was a root-and-branch review of all services. This gave us a clear picture of what we were paying for and (having decided to retain services) a chance to look at the best way to deliver at a reduced cost. Moreover, our services had to align with, and be guided by, our resilience agenda. We wanted to ensure that residents had a choice – not just 'take it or leave it' services – and that money was spent to support them in ways they wanted. This was in line with the national government's experiment with personalised budgets for those receiving public services (particularly care), to enable recipients to determine what support they got. These demands, and the need to deliver annual savings of £30 million, kept us up at night!

We have described elsewhere how a new approach to the provision of renovation grants to support disabled people saved money and improved service, cutting service costs by 40% without affecting the scope or quality. Where we could, we looked for ways to deliver a better service for the same price or the same service at lower cost. Using the small mutual/co-op approach outlined in Chapter 3, we fundamentally reviewed the service. This gave us an understanding of what we were paying for in a way that was, in our experience, unique. Before this approach, we'd known the total spend but not how much of it was productive; nor what each pound bought.

Occasionally, there were some wholly unexpected results from concentrating this level of attention on a service. There were times when we increased costs. Not many, but when they occurred it was the right thing to do. For example, in common with many councils, we operated a framework structure for the engagement of domiciliary care workers. This is a simple and cost-effective way of engaging staff. There was a difference of something like £6 an hour per person between the cheapest and most expensive agencies. Essentially, various agencies registered to provide domiciliary care staff at an hourly rate. As long as the agency could show that it met all quality standards, when new work was available it would go to the lowest bidder on the framework. New work would be offered first to the least expensive agency, if they were unable to take on the additional work it would then be offered to the next agency, in ascending cost order and so on, until one accepted. This was fine, save that we were increasingly aware that care workers, who were on low wages, suffered the added problem of travelling between jobs during their own time. That is, they spent time on a work-related activity for which they were not paid. We therefore unilaterally decided to set our own threshold minimum hourly rate, which was roughly in the middle of the range. We increased the payments to agencies paying less to ensure that hourly rates were raised to the threshold. The more expensive agencies continued to invoice Newham at higher rates. It was part of a stepped progression to ensure that all care staff were paid the London Living Wage that accounted for work-based travel time. The intention was to use the small business mutual/co-op approach to implement a better system of social care, boost wages, and thereby improve the quality of care across the board.

One of the challenges with the broader mutual/co-op initiative was that we constantly had to ask whether we wanted to save money or improve services. But in adult social care we were clear that unless we improved staff wages and set about creating something of a career structure, we would not achieve the service levels we desired. Consequently, as we reviewed the service, the aim was always to drive down costs and plough savings back into better wages.

Guiding principles

There were two significant drivers, to which we have already alluded. The first was local, in the shape of our resilience agenda. Any proposals for changes in service delivery would be judged against their contribution to personal or community resilience. The second was national, in the form of the personalisation of services, and included the drive towards giving the people we supported a greater say over their lives and how money was spent to support them. This initiative was, of course, aligned with the principles of our resilience agenda. National government (which we are quick to criticise elsewhere) deserves credit for this.

Intervening early

Social services have been demand-led for as long as anyone can remember. We wanted to work upstream to prevent some things from happening (and thereby improve lives and save money) and, where we had to intervene, to do that as early as possible. This was not simply a social care issue. It involved the entire council working together, rather than as the agglomeration of various departments. We held enormous amounts of data, but we didn't exploit it to provide intelligence – an early warning, as it were – on where problems might arise.

The integration of services between local government and the NHS was another initiative pushed by the government, and another area in which the Tories failed to get it wrong! The nexus between healthcare and social care has been the subject of much debate, not least because it determines things like who pays for care and whether you can leave your house to your children. But it also made sense. Bouncing files (which are really people!) between the council and health bodies, while trying to determine who took responsibility for certain services, wasted time and failed in the primary duty to provide timely assistance to people in need. Before the Better Care Fund was introduced, Newham and the local clinical commissioning group were effectively operating a pooled budget – which meant there was no incentive for either side to 'shunt' cases that sat on the margins of responsibility.

Prevention and early intervention were key to changing the way in which we delivered services. We were early adopters of telecare equipment. Telecare services were hotly contested by the usual opponents of change, but the equipment used has changed remarkably over a decade and has proved to be an extremely cost-effective way to support older and disabled people to live at home. Of course, some of the people we helped would eventually need to access residential care. But if we could extend by years the period in which people could live independently at home, the savings to the council would be considerable. The potential for an extended, active and independent life was no small benefit either (hint: this was really the big benefit!).

Earlier in this book, we showed how we brought together elements of the local authority, the NHS and the voluntary sector to create a seamless support package. We discussed this in relation to facilitating hospital discharges at the most appropriate time, ensuring that patients would not be kept on hospital wards when there was no longer a medical requirement for them to be there. But the same service was applied to adults who had recently become ill or who were disabled. The aim was to support and equip people through difficult periods, or to enable them to manage changing circumstances. The Enablement Service was free for six weeks. If support was needed after that, it was offered under the existing charging policy.

Supporting people to live in their homes was generally the best outcome for residents. Few of us want to go into residential settings if we do not have to. But there was a major financial incentive to support people to live at home, which generally cost a fraction of residential care fees. So, we saved a considerable amount of money.

Aligning all council services

We know that debt is often a precursor to major social problems. Debt leads to depression and anxiety, and these mental health issues strain relationships with partners and children. Children internalise their parents' distress and often express it at school by misbehaving and maybe even getting excluded. Then landlords, hire purchase shops, and bailiffs come demanding money from people who do not have any – and that often leads to huge, life-changing moves, crime, or the use of loan sharks who further the debt spiral.

We weren't in a position to predict everyone who would be affected by debt, but we could make a start. When a Newham tenant got two weeks or a month behind on their rent, instead of sending computer-generated letters demanding payment, we asked what would happen if we sent a person round to see whether there was something the council could do to help. That help could come in many forms: debt advice and support from MoneyWorks, liaising with schools, providing respite, supporting finding employment through Workplace, or getting mental health support from a GP or a talking therapies scheme. The idea was not to prescribe a set solution or 'just' demand payment, but to offer the community's support when one of our number was in need.

We anticipated a cost benefit to the council, nonetheless. It would not be immediate, but if this model worked, we expected to see a reduction in demand for services, with a consequent saving across adult and children's services. Overall, we recognised it might be costlier in the short term. But in the long run, we would be purchasing a very different package of support that would aid residents in developing greater resilience. Alas, this initiative was not followed up when we left office, so we don't know how successful it would have been.

Care homes

One area for which we explored the idea of a radical change in service delivery was care homes. The cost of providing residential care for elderly and vulnerable residents was significant. Providers constantly demanded more funding, and their demands had some merit. They were, after all, supporting some of the most vulnerable people in our community. Nonetheless, when budgets were being cut, we had to explore new ways of commissioning services.

We never favoured salami-slicing approaches to cutting costs and, in the context of purchasing places in residential homes, they wouldn't have made sense anyway. Care providers nationally asserted that they would be unable to remain in the market because their incomes barely covered their costs. A little research confirmed that capital costs were partly to blame for keeping overall costs high. It certainly wasn't the wages paid to staff. Given the council's ability to raise money from the market at historically low interest rates, an initiative was launched to buy out some of the providers who were constantly pleading poverty. The aim was to anchor the accommodation costs and then seek and develop small businesses to run the homes. And then came the revelation. None of our providers wanted to sell. Not one. Despite whining about poverty, they were happy with a guaranteed income and an appreciating capital asset. It transpired that land and property acquired, say, twenty years before had increased in value significantly. The owners or providers then took out loans on the increased value, which went to the directors – not once, but several times – turning an easy profit for the owners, but burdening the business with growing debt which then had to be supported from the same income source. Providers could honestly say that their costs had increased. But they were far less candid about the causes!

The high cost of residential care remains an issue for councils, and there is an opportunity for local authorities to enter the market and outcompete the private sector. They would not run the homes: our small mutual/co-op programme has shown how delivery can, when incentives are properly aligned, save money without negatively affecting the service. The public sector could provide the capital assets and, in doing so, drive down underlying costs.

Section 2: children's social care

This was perhaps our most challenging area of work. It is difficult to determine whether the work we undertook in children's social care made a difference, or whether it caused harm. There was almost nothing available that could help us understand the efficacy of our interventions.

What was clear about the system when we took over was that there was a lot of recording and bureaucracy, but very little precise information about whether we were solving any underlying problems. Professor Eileen Munro's government-commissioned review of child protection, published in 2011, identified four key driving forces across the system:

1. The importance of the safety and welfare of children and young people, and the understandably strong reaction when a child is killed or seriously harmed.
2. A commonly held belief that the complexity and associated uncertainty of child protection work can be eradicated.
3. A readiness, in high-profile public inquiries into the death of a child, to focus on professional error without looking deeply enough into its causes.
4. The undue importance given to performance indicators (PIs) and targets that provide only a partial picture of local practice, and have skewed the focus towards process over the effectiveness of the help given.

Throughout this book we have argued for the importance of measuring results and of the scientific method. Indeed, the scientific method requires some way of measuring improvement if we are to progress, and the measures must not be excessive, or else progress will be lost in the noise.

But, as Professor Munro noted, existing PIs at councils skewed attention to process over outcomes. We would agree with this, although we feel that some attention to process is sensible. For example, questions such as 'How stable is a placement?' or 'How long do children wait for a decision?' But children's care PIs were a partial measure at best, and certainly did not tell us what impact we were having on the children and their families.

This left us with two possibilities: either we needed better PIs that would enable us to measure intervention effectiveness, or we could not identify such PIs. If we are not sure whether we are doing a good job in children's social care, why do we do it? How can we be sure that we are not doing damage? Remember the Hippocratic admonition: 'First, do no harm'! This was recently underlined by the government's chief social worker Isabelle Trowler, who said that not only are too many children being taken from their families, but too many families are subjected to unnecessary formal investigations. To put that into context, the number of families subjected to a formal child protection investigation in which no further action was taken more than trebled from 43,400 in 2010 to 134,620 last year. Almost one hundred thousand additional investigations! So, either there has been carnage within our families, or social services are out of control. (Or, of course, social services in 2010 were failing massively.) Pause for a moment and reflect on this. Children are taken from their families unnecessarily. Yet we know that stability is essential for young children. Families suffer the considerable mental anguish of undergoing a formal investigation. In the pursuit of the noblest of aims, we ill-use children on an industrial scale. Inevitably, this leads to the question: is the remedy worse than the illness here? But the unfortunate answer is that we just don't know.

Professor Munro identified the problem of high-profile cases focusing on professional error. It is widely accepted that social work became more risk-averse following the death in 2007 of Peter Connelly (known as 'Baby P'), who died after suffering more than fifty injuries over an eight-month period, during which he was seen by social workers in Haringey, North London. The increase in intervention seems to be driven by public (and sometimes tabloid) pressure arising from cases such as this. This is a recurring pattern. In Britain roughly one child a week is killed at the hands of a carer, a parent or a step-parent. We are familiar with the names of Peter Connelly and Victoria Climbié, but remain unaware of so many others. Reports into the high-profile deaths of some children have led to pages of recommendations. But what we remain unaware of is how well those recommendations work in reducing the number of children killed unlawfully in their home.

When any child is killed or seriously injured, the authority must conduct a case review. There are now thousands of these sitting on shelves (or computer discs) across the country. Our best endeavours have failed to uncover any analysis of these reviews; any attempt to understand the commonalities (and therefore the steps that might be taken to intervene in different ways or at different times), or to identify the factors which might genuinely indicate that children sharing certain characteristics are at higher risk. Many are seemingly self-evident but, if so, why does the rate of child death from maltreatment remain so consistent? Either we know and are failing to act, or we don't know, in which case we should be willing to find out. The other thing to stress is that 'safety' becomes all-important (in theory, at least). We are not talking about 'safeguarding', but about the way in which a desire to be immune to criticism seeps into our policy and practice when it comes to children and young people.

When we were young we benefited from what we can only call 'benign neglect'. Both authors had two parents and siblings. One was brought up on a council estate and the other in army family quarters. The children in our families were allowed to roam and get into minor trouble without the police being involved. It is a freedom that we seem to have lost, certainly in our inner cities. The contemporary awareness of predatory abuse has, in part, conditioned our responses. Schools have become virtual fortresses – at receptions, people are received via intercom rather than in person. We are highly risk-averse. In part, this is obviously because we want to protect children from harm. In part (and we suspect that this is true to a higher degree than would be generally acknowledged), it is because we don't want to be blamed if something goes wrong, or even criticised if something – possibly, somewhere – *might* have gone wrong. The blame culture fostered by, but not solely the province of, the tabloids often conditions policy responses.

The time has come to ask whether this is the best way of keeping our children safe, whether the focus on 'safety' creates more harm than it prevents, and whether the 'safety' mantra prevents millions of kids from developing the resilience that is important in life. If we are to break out of what has become a vicious circle, we need a few clear measures defining the outcomes we require, and then a series of pilots to see what practice might result in the desired outcomes. Perhaps it is time to focus on developing resilient children?

In our view, a clue to the problem is in the name: everybody still refers to social *care*. Not social 'let's challenge kids to do better', not social 'let's work on the life chances of disadvantaged kids by providing a decent education and skills offer', and certainly not social 'let's build the resilience of disadvantaged kids'. No – it's 'Let's *care* for, or look after, the poor little mites.' This, we argue, is why children's social care often fails, and has become the vanguard of the woke. We believe – and there is plenty of supportive evidence – that the early years of life are critical, and our record on education in early years is outlined elsewhere. But we also think that 'safeguarding' does what it says on the tin: it safeguards at the cost of everything else. Or, at least, it tries to. As the national statistics suggest, this approach doesn't always 'safeguard' anyway. For all of the inquiries and reports, children continue to be killed by the people who are supposed to care for them the most. We understand, of course, that sometimes children are at serious risk and that action must be taken. But a policy approach based disproportionately on a small number of high-profile and terrible cases now affects the mass, and so everybody suffers an atmosphere that inhibits children's growth. Is it any wonder that we now emphasise 'safe spaces' and have an epidemic of mental health issues among children? We have mused on the apparent determination of our society to prevent children and young people from developing life skills, and while the connection is unproven, we note that our parents' generation was involved in an existential struggle: to them, a 'safe space' meant spending all night in an underground tunnel or bunker. Today, a 'safe space' requires our children's generation to be sent to a privileged institution and protected from hearing opinions they don't like!

But that is to digress.

Without a proper method of measuring the success of children's services interventions, we are doomed to repeat the failures of multiple councils such as Doncaster, Rotherham and Lambeth. Yes, that's correct – Lambeth, where, thanks to modern exposure of scandals such as the abuse at Shirley Oaks Children's Home, we now know that the hard Left of the 1980s demonstrated a callous disregard for children, while at the same time virtue-signalling in spades, before the term was even invented.

In truth, during our time at Newham we struggled with the reform of children's care services. Not for want of trying, but while we improved process measures and some elements of the bureaucracy, we did not really get to grips with underlying problems that continue to blight the sector across the UK. Instead, we adopted an approach that said that there were many areas of council work in which we could help to improve young people's life chances. If resilience could be encouraged – not only for young people, but also for their parents and carers – we believed we could create better environments in which young people could flourish. If people get a job, their view of themselves improves. We reckoned that must rub off on the family. For us, childcare was about more than strange measurements of social services performance. But we did believe that improving social care was a good idea. Having recognised some of the weaknesses in the sector, we were developing a risk model using our data warehouse and intending to pilot different approaches to improve performance. Our aim was to develop a better, more objective approach to determine which children were genuinely at risk and thus avoid intervention in families who did not require our interference and allow our resources to be targeted at those who would benefit from help. Unfortunately, after our departure this approach was not continued and the current haphazard system continues.

Two problems underpin the approach of any local authority to child protective services: guilt and shame. Currently, the number of children processed via social services depends entirely on when the last bad case was publicised. Families are torn apart or, at the very least, put under dreadful pressure – and these are not usually the most resilient of families. In addition, the certainty of social services that their actions are always right and the fact that actions are not generally scrutinised in public lead, as they inevitably must, to abuse of power. Regardless of how conscientiously they acted, irrespective of the pressures they were under or the policies they followed, when a child known to social services is injured or dies, the social worker and their manager (and the manager's manager!) are at fault and their guilt is proclaimed across tabloids, TV and social media. Who in their right mind would want to do such a job and put themselves in that position? We want professionals to make decisions. Some of those decisions will be wrong, inevitably, because we haven't yet designed the perfect human being (or computer). And neglectful and violent parents lie. Social workers carry a bag-load of competing considerations in addition to the best interests of the child: accusations of racism and condescension; the limited budget of the department;

unwillingness to repeatedly face verbal abuse from adults in the family; time pressures on a worker with a caseload that is too large etc. Far better to simply follow the guidance and avoid controversy. But if we are to protect children, we need adults willing to make decisions (knowing that they will sometimes be wrong), and managers and politicians who will back them up and not throw them under the bus to appease tabloid witchfinders. A data-driven approach, properly implemented and tested, while it will still miss some cases, will at least provide an element of transparency. We would argue that, in addition, as we learn to interpret data better it should provide a better means of identifying children genuinely at risk. At the very least, we could ensure that the state is not abusing thousands of families as it currently does.

A final suggestion. Why does the government not organise a review of existing social service practices to identify the level of abuse of families by government agencies? Then they could always say, 'We have learned important lessons' while changing nothing.

Chapter 13

A WAY FORWARD

What is to be Done?
(Vladimir Lenin)

Throughout this book, we have argued that social democracy
needs to rediscover its mojo. We hope we have made clear
our distaste (and even contempt) for those on the Left who
pursue the delusional aspiration of a world made perfect via the
destruction of the very things that have brought us the societies
in which we live today. For all their faults, Western democracies
provide the highest standards of living and the freest and most
socially liberal societies in history. We need to constantly remind
people of what has been achieved. Of course, there is much still
to be done, and systemic problems continue to damage people's
lives. The answer to these challenges is not to tear everything
down, but to fix the problems.

Perhaps one of the reasons why revolutionary groups
excite the young is their certainty. In this book, we have tried
to show that our preference is for incremental change that
allows the chance to test theories as they are put into practice.
Many of them will be wrong: they won't work, or at least not
in the way they were envisioned to work. The point is to test
how well they work; not by recounting the 'lived experience'
of the loudest voices, but by measuring that of hundreds or

thousands of people. When we tested our policies in practice, we did so because we wanted to know what effect, if any, they would have; specifically, did they work to solve the problems we had identified? The alternative is effectively to draw up a wish list and spend money. That is an awful way to use scarce public resources supplied by taxpayers. Even today, you'd be surprised by how many councils and government departments spend money on 'good ideas' without reviewing their experience and then implementing their improved understanding before they move on to the next 'good idea'.

The current vogue for the rejection of objectivity will hopefully soon pass. As a means of determining social or economic policy, it is plain idiocy. In rejecting objectivity, the proponents of postmodernism have not replaced it with a better alternative. Instead, they have asserted that, because there is no perfectly objective solution, any solution is of equal value to any other. It isn't. They're wrong. As we entered the second decade of the twenty-first century, several tendentious assertions entered the language of the body politic: that a woman could have a penis; that nations with an ethnically white majority were white supremacist; that we were required to address individuals in the plural etc. History was rewritten. It was as if we were suddenly required to interpret the actions of people who lived two centuries before us through the lens of the twenty-first century. Because none of our predecessors could hope to match the informed condescension of the current crop of graduates in grievance studies, they were inevitably found wanting; not for what they did, but because they failed to see the world through this century's intersectional spectacles. How else do you account for the fact that Abraham Lincoln is reviled by our current crop of social justice warriors? Or that a genuine nurse and innovator of medical care and the analysis of data to save the lives of the infirm is somehow considered less important than an entrepreneur and purveyor of quack medicines? Mary Seacole was no less patriotic and her concern for the dying and injured in the field moved *The Times'* correspondent to write of her in the most glowing terms, but her contribution to nursing was somewhat more dubious than Florence Nightingale's.

The historian David Starkey made an interesting observation in arguing that we are the product of our past, both good and bad. He noted that the mark of a healthy psyche and society is probably the ability to incorporate both parts of our history. Nowhere is this more graphically illustrated than along Whitehall, home to the corridors of political power. To the north, near Trafalgar Square, a statue of King Charles I sits atop a horse, looking down towards the Palace of Westminster. Outside the Palace stands one Oliver Cromwell, hero of Parliament and regicide. The polar opposites in one of the bloodiest and most divisive periods of English and British history. But both are contributors to what we are today. They, and countless thousands like them, made us what we are.

Social media, and increasingly the mainstream, have made a new McCarthyism respectable, even required, though this time it comes from the other side of the political divide. None of this was the result of discussion or agreement; none of it was the result of new learning. It was the result of the assertions imbibed by a generation from the vastly increased number of universities which instructed students not in *how* to think, but in *what* to think. The benefit of all this new thinking is that, as we write. Formerly mediocre male athletes now win gold medals as exceptional 'female' athletes, and girls are excluded from their sports changing room because they are uneasy about sharing that space with the owner of a penis. For us, the gender pronoun discussion is yet to be settled. A complex, difficult and often heartbreaking process (for a very small number of people) is reduced to the recitation of a new mantra. It is not by accident that commentators increasingly see the woke emergence as a new religion, or some compare our current culture wars to Mao's Cultural Revolution in China.

Before democracy, Parliament, the Great Reform Act and widespread suffrage, at times of enormous wealth division Britons were able nonetheless to regard themselves as free. Not all of them, and not all of the time. But the autocracy of the historical regimes of Europe and the passionate denunciations of the utopian revolutionary regimes that followed them were anathema to the inhabitants of these islands. Between 1789 and 1850, France suffered three revolutions, the Terror, and subsequent restorations. Within the same period, Britain had the Peterloo Massacre and the Great Reform Act. In our bumbling way, the rule of law emerged to moderate the worst excesses of government and landowners, and people (generally) experienced both the freedom to do as they wished and equality before the law. It is that sense of freedom that now appears to be under the greatest threat.

Society at the beginning of the twenty-first century is different in many ways from that at the beginning of the nineteenth. Both centuries were/are times of enormous upheaval. Post 1945, Western Europe and North America have created areas of relative stability and almost uniquely recognise the value of human life in their institutions and behaviour. Again, if you do not believe this, look at what is happening in Ukraine as we write this book. There, an emerging democracy is fighting for its independence against a de facto nineteenth-century autocracy (albeit with modern weaponry). Alternatively, look at Venezuela. Ten years ago, the South American state was the great new hope of the radical Left, but today, like so many of its predecessors, it has turned in on itself. Venezuela's greatest export is now its own people.

One of the problems of the harder Left is a tendency to view the world through a single lens. For the longest time, this was crudely expressed as a concern for the poor or the oppressed. Advocates of this flawed approach too often ignored the fact that increasing numbers of people (initially in the West) did not fall into these categories. No problem. The Left simply changed the lens and expanded the number of categories to include almost everyone. (Except for able-bodied white men, but then they are 'just' 40% of the population.) In their narrative the Left often ignore vision, risk, enterprise, effort, training, deferred gratification, and education, and use the reality of poverty to create a narrative of blame and oppression. But without those capabilities people will become poorer literally and spiritually. We want a society that can support its weakest members, but we also need a society that can generate wealth. As the authors of this book, we recognise the importance of generating wealth and support policies that will do so. We also believe in a muscular state, but that muscle must be used effectively to deliver the services that people want and politicians promise.

There will always be a tension between liberty and equality. When you free someone to do their best, there will be unequal results. It is the task of governments to support the drive for equality with minimal impact on liberty. Full equality will never be realised with such an approach (nor do we think that it is desirable), but the past century has shown that we can improve the lot of every citizen and make it possible for many to experience significant improvement through their own effort. We have argued that inequalities are not just those of income and wealth, but also those of personal capacity. And we want societies that encourage ambition and innovation, for which there must be a reward. Without that, we would all be the poorer. We have argued that the best way to create greater equality is to support people in developing the skills and ambitions that will yield them the best possible life; one in which they are in charge of their destiny and allowed to choose how they spend their time and money. As a country we have experimented (with a degree of success) with the welfare state, mitigating the worst effects of poverty, but now we need to add a determination to develop resilience alongside that safety net.

At the same time, we must challenge the inertia of the bureaucracies that work against the very things we are trying to achieve. That is the task of social democracy today. Question: how many bureaucrats does it take to change the world? Answer: they don't want to change it. Those who genuinely believe that social democracy is a force for good need to show courage and exhibit the benefits of interventionism by driving improvements across the public services in vision, cost and delivery. We know that doesn't sound very exciting and it won't bring the masses onto the streets – but perhaps when today's wannabe revolutionaries have children of their own, they will appreciate safe, clean streets and a decent education for their offspring. This approach requires political bravery because social democracy has fallen out of favour in Britain over the past decade. It has been squeezed by the forces of neoconservatism, Jeremy Corbyn's statists, the painfully woke (and at the same time centralised) Labour movement that has lost touch with the reality of the working class, and by whatever it is, philosophically speaking, that the Conservative Party actually stands for today.

We hope this book will help to initiate a campaign to restore social democracy to our politics. Because, as we like to think we have shown, when it is sensibly applied to public policy, it can be a radical, reformist and life-changing force for good.

To summarise our position:

- You need vision. 'Where *there is* no vision, the people perish' (Proverbs 29:18).
- The scientific method works – so apply it.
- Identify the objectives and the measures necessary to deliver – but keep it simple. Too many measures simply won't work.
- Provide incentives to encourage the behaviours you want.
- Devolve to the lowest possible democratic structure.

In general, we would argue that it is right to devolve to the lowest democratic structure, but for national government to set a few key measurable objectives before leaving local people to determine other desirable objectives. (But not too many!)

The current reality is that many levers in health, local enforcement, employment, education etc. lie with councils while government agencies operate substantial budgets in these areas without ever truly engaging locally. Delivery is, at best, patchy and much of the resources ploughed into services are wasted. We have tried to demonstrate the reasons for government failure to deliver. This is also true (though to a lesser extent) of local government. A substantial bureaucracy required to deliver a myriad of services without any real clarity on outcomes is a problem waiting to happen. As we showed in Newham, there is a great deal of waste in the system and outcomes are not necessarily what voters or politicians want. This mismatch of control at the centre and potential leverage (or opportunity) at the community level needs to be addressed if Britain's public services are to achieve a true resurgence that consistently improves areas.

Under current arrangements, in which government or sub-national bodies (but not councils) pull purse strings, some kind of 'fig leaf' participation system is often created. But since these sit outside local democratic structures and are not integrated with other delivery systems run by councils, they have little legitimacy or voice. Setting up and running these separate structures always involves inviting a man and a dog to a meeting, and the dog is usually the smartest mammal in the room! Generally, the civil service does not want to listen to what local people think – so the lack of local participation and accountability suits Whitehall. That said, councils also fall foul of poor consultation with residents, so we should not assume that town halls will always excel. There are many pitfalls at the local level, too. In our experience, consultation 'events' are often set up to sell an idea to residents (or voters!), rather than to listen them. Either that, or local meetings often become self-selecting echo chambers of the initiated. There is no guarantee that what people want locally will be delivered by those in charge; they don't always listen or even have the structures to enable them to listen.

So, what follows is a set of proposals for how we might better organise things. The staggering failure of the current system demands that we do *something* to improve it – and quickly.

As we neared completing the draft of this book, the UK government was criticised for taking no decision regarding a further response to the Covid-19 crisis which, at the time, still dogged the UK. We can argue as to whether the government was right or wrong, but the point we want to make is this: *taking no action is still a decision.* Far too often, the risk of a particular action is assessed but this does not include an assessment of inaction. Failure to deliver in a host of ways is (as we have tried to demonstrate throughout this text) a disastrous place to be.

So, if we ruled the world – other than every day being the first day of summer (sod spring!) – what would we do? Firstly, the government needs to stop micromanaging and get some perspective. There are many areas in which the national interest needs to be pursued at a national level – defence, foreign policy, fiscal policy etc. But what we are discussing here are the right policies to follow when delivering services within a local area. Here, the government cannot help itself. Health, education, policing… central government wants to dictate through a civil service that believes that only Whitehall understands the truth and only civil servants know how to deliver. (Evidence notwithstanding, of course.) The national government has the democratic legitimacy to set national standards and goals, but its failure has been in attempts to deliver locally through national organisations – whether through a dysfunctional civil service or an overly bureaucratic NHS. What it ought to do is establish the *framework* for delivery and the outcomes that are required, ensure that people do not game the system, encourage pilots, ensure that there are incentives that support the delivery of the services sought, and intervene where services are failing or coasting. But national government needs to learn to let go of local delivery.

The argument usually raised by decent (generally non-woke) Lefties is that if you go down this localist route, you create a 'postcode lottery' whereby some areas deliver better services and outcomes than others. We have a simple answer to this point: wake up and smell the coffee! There is currently 'postcode *determinism*' resulting from central control of key services that maintains unacceptable status quos in things like health outcomes. A lottery would imply that – occasionally, perhaps – poorer areas might do better!

In addition, we would argue that every proposal outlined below should be appropriately piloted (which also means recognising what doesn't work) and amended to reflect learning.

But enough of the theory. Political books are full of 'what we should do'. We have tried to focus on how we can *deliver* what we should do. Let's get down to practicalities, and the areas of reform we'd like to see implemented by progressive, social democratic movements.

Employment and benefits

Workplace started with the people providing the jobs: the employers. The person seeking work needed to be suitable for the employer. Why else would an employer take somebody on?

Following the regeneration work we had done, we believed that jobs would be created locally. But the experience at Canary Wharf in Tower Hamlets next door showed that residents would be outcompeted. So, we developed an approach that involved building trust with employers and ensuring that support for residents was of sufficient quality to give them a decent chance of getting a job. Key to this was recognising that employers do not have a duty to take on difficult employees. Too often, national employment programmes have focused on trying to combat unemployment by forcing square workers into round jobs – for example, people who lacked the skills for the only roles available locally. This approach effectively asked employers to take unsuitable candidates. It wasn't for us. Workplace helped into jobs everyone who wanted to work – so employers had a good selection of quality staff. But we threw nobody under the bus. We also supported harder-to-place people into jobs with the same employers. We just worked harder to find relevant skills matches. This approach worked, essentially because there was a simple feedback mechanism to ensure that we listened to both employers and potential employees.

In addition, as Workplace developed an employer- and person-centric approach, Whitehall's Department for Work and Pensions (DWP) demonstrated just how *not* to do it. At one point, the DWP offered the East London boroughs a devolved employment programme that involved the department specifying the contract and outcomes. You will recall from Chapter 3 that Newham declined to participate. This was on the back of a previous initiative under which the DWP invited companies to bid for work as employment brokers helping people into work. We encountered the ridiculous situation whereby one of the successful bidders approached the council asking if we would take their applicants, in return for which the department would pay them. So national government were offering to pay private companies to place people in local government and the NHS. Of course, they could have just asked us to do it and paid us for it. We told the private company where they could go and assured them that we were perfectly capable of recruiting without their assistance.

We believe that the human cost of unemployment is enormous and unacceptable, and that government is there to support people to live better lives (hone resilience). That was the attitude we took in Newham when we established the Mayor's Guarantee. We did not know what the price in pounds sterling would be, but we certainly knew the human value. However, to assist the cynics, if someone does get into work, there is an obvious saving in benefit costs. The tax gain for the national government is also considerable over a lifetime; never mind the savings from better health. It really is a no-brainer.

So, the government needs to answer this question: what is it worth to get somebody into work? What are the gains from getting someone on invalidity benefit into work? With some foresight and innovation, the government could easily work this idea into a reward system to provide incentives to local councils. We would argue that the Workplace approach to supporting everybody who wanted to get into work was the right one. It meant that instead of asking employers to take only people furthest from the job market (a big ask when you are running a company), a mix of people were offered – all capable of doing the job. The reality was that employers were happy even while many people furthest from the job market were finding gainful employment. In addition (and importantly), someone who has recently lost a job should be supported in landing another. The original concept of the welfare state – to help people get back on their feet – should guide us as we support people back into work as quickly as possible. These are often people with limited resources who need to earn.

Having said that we think that Workplace's example should be followed nationally, the whole thrust of our argument is that each area should assess the best way to do things and learn from examples elsewhere. If other people have different – and perhaps better – ways of doing things, then let us all learn from them. We're immensely proud of what we achieved with Workplace, but other systems may work equally well and some amendments to our approach might be necessary to meet different circumstances in different areas.

An approach to supporting people into employment should include some of the money currently spent on keeping people inactive. While we would support the idea of a basic level of benefit, the ability of councils to leverage substantial elements of the benefits budget to help people into employment is potentially a game changer. We should trust local politicians to develop an approach to benefits that works to the advantage of local people. The national government should start with generous payments to councils for getting people into work, and then refine the process as it develops into a clear system for sharing any profit. Councils should be able to modify benefit rules locally to support employment aims and outcomes. In other words, councils should be able to use benefits budgets to support people into work in imaginative ways. An example in Newham was the Mayor's Guarantee that nobody would be worse off in work than they had been on benefits. This had the effect of reducing psychological barriers to work – though there was no government subsidy for this.

We are in favour of positive and negative incentives. Where councils fail to deliver, neighbouring councils should also be allowed to take over crucial local services and brand them appropriately. Carrot and stick: if one council can't deliver, look at how much better the neighbouring (often hated) council is! Remember, a common definition of 'partnership' in the public sector is 'the suppression of mutual loathing in the pursuit of public funding'. How much sweeter if additional funding comes at a cost to a loathed and incompetent partner or neighbour!

We say this with tongues partially planted in cheeks, of course. But we would stress that any successful employment and benefits operation must work such that councils can make a surplus to be used as they see fit. Incentives work for individuals and for organisations. If the government seeks to take too much of the gain from successful programmes, local incentives will be lost. Government, and Whitehall, must learn not to kill the golden-egg-laying goose.

National minimum wage

National minimum wage enforcement is a joke. If employers do not pay the minimum wage, they should pay for their exploitative behaviour.

Local authorities should have the power to enforce this law. Initially, to get things started, the national government should provide a one-off budget to local authorities who would determine how to enforce minimum wage compliance across their area and make the exploiters pay for that enforcement. Allowing councils to retain (enhanced) fines levied against criminal bosses who exploit workers would help finance the whole operation. We could, tomorrow, reduce levels of non-compliance massively. But this would require giving local authorities powers and a financial regime that incentivises action on their part.

In Newham alone, 20% of workers are not paid the minimum wage. This means that taking no action simply perpetuates support for, and the existence of, abusive bosses.

Debt

The purpose of creating MoneyWorks was to provide affordable credit to residents who did not otherwise have access to it, to do so in a way that could be replicated across the country, and to create a sustainable model for how local authorities could assist with debt management.

We have described elsewhere in this book how MoneyWorks made a difference and how the information we gathered about customers could be used to provide a product to similar people. We intended to create a credit scorecard that would have identified a group of residents who were likely to repay their debts – and hence could have made affordable credit available over a longer period. If this scheme were launched across the country, it would be possible, after some initial losses (a necessary part of taking some risk to identify those who will repay and those who will not), to set interest rates at a low level, but one sufficient to avoid any significant long-term losses.

We know that access to affordable credit would make a massive difference to many people's lives, not just in Newham and its neighbouring boroughs, but across the UK. In the grand scheme of things, running an effective credit management offer to support many poorer residents is surely something in which a progressive and socially responsible government should invest? The way is open for any government that wishes to change the lives of many striving UK residents and make those people's difficult lives a little easier. Since the people identified by our debt model were those most likely to pay back a loan, such schemes would target the strivers and support the development of resilience; a real levelling-up initiative. In our view, the government should run several pilots to establish the best way to implement MoneyWorks across the country. We argue that 'proof of concept' has been established, so future pilots should focus on how to implement the offer most effectively. However, even if the government wanted further proof of concept, that would be a step in the right direction.

A localised system of affordable debt for a whole new tranche of people and families, removing them from the clutches of rapacious and evil loan sharks; that would be an outcome of which any government would be proud. We also believe that this sort of system would put out of business many insalubrious usurers who prey on poorer people, because those who repay form a key part of MoneyWorks' customer base, and such customers will migrate towards councils. So, what are we waiting for?

Policing, enforcement and the justice system

The police will never prioritise certain areas unless local leaders or residents have louder voices. They are currently turning a blind eye to all sorts of antisocial behaviour.

Poorer areas tend to have poorer environments. Crime, drugs, and rubbish dumping are unfortunately all too common in inner-city neighbourhoods. The failure of police forces to prioritise 'everyday' crimes or antisocial behaviour undermines the efforts of law enforcement.

An excellent example of the pointless misuse of resources was the decision to record 'non-crime hate incidents' – nationally, 120,000 were recorded between 2014 and 2019. This is not something the working-class Somewheres asked for. Rather, it is an obsession of the woke chattering classes who tend either not to live in Newham, or to live in the wealthier parts of the borough. Yet the environment in poorer areas with high levels of environmental crime is not adequately policed or monitored. In all our time at Newham, no resident ever asked us about the number of non-crime incidents recorded by the police. But they did ask us for more local policing and enforcement. Frequently and loudly.

At some level, we could understand failures to tackle low-level and persistent crime if the police were successfully investigating murder, rape and other violent crimes. But increasingly, official figures show that serious crimes often go unsolved. Actual crime-solving has collapsed dramatically – particularly for rape and other sexual offences. In 2020, just 1.6% out of tens of thousands of accusations of rape or attempted rape led to charges against an alleged attacker. Even Cressida Dick, the former head of the Met, described national detection rates for some crimes as 'woefully low'. Our response? Start focusing on everyday crimes (while persisting with serious investigations). Low-level crime blights many more lives and residents' perception of policing is often based on how well everyday activities are investigated. Taking the Newham example, is it not evident that local authorities, or those who vote for them, should have the capacity to determine at least some local policing priorities, and thereby ensure that the people who pay for the police have some say in how they are deployed? Trust us; this would result in more focus on local crime, and the accountability would most likely lead to improvements in local conviction rates. As Newham demonstrated, combining local authority enforcement with effective police deployment can make a real difference to an area – but only if local politicians are prepared to take the necessary difficult decisions to enforce. If they are handed these powers, it will be hard for them to hide from residents' concerns and avoid responsibility.

To us, these decisions and reforms are not actually difficult judgement calls. Local people want action. But we also know that taking such action would irk the woke, who would prefer instead to defund the police, stress the 'tough on the causes of crime' mantra and ignore the equally important 'tough on crime' bit. As is often the case, the USA has been there before the UK and provides us with ready-made examples of successes and problems including those brought about by woke concerns. It is difficult to discern a single programme of action within the Black Lives Matter (BLM) movement, not least because there are many different agendas running alongside one another. However, one of the most clearly articulated demands was to defund the police. The strength of that demand was such that an outside observer might be forgiven for thinking that its biggest advocates were African Americans. So, it might come as a shock to learn that, when Gallup polled attitudes across three cities in 2015, black Americans were far more likely to want a more significant police presence than either non-Hispanic whites or Hispanics (38% wanted a greater presence, compared with 10% who wanted a smaller presence and 51% who wanted no change). Gallup's survey also found that 58% of black Americans had a favourable view of the police. This was a smaller percentage than for the white population at 73%, or Hispanics at 70%, but is still a significant majority of the black population. This is not what you would glean from the voices at BLM rallies. But as we have said before, if you have a political axe to grind, the narrative is often more important than the evidence.

In reviewing the major US cities that enacted police defunding programmes, Michael Shellenberger noted the results throughout 2020/21. 2020 saw a national (US) increase in homicide rates of some 30%. In the wake of BLM-inspired defunding, a dozen major US cities have recorded increases of 30–80%. Additionally, Covid, defunding, and a collapse in police morale have led to a major drop in arrest rates for serious crime. America's policing is in crisis, at least part of which has been fuelled by an overreaction to the demands of the woke who espouse defunding programmes. (There are, of course, many other contributing factors, including America's history of and complex relationship with firearms.)

There are no easy answers to what is happening with policing in the US or here in the UK. So, to implement lasting, effective and achievable change will require sweat and toil on the part of policymakers, leaders and residents. But as far as the woke are concerned, it is easier to hold another demonstration or burn down a building – like that will help! We take a more balanced view, which is that both parts of the Blairite mantra 'Tough on crime, tough on the causes of crime' are correct. Unless criminals believe that there will be effective enforcement against them, they will have no incentive to change their behaviour. And that means that talk of defunding the police should be treated as the cynical rantings of wannabe woke politicians playing to their gallery, not a programme for action. Instead, we should focus on reforming policing and aligning it with the concerns of the wider population. The introduction of police and crime commissioners was a nod to improved democratic involvement within policing, but it was, in effect, a tier of bureaucracy on top of existing tiers. A classic British response: 'Let's set up another committee!'

We feel the need here to stress that if we want to see any real impact from reforms, they must integrate with existing set-ups. Local police organisations must reflect local democratic structures. Rather than create new structures, adapt the policing organisations to reflect the existing ones. Hence, the importance of having borough (police) commanders for each London council. Ideally, nationally the government should follow what Newham did and make available to councils a number of police officers who can be tasked locally. Of course, the existing police organisation would continue to employ them (and thus ensure ongoing professional standards), but the local authority, with its democratic mandate, would be able to deploy those officers in a way that best reflects community concerns. One advantage of this system is that the officers could continue to provide intelligence to support other police activity.

For their part, and to assist with improved accountability, councils should be required to outline how they plan to use their policing resources and what results they expect from them. If the national government is to commit resources, then it is not unreasonable to hold local authorities accountable for the results they do (or do not) deliver. In this way, national government would actually exercise more power over delivery than it currently does. Local authorities should also have the right to pay for more police officers if they wish. If a council wants to flood an area with police to protect its citizens, why would we object if those citizens, through the council budget, are effectively paying for the extra resource?

The whole point of this effective devolution of accountability would be to tackle low-level crime, leaving the core police free to reorganise and deal with more serious crimes. The current arrangement seems rather bureaucratic to us. Of course, since local policing would be truly 'local', police forces would then be free to change their approach to tackling more serious or specialist crimes, and any new structures need not be based on council areas or boundaries.

We have not covered the issue of the justice system in this book, partly because we feel that we criticise enough vested interests without taking on the judiciary as well! But it is a fact that when the police do decide to arrest someone for an environmental crime in a poorer area, you can bet that the fine involved will be derisory. One of the challenges Newham faced when introducing the private sector licensing scheme was that the fines handed out by magistrates were initially meagre. So, a process of education was undertaken to let magistrates realise how serious some of these crimes were. There was a positive response that acted as a deterrent, so it can be done. But reforming cultures within the justice system can be like pushing treacle uphill.

Education

The Blair government made a huge and positive difference in the education sector. The improvement in schools, particularly in London, was spectacular. The lame excuse that poorer children were ineducable (we used to hear this ad nauseam in Newham; usually from Trots and 'educationalists') was demonstrated as the nonsense we had suspected it to be all along. And the rhetoric of Blair's government also made it easier to win local battles for those within local authorities who had been fighting against poor standards in schools.

For us, the key to school improvement was leadership, and that was linked to the quality of teaching and a focus on standards. Schools are effectively small businesses which, once there was national clarity on desired outcomes (five GCSEs at grades A to C, for example), saw significant improvements. The approach we proposed does work! Unfortunately, as the years went by, people sought to game the system by, for example, concentrating on borderline C/D-grade students, demonstrating our broader argument that it is necessary to keep policy outcomes and unintended consequences under constant review. The basic education model was right, though: decide what you want to achieve, not too many measures, and then focus on attainment of those outcomes, all the while looking out for the gaming of the system that will inevitably follow.

But in recent years, national government has taken more power over education and increasingly removed local authorities from the equation. They are ever more fixated on structures: academies rather than local education authority schools etc. In Newham, the form of school governance was secondary. What mattered was results. We were perfectly happy to convert to academies, but also argued that it should be possible to convert failing academies (of which there are many, though not at that time in Newham) back to local education authority schools if that was what worked.

While we were in charge in Newham, we proved to be more ambitious than the central state. However, the central state has also been more ambitious than local government on occasion – just look at what happened with the Inner London Education Authority. Local challenge from determined politicians can be beneficial to education. But where that is lacking, the national government should intervene. And there should be nothing to stop one local authority from running the schools in a neighbouring council, so long as there are appropriate incentives.

We would argue that national government should provide local authorities with both the resources to challenge school standards, and powers to intervene. But we would also want to retain government oversight to ensure that there is always a push for improvement. But this would involve a significant reduction in the Education Department – let schools decide how they should be run; what matters is the results they achieve with young people. A genuine partnership aimed at improving standards would be ideal.

There is a further price to be paid for taking councils out of education. In Newham we undertook many initiatives that impacted on standards: the early years programme, free school meals, the Every Child programme, the phonics/one-to-one tuition initiative etc. Most of the cash for these came from outside our education budget because we thought they contributed to our resilience agenda. The ability to run different initiatives (as we did in Newham) could, if properly supported and evaluated by government, lead to improvements across the country. We would argue that all of our programmes mentioned above should be implemented across the UK. But where is the mechanism to enable this sort of experimentation? It does not exist and, until central government stops trying to run schools from Westminster, it never will. In our view, the government needs to make substantial sums available to encourage pilots, to ensure that appropriate research is undertaken and that the learning from pilots will eventually make it into our schools. In Newham, we did this with our own cash and not education money from the government – but that is because we believed that building resilience was our primary role, and that helping our young people to learn was important enough to spend money on things that improved their learning.

Does the current system work? Well, the failure of direct government control of education can be seen in the present failure of white working-class boys to meet educational targets. And we are failing these youngsters without the outcry there ought to be, mostly because the woke who run the education establishment, and the chattering-class commentariat, do not see them as a priority. Some might claim that the woke middle classes have stopped caring about the white working class; a dangerous mindset, given the proportion of the UK population involved. Of course, there are those who argue that, for generations, women or citizens from a variety of ethnic backgrounds, for example, have been discriminated against, and we are only complaining now because the boot is on the other foot. It's a point of view. But we are against all forms of discrimination, and always have been. If we are true to our principles, we must call out discrimination now when we see it against white working-class boys; the new forgottens or left behinds of the education system. Note, however, that we do not want to treat this group as a homogenous mass. Instead, we want to find out what the problems with their learning are, and then look at ways to address those problems. We do not want another oppressed group to be supported by people interested in maintaining problems.

This issue is one of those pernicious ways in which language has been twisted for political ends. We currently focus on the 'rights of' or the 'oppression of' groups, implying that a concern for groups equates to a concern for people. It doesn't. Much current discourse requires heroes and villains; an oppressor and an oppressed. And if they don't exist in reality, they are simply invented. In a world in which objectivity is shunned as a racist obsession and rationality as a white fixation, it underpins a narrative of the struggle against 'oppression'. But of course, in the minds of the woke the setting of this 'oppression' is not countries with overtly racist political governments, those where gays are thrown off rooftops, those that enslave members of their own population, or those where genocide is endemic. In too much woke analysis, such 'oppression' must be resisted in countries with the most significant levels of personal freedom in history. Those where welfare support exists to an extent unimaginable to past generations; where healthcare is generally available to everyone, and opportunities exist for personal advancement to a broader range of people that at any time in history.

The vanguards of this woke movement often emerge from the state/taxpayer-subsidised dens of oppression we know as the humanities departments of our universities. These champions of the downtrodden waste little academic time on such minor matters as the incarceration of one million members of a religious minority, the wholesale murder of an ethnic minority, or the embezzlement of a nation's resources to fund the private lifestyles of despots and dictators. Instead they have more important academic concerns, such as whether the barista in a coffee bar looks at you in the 'wrong' way, or somebody might refer to you as 'he' just because 'Mr' is written on your credit card. This perversion of priorities (not to mention meaning) is truly Orwellian. Many statists, still schooled in the fantasies of the (Soviet-era) hard Left, were slow to criticise Russia's murderous stance on its neighbour Ukraine when Putin invaded. Stop the War's muted criticism of the invasion was lost in its 'analysis' of the reasons why the West had caused it to happen. Policy based upon ideology rather than empiricism risks harming real people. Just look at the Tavistock clinic's attempt to feed puberty blockers to children, or the increasing number of young adults who now want to detransition only to find that they are scarred for life both physically and mentally. It can also cost lives. In our chapter on health, we showed how attachment to prevailing orthodoxies wrongly identified those at risk of contracting TB and, as a result, put lives at risk.

Health

In the UK we have created a vast health provider. Actually, that is probably untrue. We have created a vast network of mainly public facilities that identify and treat illness.

The NHS has been described as the closest thing that modern (largely secular) Britain has to a national religion. There are very few of us who are not grateful for the service that we, or members of our family, have received from it. In the USA, the greatest cause of personal bankruptcy is the cost of medical care. That is a worry of which Britons have been entirely relieved. Though Britain is not the only country where this is true, there is much to celebrate about our health system.

But we have three concerns. The first is the enormous bureaucracy that underpins the NHS and is made worse by a multiplicity of regulators. The second is that the NHS is not as good as we like to think. On a whole number of indicators, Britain's health service does not do as well as some of those in comparable European states. For example, Britain is a mid-ranked nation in the performance tables concerning death from stroke, heart disease and a range of cancers. A third point we'd make is that the NHS is *not* a health service. It is largely a *treatment* service for those who have been injured or become ill.

In the nineteenth century the massive improvement in health (by the eradication of preventable disease) came not from doctors, but from innovative councils. Local councils forced and introduced improvements to clean water, sanitation, and public health; improvements that have boosted life expectancy even more than advances in medical technology. Nevertheless, the creation of a national health system, free at the point of access, was a tremendous social democratic achievement and one of which we should be proud. It's just a shame that when it was set up, the prevailing orthodoxy was that the government should deliver at the national, rather than local, level. But, as happens with so many bureaucracies, the NHS now feeds off itself and its bureaucracy continues to grow, to serve and perpetuate itself. If the NHS were set up today, would its mission be the same? Would it be leaner or as bloated? Why would we choose this model over, say, the French hybrid public/private model?

If the nineteenth century saw health improvements as a result of councils improving physical infrastructure, the twentieth saw the development of a range of drugs that were little short of miraculous in their effects. Perhaps the challenge for the twenty-first century is to transform healthcare from something that just treats illness and injury to something that better promotes *health*. Increasingly, there is a recognition that many leisure and community facilities provided or supported by local authorities (whether directly or through third-sector organisations) can be important contributors in supporting people to become healthier – though the word 'leisure' does not properly reflect the importance of its contribution to health. Yet even as the NHS makes greater use of these facilities, they generally remain an afterthought. If we really want to be healthier, then these facilities, provided/funded in the main by councils, should be a core part of the health offer. Many wealthier people choose to purchase access to private leisure facilities, but the reality is that the local council offer often supports poorer people where the need for this sort of health initiative is greatest.

The integration of strategic health planning needs to go beyond the realm of medical professionals to include more public health and 'leisure' elements of council work. It also needs to incorporate the work of adult and children's social care departments. Willingness to think radically about the future of the UK's health seems to be absent among our national politicians, for whom healthcare debates too often boil down to boasts about who will spend the most on hospitals. But at a local level in Newham we tried to make integrated care (adult social care and primary care) work. Our success was demonstrated by the fact that, through the Better Care Fund, we had the greatest degree of financial integration in London. We were also willing to interpret our role flexibly, such that the problems of another organisation (the clinical commissioning group) were ones we shared. The people affected were the residents of our borough and we were their representatives, so it made sense for us to be involved. In partnership with the CCG, we were in the process of completely reimagining the provision of primary healthcare facilities across Newham. As we have explained elsewhere, the intention was to create hubs serving enough residents that all necessary support facilities would be included; Workplace, MoneyWorks, community facilities, gyms etc. A health hub financed by local government borrowing that would have made a surplus to be reinvested in social care – what's not to like?

To truly take Britain's health services into the twenty-first century, the national government should specify the sort of primary healthcare provision it wants. We liked Lord Darzi's 'polyclinic' idea, so we'd like to see large sites serving a specific number of residents (an ideal of fifty thousand has been suggested to us by people who know something about this), with national government specifying the minimum facilities provided. Many GPs no longer wish to run a business, but would rather function as doctors. Well done them, we say! So, let's pay doctors to doctor, and health office managers to run offices.

But if the government is to follow this course and devolve new responsibilities to local authorities, it will also need measures to check that value for money is obtained. We already have, via the National Institute for Health and Care Excellence, the concept of a quality-adjusted life year (QALY) – a generic measure of disease burden that helps to assess the value of medical interventions – so the creation of appropriate targets should not be beyond reach. But striking the right balance here is important: we would stress that the more measures a society has, the less likely it becomes that change can be delivered.

Additionally, as we outlined in our education chapter, there is a role for local initiatives and trials. Properly incentivised local contributions can be made not only across primary care, but also to the improvement of mental health care. Councils running the local facilities and linking these to local 'leisure' facilities to provide effective non-medical preventative and rehabilitative support can open up a range of new options that avoid the bureaucratic hurdles of transferring between organisations. This might even lead to better health outcomes. Who knows – we might get joined-up thinking. At a time when we want people in work to generate growth, we might think it worthwhile to pay for simple operations or more physios to get people back to work, earning money and paying taxes sooner, rather than leave their health to decline and their challenges to increase as they sit around waiting for treatment.

Summary

We hope that, through this chapter, discerning readers have recognised the potential for a similar approach to the problems of delivering different services across a local area. Across health, policing, benefits and employment, we argue for empowering and implementing local approaches to things that can be delivered locally based on existing democratic governance structures. For goodness' sake, don't go inventing new structures or bureaucracies; use existing structures wherever you can! This would then leave the government free to organise the residual services according to their nature rather than geography. For example, we do not envisage a role for local councils in stroke care. There is sufficient evidence that specialist regional response units make sense and, if they are not entirely efficient, the saving of lives can be a sufficient argument to spend a bit more. Equally, we believe that specialist rape investigation units should be established on a regional basis.

This brings us back to a critical point. Doing nothing is a decision to continue with the current problems. Where people find our proposals radical, we would reply that they are the only way to deliver services for which people pay at a sensible cost. The alternative is to continue increasing the size and ineffectiveness of our bureaucracies and the public's disillusionment with democracy.

Following the path we have outlined would result in the devolution of resources to localities. If that is done in a penny-pinching way, we will end up with the same miserable results we got with the implementation of Universal Credit. National government should kick-start this process with resources that enable councils to benefit from implementing this new approach, but with a clear plan to reduce central resources as local benefits and savings accrue. As a lubricant to change, perhaps the national government could even take a small share of those savings to invest in other services?

That should give the Whitehall wonks something to think about. After all, if our proposals were to be adopted, then lots of civil servants would have nothing to do.

ACKNOWLEDGEMENTS

As with any enterprise, there are many people who contribute to its success. Inevitably in recognising the contributions of some of them there will be those that we leave out (especially those who were there at the start) and the dividing line will be arbitrary. Apologies to those we have missed – we owe you a beer.

However, there are some whose support for this volume and others who were key to the success of the work we did in Newham and we would like to recognise their contributions.

There will be those who recognise the name of Sir Cyril Chantler, but for those who don't he is a physician with a lifetime of service to the NHS and his contributions have been at the highest level. We were lucky to have met with and collaborated with him on some of the key areas of our work, again, those who know him may recognise his influence on the work we describe bringing health and local government closer together. Moreover, in the production of this volume he has been unstintingly encouraging and we are grateful for his friendship and support.

At Newham, we were part of a team and over 20 years many politicians contributed to the success of the council. There are some whom we would like to note because without them, the work would have been much harder. To avoid hidden messages of some form of hierarchy, we list them alphabetically. Hanif Abdulmuhit, Jose Alexander, Andrew Baikie, Christine Bowden, Paul Brickell,

Ian Corbett, Jo Corbett, Richard Crawford, Unmesh Desai, Lester Hudson, Alec Kellaway, Joy Laguda, Pat Murphy, Quintin Peppiatt, Lakmini Shah, Ted Sparrowhawk and Stephen Timms.

There were a number of Chief Executives who brought both their energy and experience to the role. We would like to recognise them and in doing so, recognise all of those who worked with them; Wendy Thompson, Dave Burbage, Chris Wood and Kim Bromley Derry. There were also a great number of officers who contributed (especially those in the Mayor's Office) – too many to list but thank you to all of them.

In the field of health and social care, Steve Gilvin, then the Chief Operating Officer of the CCG was a genuine partner and always a pleasure to work with; Matty Peacock gave form to the joint venture which would become Health and Care Space Newham, and Grainne Siggins who combined vision with genuine concern for people and considerable management skills. We are indebted to Shanti Vijayaraghavan for her sound advice with regard to diabetes care.

The transformation of thinking and operations in enforcement, which was necessary to deliver on much of our agenda was due to the expertise and focus of Nick Bracken, who brought his long experience of law enforcement to the borough.

In the production of this volume we would like to thank Mark Conrad who took on the task of editor and has remained both a friend and collaborator in this project; Tim Waterstone, whose sound advice was instrumental in giving this volume its particular form; and to Jane Sherwood, Norma Sparks and Frances Gordon who willingly shared their thoughts and experience.

We'd also like to thank both Zoe Power and Jill McWilliam for their support, their wisdom and their work on this project.

It goes without saying, many of the ideas and initiatives were the product of conversations shared and work done jointly. All of the above, and others shared in that process. Any success we had is shared, any cock-ups are down to us.

ABOUT THE AUTHORS

Sir Robin Wales joined the Labour Party in Scotland aged fifteen. Elected as a Labour councillor in Newham in 1982 he subsequently served as leader from 1995–2002 and then as the first directly elected Labour mayor in the country from 2002–2018. As a member of LOCOG he played a significant part in the 2012 London Olympics.

Clive Furness joined the Labour Party when he was twenty-one and served at every level of his constituency party. He was a Newham councillor for twenty-one years. He spent most of his working life in the voluntary sector, working with homeless people and those with mental health problems. His thirty years of voluntary youth work saw him receive the BEM. He is a deacon of his church in Plaistow.